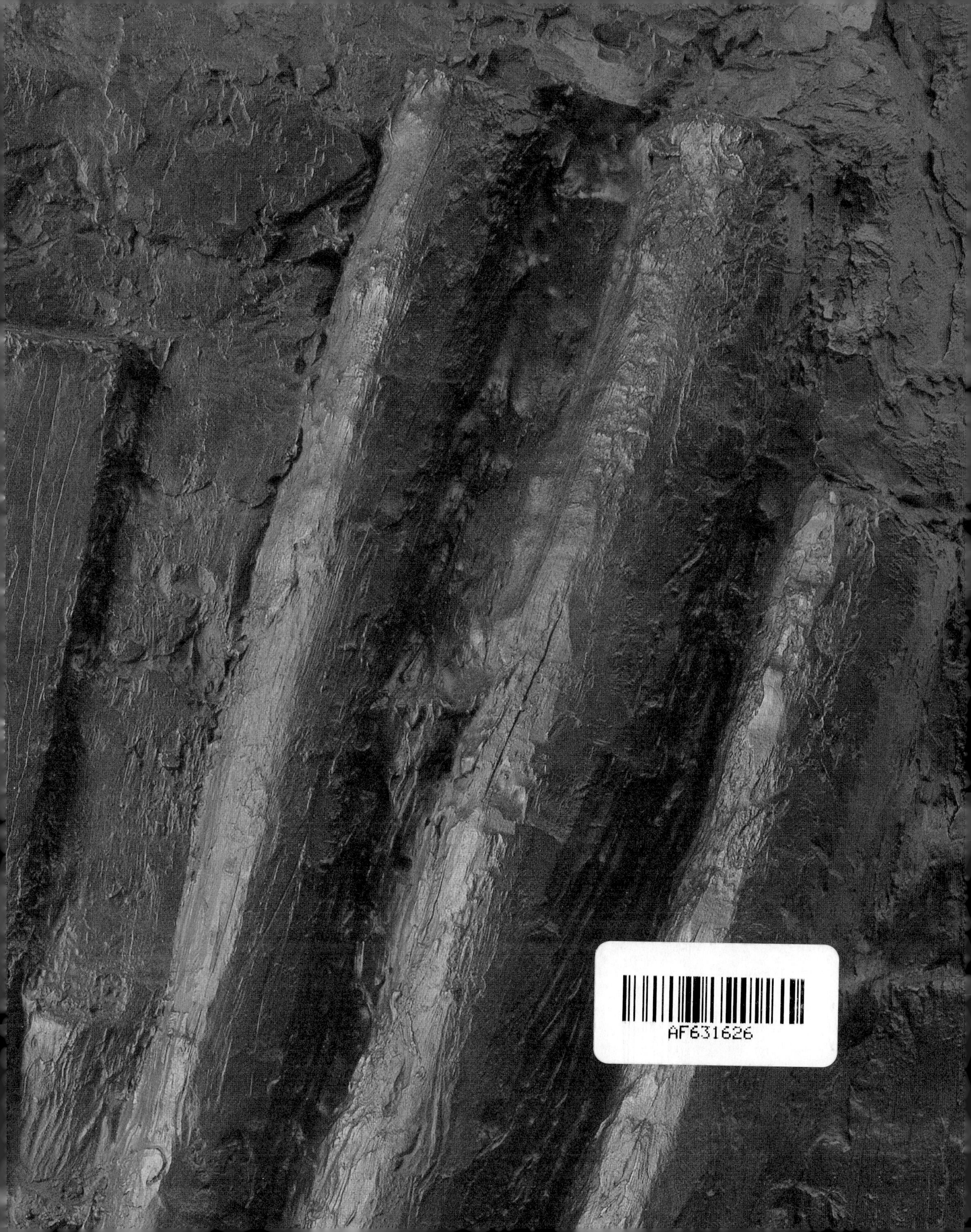

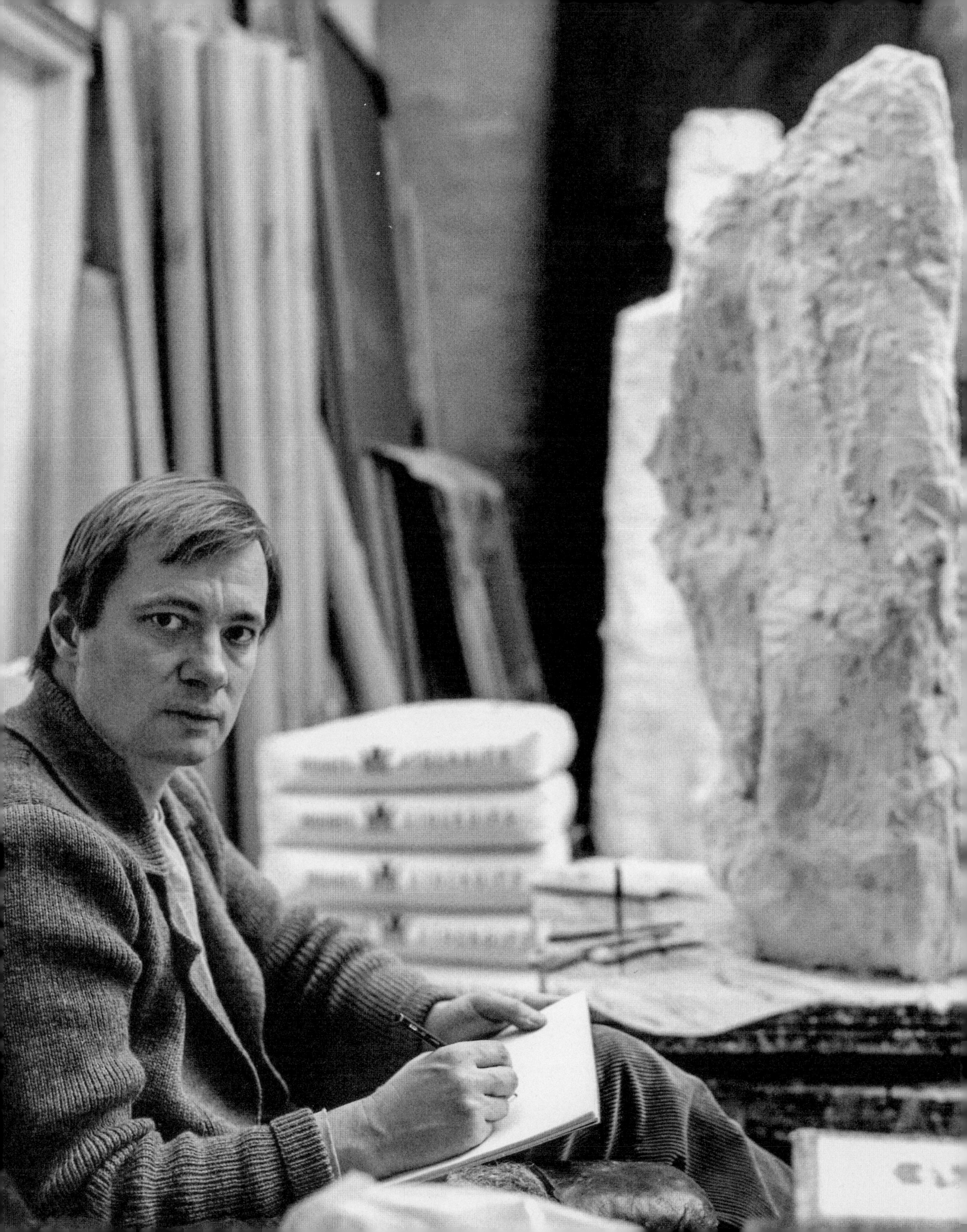

Per Kirkeby Bronze

The Louisiana holds the biggest collection of Per Kirkeby's (1938-2018) work anywhere. We have followed the artist and his work over many years. In the last two decades, the museum has mounted two comprehensive exhibitions of his work – *Paintings on Masonite*, in 2002, and *Per Kirkeby Louisiana 2008*, celebrating the artist's 70th birthday. The first exhibition took a look at Kirkeby's early work and its Pop-inspired imagery that once seemed capable of embracing the whole world – from the Vikings to the Maya, Prince Valiant to van Gogh, science to fairy tale. The 2008 exhibition was a retrospective, bringing together a great number of key works from international collections to establish a big picture of Kirkeby the painter.

Per Kirkeby – Bronze looks at the artist's bronze sculptures, which first saw the light of day in the early 1980s. He kept on making bronzes for the remainder of his career, ultimately working on a monumental scale, which is richly represented here. The exhibition also looks at Kirkeby's overall artistic process, examining the role of the sculptures not only in the artist's work but in how he worked.

Telling the story of Kirkeby's art, the exhibition spans sculpture, drawing and painting, complemented by the work of other artists with whom Kirkeby had a dialogue, including Willumsen, Giacometti, Fautrier, Leroy and Jorn.

As curator of this exhibition, I would like to thank Galerie Michael Werner in Berlin and Michael Werner personally, Galleri Bo Bjerggaard in Copenhagen and all the lenders without whom this exhibition would not be possible. Heartfelt thanks to the writers of this catalogue: Helle Brøns, Erik Steffensen and Ulrich Wilmes. Finally, I want to thank Ane Hejlskov Larsen for her great work in producing the catalogue raisonné of Kirkeby's paintings. While there is still a way to go, the work she has done so far is an invaluable contribution to the continuing engagement with one of Denmark's greatest artists.

Per Kirkeby died in 2018. He is missed as a friend and an artist. I can think of no better way to remember him than by making another journey into the world of his art.

Poul Erik Tøjner, Director

Foreword

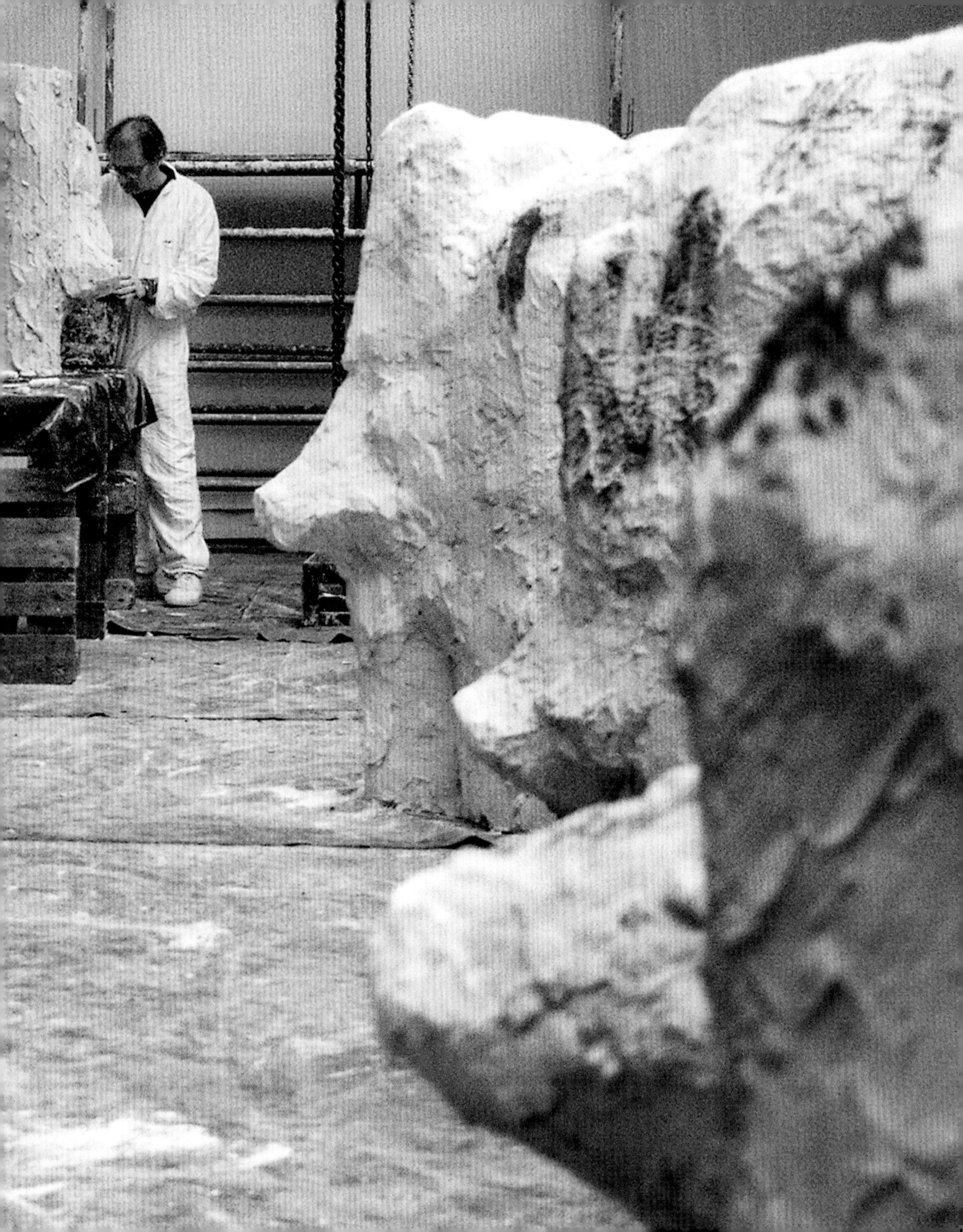

Introduction
Per Kirkeby – Bronze

Poul Erik Tøjner

An exhibition of Per Kirkeby's bronzes should, of course, be a presentation of the work in its own right. But what does "in its own right" really mean, when everything the artist did over a long productive life is intertwined, over time becoming the aesthetic universe of his oeuvre? This exhibition recognizes that Kirkeby's bronzes are perfectly capable of standing on their own. One, the large sculpture *Gate II* (1987) (p. 45), has for decades held the corner of the Louisiana's park where wood and open lawn meet at the edge of the bluff. However, any exhibition is also a take on, and an intervention in, the material, the work. Which takes us somewhere else, where Kirkeby's sculptures are more than just another part of the Louisiana's collection, alongside works by Moore, Calder, Ernst, Serra, Kwade, Lichtenstein and others. Presenting a large number of the artist's bronzes, *Per Kirkeby – Bronze* is also the story of how the artist worked and the role that the bronzes came to play for him. In turn, it makes us wiser about all of his work. And not just smarter academically. If an exhibition is about showing not lecturing, becoming wiser about Kirkeby's work simply means expanding our experience of it.

There are many signature elements in Kirkeby's imagery, their number increasing over the years. Once we see them, we cannot unsee them. And why should we? They are there for a reason. The reasons are many, even more so because the artist's existential history dovetails with the history of his era. Together, they make up Kirkeby's world, which we are now entering – through a bronze gate, as it were. Kirkeby was big on gates and their multiplicity of meaning: entryway, threshold, exit – yearning, overstepping, departure. "Venter på et klart tegn" (Waiting for a clear sign), he wrote in the corner of a drawing of a gate, in the early 1980s when perplexity was dictating his artistic agenda, or maybe lack of one.

In the late 1970s, young Kirkeby could look back on a productive period as a poet, filmmaker, performance artist, travelling geologist, painter and more. The list reveals an unusual and highly personal blend of inspiration from American Pop art and Minimalism, illustrated classics, archaeology from the land of the Maya, Grundtvig's Church in Copenhagen, the local alternative to the academy, Eks-skolen, the life of van Gogh, and westerns – all expressed in the signs of pictorial language, and with signs aplenty. Everything is a reference. Some make sense; others create meaning, new meaning through unexpected clashes. The artist's personal biography and an infinity of historical and contemporary role models are fed into his image duplicator – in machine formats: masonite boards measuring a standard 122 × 122 cm.

The artist is facing a possible international career, but the road ahead will not be paved with brightly coloured hard board. The new age and the new space, Europe, call for oil on canvas, real painting. Preferably, representational painting, like the work of the painters who became Kirkeby's colleagues and competitors: Georg Baselitz, Markus Lüpertz and A.R. Penck, all affiliated with Kirkeby's new, German gallerist, the unerringly discerning and influential Michael Werner.

Figurative painting. How do you go about that, when clipping figures from the existing images of pop culture is no longer enough? A great many historical forms seem passé; history painting and portraiture are things of the past. The younger Kirkeby had often polemically returned to the neo-realists of the day, who painted photographically, which is of no interest whatsoever to someone looking for the stuff of pictures, pictorial matter. The artist is in crisis. Not that he does not paint. The years around 1980 are productive ones. But he keeps turning out landscapes. And not even landscapes the viewer can inhabit. Wind and weather, mainly. Gestures, swirls, crosshatching, abrupt shifts, a space of movement or of being moved. Nature, we will call it for lack of a better word.

Figure, 1983
Plaster, Kirkeby's studio in Copenhagen, 1983

5

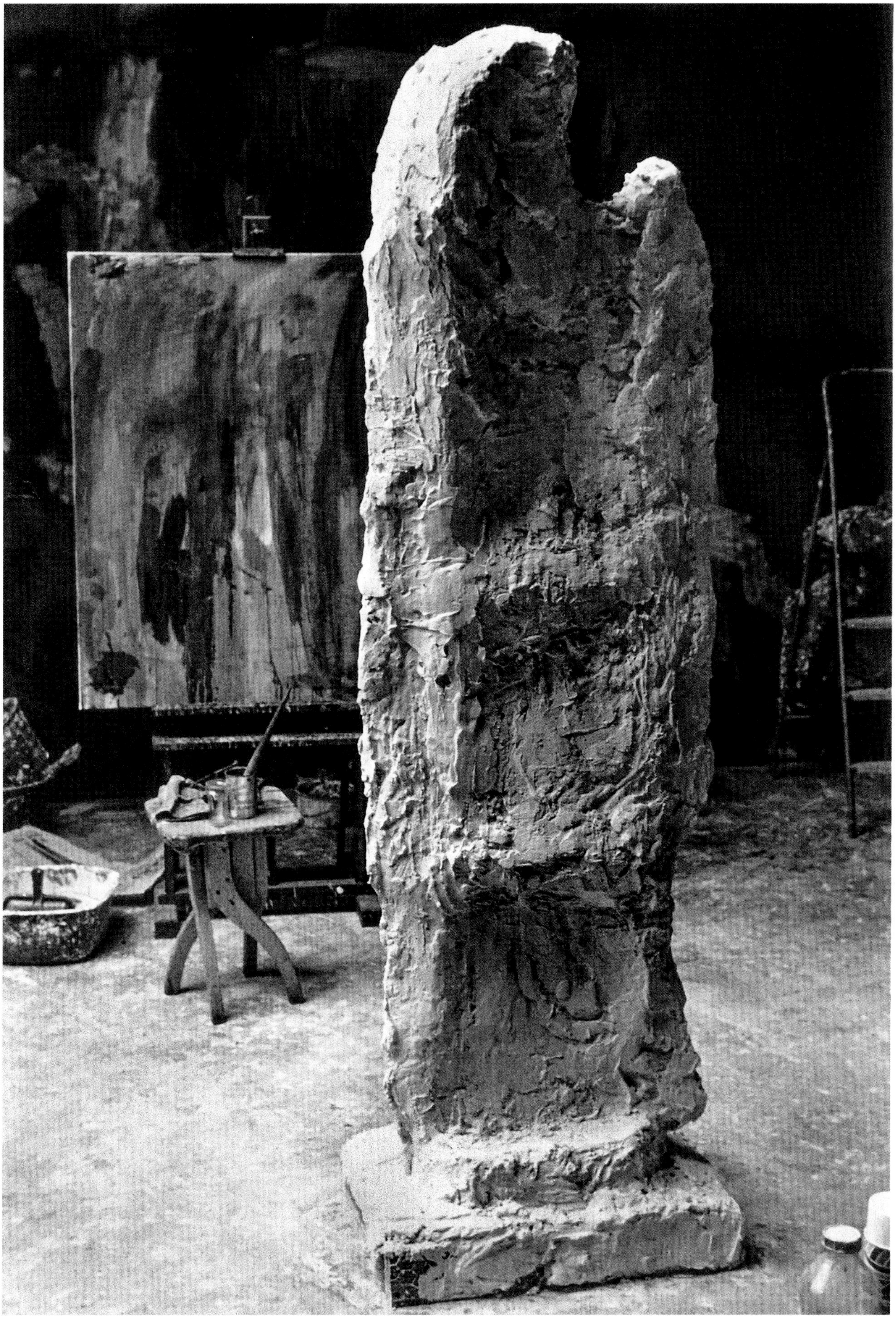

What should Kirkeby do? Artistic crises are a good thing, not least because all good art is crisis. The artist is waiting for a clear sign, and something is bound to come up. Kirkeby is struggling with two crises at this time. One is simply putting a figure in the picture. The other is deciding what that figure should be. Not the who, but the what. Anything, it seemed, could be poured into the image duplicator of the masonites, because the import of images was the whole point (though Kirkeby did, over time, see the obvious structures and themes underlying his choice of subjects: love, adventure, dream, yearning). In painting, however, the subject cannot be an occasion for painting, the artist reasoned, because the subject has a not insignificant story. So, what are meaningful subjects, now that the history of art can no longer be counted on to provide certified subject matter? How do you manage and master the balance between figurative presence and disappearance in painting that Kirkeby would eventually manifest as layer upon layer?

An intellectual breakthrough came in the early 1980s when Kirkeby appropriated the work of Auguste Rodin. Later, during a 1985 visit to the artist's museum in Paris, Kirkeby photographed his way through the collection.

From a strictly photographic point of view, these are mediocre pictures – blurry, crooked, grainy. Clearly, something else is at stake. The visit provided a vital artistic experience. For years, Kirkeby had been preoccupied with Rodin's famous *The Gates of Hell*; there is a cast outside the Kunsthaus Zürich, another in the Metropolitan Museum. Rodin worked on this sculpture for decades. It is grist for Kirkeby's mill. For one, it is a gate, a piece of architecture (Kirkeby made his first brick sculptures back in 1966, and architecture is foundational to everything he did), with all the attendant symbolism of a gate. Second, it represents the grand artistic project *par excellence* – what might, in a dramatic figure of speech, be called "the artist's struggle to extract a figure from the material." This consumed Rodin. Witness his many sculptures of figures seeming to grow out of the stone or the bronze, as in the work of Michelangelo. Third, in the Paris museum, Kirkeby noted how Rodin worked with fragments of bodies rather than classical statues (which he also mastered), and how those fragments are nonetheless perceived as whole figures. A head without a body is still a body. So is a shoulder or torso. They are corporeal. The point is that the whole figure can distract from the body itself by pointing to character and all its immediate anecdotal qualities (who was this person?), whereas the fragment can point to corporeality itself, the flesh, the body, presence rather than absence (no small feat for a fragment). That is Kirkeby's cardinal insight from the Musée Rodin. His paintings begin to look like the photographs he took at the museum: foggy spaces with corporeal volumes – a leg, an arm, a shoulder. Paris was well worth a mass. The road to Kirkeby's new paintings goes through Rodin and sculpture, the first stops on the way.

Kirkeby's take on the figure in the early 1980s is both visual and tactile. In his drawings (always leading somewhere, they are like travelling papers for the artist), he seeks basic forms, which he also models in clay or plaster. "Prototypes," he calls some of these drawings (p. 17). A face in profile, lip and nose, thighs, abdomen, arm, head – this is Woman, with the artist's then wife, Vibeke, at the core of his fascination and work.

Drawing in sketchbook, 1984

→

Contact sheet with Per Kirkeby's photos from the Rodin Museum in Paris, 1985

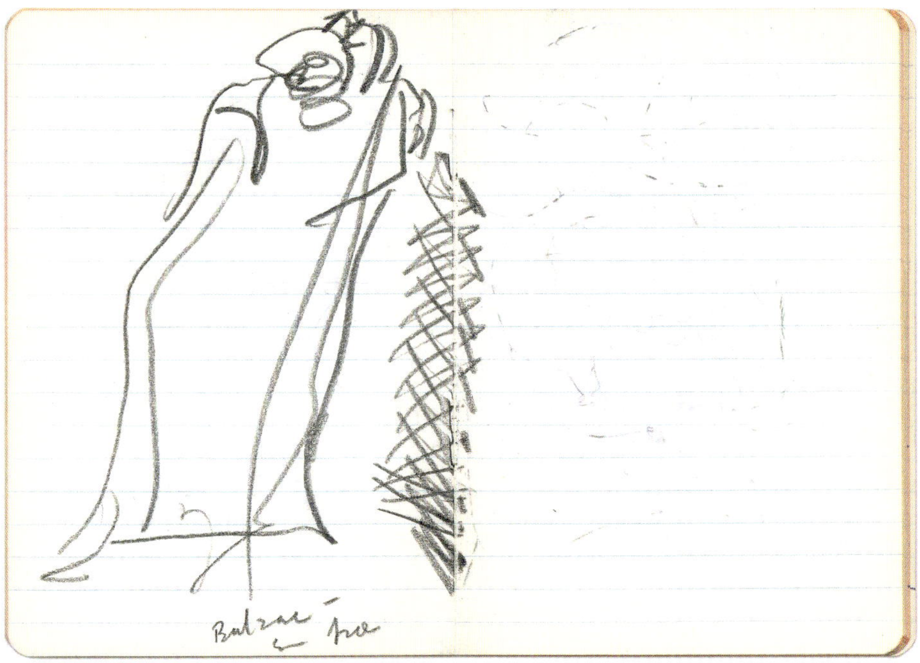

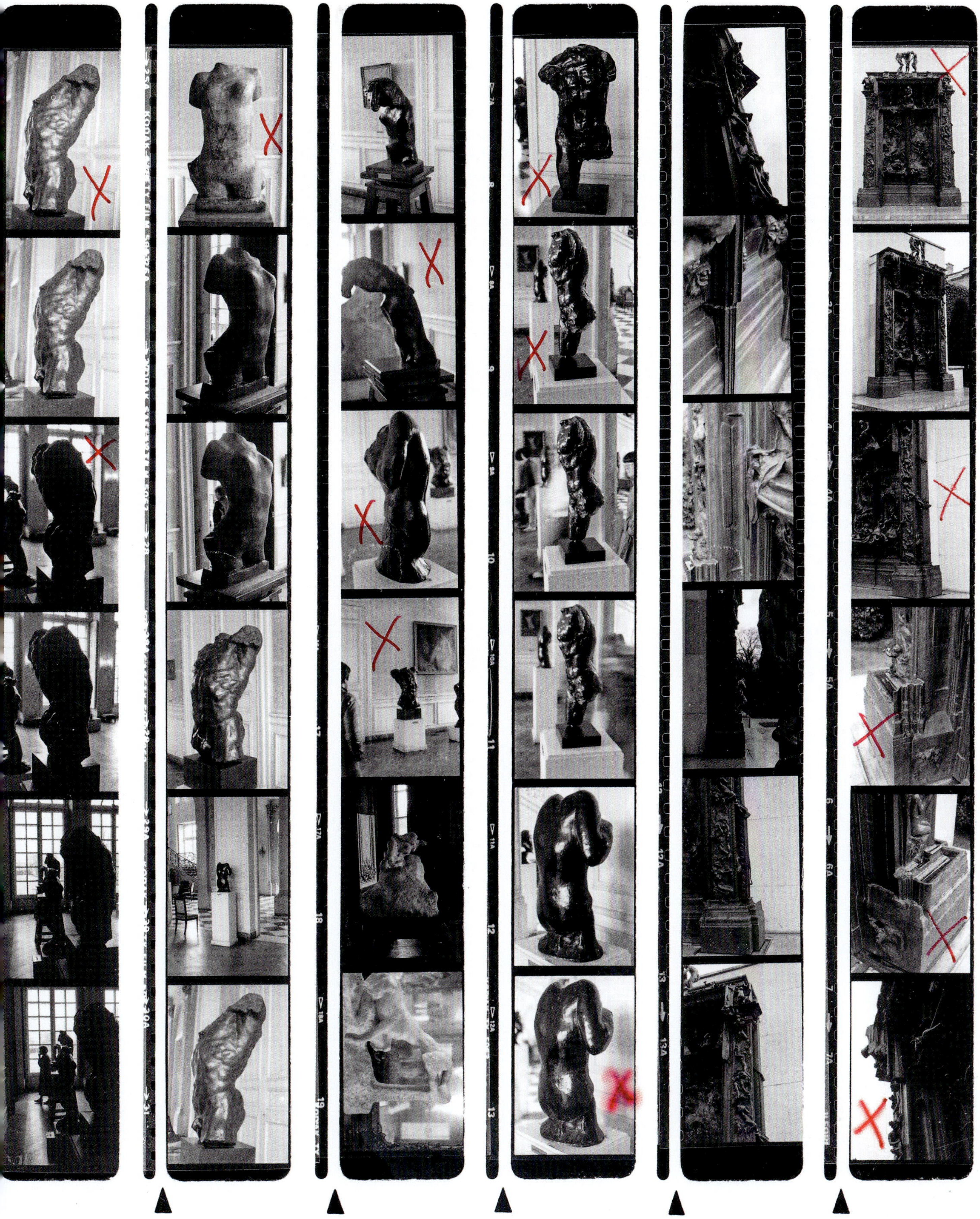

The artistic exploration of possibilities is undoubtedly erotic in origin, though that rarely shows in the finished work. Kirkeby sees in a new way. And what he sees he roots in sculpture – a highly physical process, where the work instantly closes, at the exact point when it is converted from plaster to bronze. This is a relatively new step for Kirkeby, who had always cherished the perspective of correcting, erasing and overpainting. When he works in bronze – and later when he substitutes oilstick for chalk in his blackboards, pictorial heir to the masonites – a more consolidating rhythm enters his work. His many scale models, some made in terracotta and later cast in bronze, testify to this, as well. Things are completed in an entirely different way now. Which is a boon, especially for searching souls.

Kirkeby often returned to these "formative years" in his painting, as the bronzes gave him a grasp of the figure that fed back into his paintings, ultimately providing a structure elevating them from gesture on canvas to something more substantial, fundamentally shaped by the science, geology, in which the artist was trained. "The sculptures are marching," Kirkeby said. A German critic dubbed this phenomenon "painter's sculpture," not just because a painter was doing sculpture but also because Kirkeby's (and other painters') treatment of the bronze surfaces looks painterly, like frozen brushwork. Kirkeby later signed off on this when he made his largest sculpture ever, *Sculpture for Copenhagen* (1997) (p. 98), which looks like nothing so much as a giant painting in bronze.

The figures are marching. But their entry into his paintings does not result in outright figure painting. What it does is free Kirkeby to approach landscape in a different way than before. Figures create space, and space creates landscape. This newwon security enables Kirkeby the painter to saturate his pictures with colour (the matter of colour). Many of us are familiar with these paintings, not least from the Louisiana's collection. They are big and immensely assertive in their beauty. We could say that the bronzes were a midwife for the artist. Bronze was *the* genre for him. But only in the beginning. Once Kirkeby had conquered a new field, he never abandoned it again. He kept iterating and expanding established practices. In his work, and in this exhibition, we see themes passing from drawing to etching to blackboard to sculpture to painting and back again.

No sooner did Kirkeby's early bronze sculptures march into his paintings as half-visible fragments of bodies than he expressed this newly conquered landscape of logs, stumps, caves – light and darkness in space – in bronze. His standing figures are barely distinguishable from standing trees. For the artist, nature and body become two sides of the same coin. We return to what we came from, ashes to ashes. The geologist slowly meets the theologian, but the unfinished business between the images – cultural and mythological images – postpones the meeting. The heroes must be forged in the fire, and these heroes are very much Kirkeby's own. In Baselitz's work, correspondingly, the heroes have given up and the picture has been turned upside down, not to create heaven on Earth but as testament to the gravity of Earth.

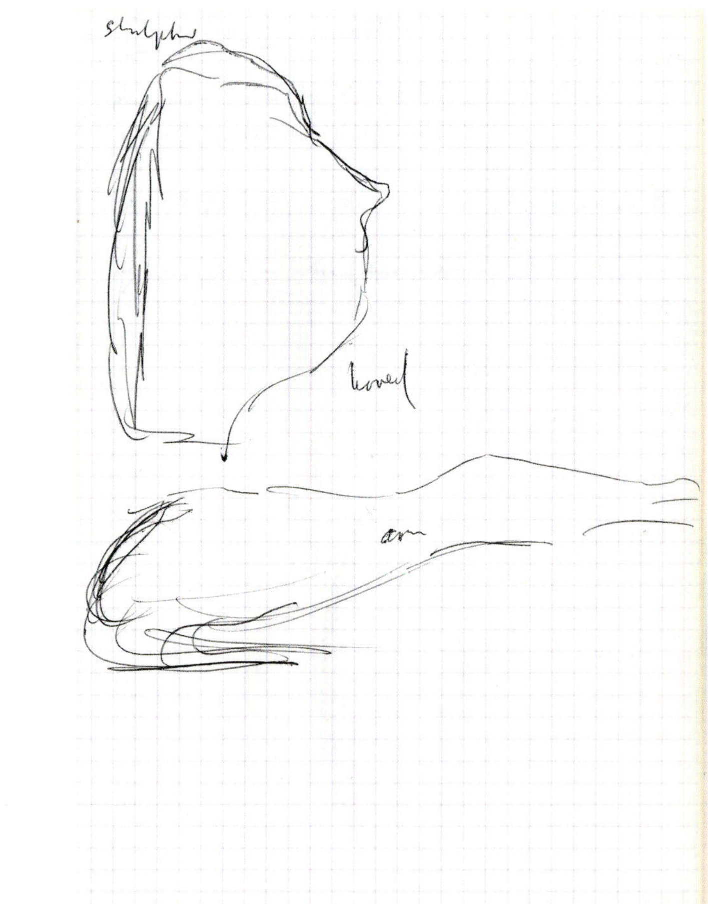

Drawing in sketchbook, 1982-83

→

Torso Offshoot, 1988 / 220 × 160 × 150 cm

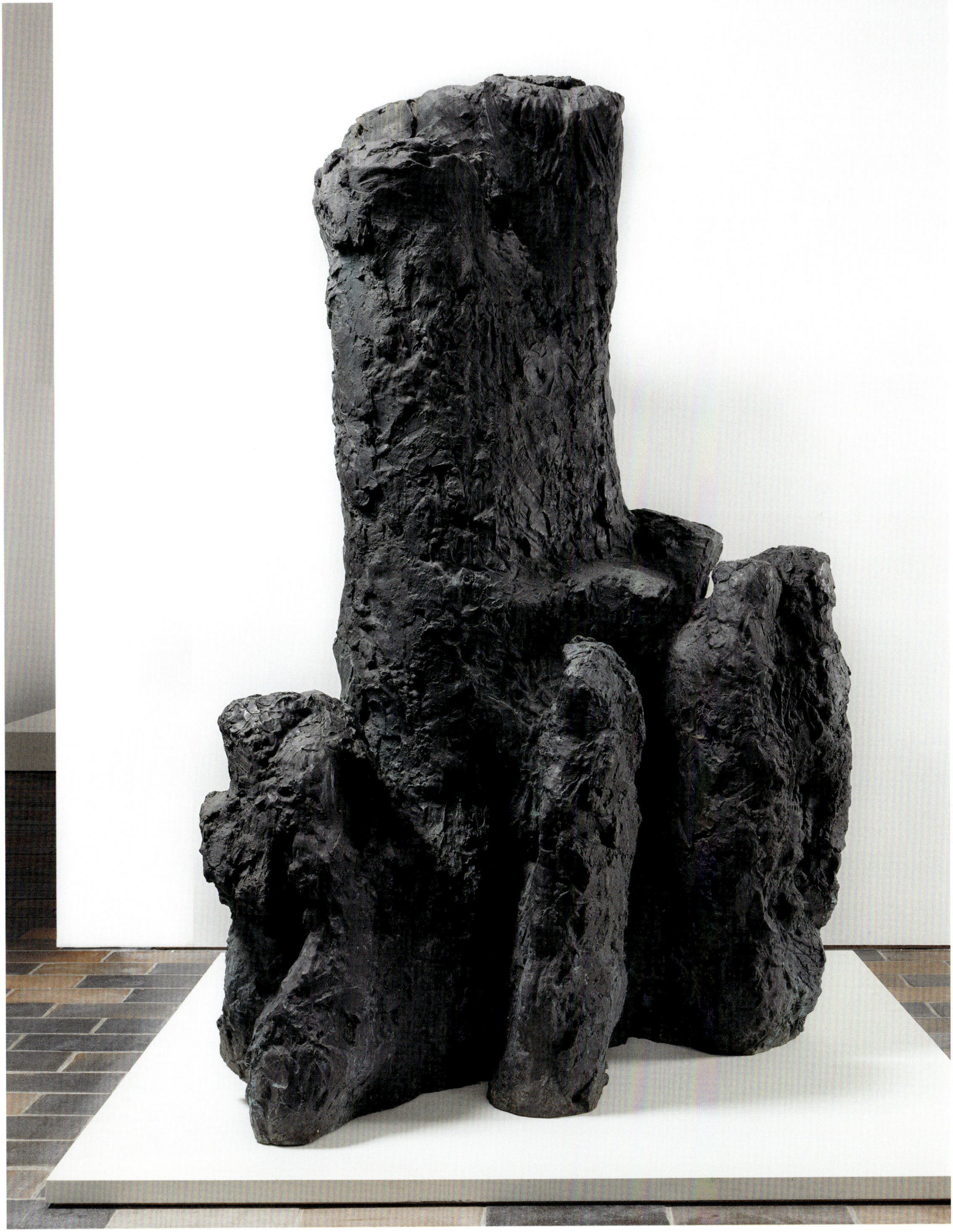

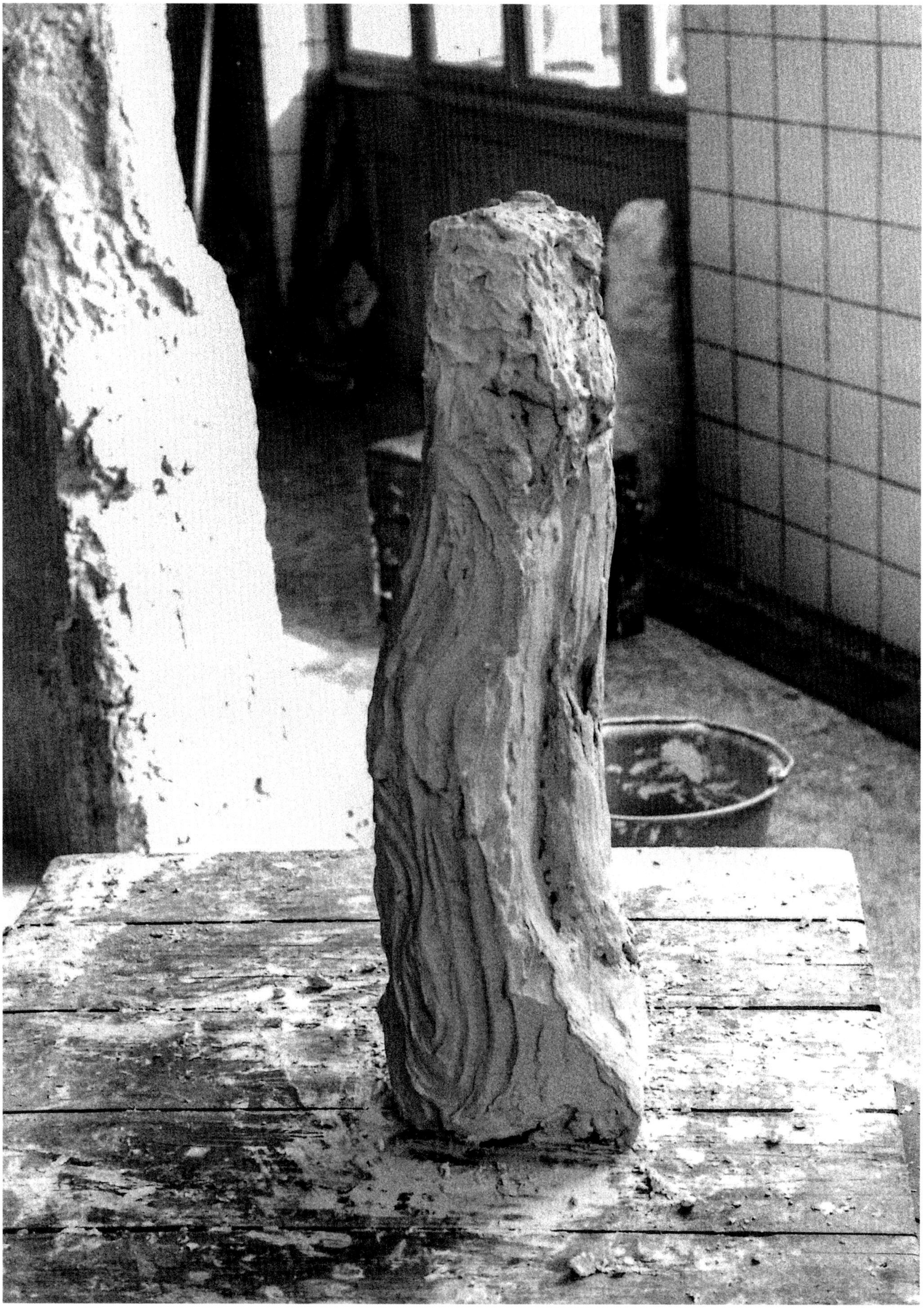

Three monumental sculptures testify to this: *Heracles*, 1991-92 (p. 54); *Large Stele* (with Jason), 2002 (p. 53); and *Laocoön*, 2012 (p. 56). You can read up on these mythological figures elsewhere in this catalogue (pp. 52-57). Suffice it here to point out that these three sculptures are both summaries of much of what is going on in Kirkeby's painting in the last half of his career and mighty manifestations of basic cultural narratives and art-historical signposts unfamiliar to most people today.
The three heroes, Heracles, Jason and Laocoön, all fare badly, in varying degrees. Heracles undergoes Herculean labours, superhuman trials, which includes fighting the endlessly regenerating Hydra. Kirkeby's artistic model for this is the Danish sculptor Rudolph Tegner's monument (p. 55) at Elsinore Harbour (Tegner himself struggled in his life). Jason was beset by trouble, and when he finally lay down to rest, he was crushed to death by falling beams, like the ones Kirkeby has piled at the top of the sculpture. Kirkeby's model here is Danish sculptor Thorvaldsen, with whom he carried on an extensive dialogue in his writing. Finally, *Laocoön*, Kirkeby's last sculpture, made over years of debilitating illness, is a both mournful and moving work by an aging artist who had always known his life was going to end, just not how. Kirkeby's point of reference is not the classical versions of the sculpture, I believe, but, mentally at least, El Greco's painting *Laocoön* (p. 56), which he included in his series of books on the great classics that had been most important to him, among them Delacroix, Giacometti, Picasso and Willumsen.
All three figures seem to be turning back into matter. Barely visible, they hold up the sculpture like a skeleton, repeating their role from the paintings, where appearance and disappearance are indistinguishable.

Sculptures in plaster in Per Kirkeby's studio on Læsø, c. 1981

A similar ambiguity marks Kirkeby's large cave sculptures. As we stand before them, are we waiting for something to appear or should we go inside? A powerful existential motif. An image of life choices per se and of the many moments in life when a person faces such situations. An occasion to think. Heavy and almost impossible to get around. Late in life, then, the artist finally articulated this cave, which had so often preoccupied him, from his first masonites to his late work. *Resurrection* (pp. 46, 77), he called his big sculpture for Frejlev Church. The cave now becomes the empty tomb. Such an explicit designation was unusual for Kirkeby, who for long periods was a classic "Untitled" artist. Perhaps it was just a sign to look in a specific direction, Christianity, which had become a powerful narrative for Kirkeby over the years, not least because of the imagery produced by the Church over the centuries.

Standing before these giant Kirkeby sculptures, we may even feel divided between experiencing them as physical accumulations of matter in space and making out meaning or familiar elements in them. What does this experience actually involve? Reading the sculpture? Or is it something else, brought on by, or perhaps even in spite of, what we recognize? Kirkeby's interest in, and personally acquired knowledge of, art history (from reading, but much more so from travelling around Europe) takes up a lot of space. Though it might seem absurd regarding monumental bronze sculptures, I cannot help but think that even they, in a sense, propel us further into history. This is a bit like Kirkeby's drawings, which are searching, as if they want to get themselves over with in order to move on to a different expression. Involving the viewer in a similar way, they have the character of signs pointing to something (else).

This is obviously absurd regarding the sculptures, because it reduces them to mere, and rather megalomaniac, signposts. Nonetheless, letting even these massive sculptures march back into the space of painting is an aid in recognizing the painterly dimension of the sculptures' material, the qualities of their folds, light and shadow – and how they hold both light and shadow. The material creates images. Incessantly. Which is not an unwelcome experience for a visual artist. Or a museum visitor.

All the same, let us dwell for a moment on the above thought that the sculptures are more sign than action. Over the years, an increasing number of signs, or emblems, appear in Kirkeby's art – in his sculpture, painting and all the other genres. The sculptures begin to point to something the moment Kirkeby lets go of the body as a universal and anonymous theme – head, arm, torso – and returns it to the great pictorial system of mythology and narrative. Mythology and narrative are collective entities shared by people within a culture. On this point, the artist is ambiguous. He raids the inventory of art's history, but he privatizes the venture in a number of ways.

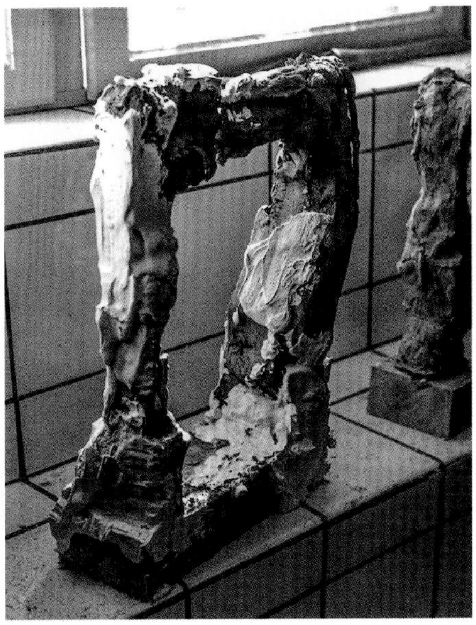

The motifs – beam, tree stump, etc. – become existential signatures on a map, *his* map. Sometimes verging on a psychological scenography of the artist's inner drama, it is resolved, transformed into emblem, language. This is evident in the sculpture series *Inventory* (pp. 90-91), as Kirkeby (re)creates all his figures in stylized form without a trace of searching, and in the *Opera Reliefs* (pp. 78-83), exhibited here in the artist's preferred black version, as a final merger of picture (on the wall) and sculpture. Incidentally, this makes the two paintings (pp. 84-87) he made while working on the reliefs the world's biggest footnotes to a work.

The two paintings, which belong to the Louisiana, are immensely interesting when discussing the experience of Kirkeby's world of signs as an act of decoding rather than immersion: the reliefs are a montage of thematic fragments from the whole Kirkebyesque narrative (four sketches for the reliefs are also on display), revealing how Kirkeby unfurls the work's etymology, telling (himself and us) where the elements are from and what they are pointing to. So do the *Opera* paintings. What do they not do? They do not offer the viewer to inhabit their sensuous irresolution, because they have none. They are like reading a dictionary instead of a novel. Even so, these pictures are important for understanding Kirkeby's work, because they identify – if, perhaps, negatively – what he is capable of doing in bronze and as a painter *beyond* the signs and the references to the history of art and culture and his personal history.

Large Head with Arm, 1983
Plaster, Per Kirkeby's garden on Læsø, 1983

Two roads open up for the viewer in encountering the clear Kirkeby – the artist of the *Inventory* series, the reliefs, in their relative clarity, and the 3 × 5 metre painted instruction board. While we can only guess why Kirkeby made the two big paintings, we can note that the experience he gained from it enabled a return to the productive, unclear world of painting as a counterpoint to the many references. Now we sense what is not there, the "painting" that opens up space instead of speaking.

In conclusion, let us swing by the great kink in art's history made by the so-called Iconoclastic Controversy of 9th-century Byzantium, which occupied Kirkeby throughout his life. The iconodules loved images and hence lost sight of the one true Creator, while the iconoclasts fought against the seductive power of images in order to direct the senses towards a higher reality behind appearances.

Kirkeby is at heart an iconoclastic painter, one who does not glorify the physical image but wants to send the viewer further, into and out of the image, in every which direction. Iconoclasm explains his distrust of realism in painting and of clearly figurative (instead of fragmented) sculpture, as well as his love of works of art in which it is impossible to tell if something is appearing or disappearing. But what about all the elements that populate his late pictures, reliefs and sculptures, as readable signs? They may seem a bit heavy-handed, like a litany of symbols. How do you escape the grip of reading and decoding, and arrive at a sensation of the picture as generous, providing more than words and signs, opening up an experience of the picture as more than vocabulary, taxonomy and periodic system?

There must be another way for the viewer, and the viewing, than immediately identifying the trademark Kirkebyesque elements in the paintings and sculptures. Lingering on the tree stumps, now that the trees themselves have been put to death, as it were, is not much of an experience. What is the other way? It could be letting the material qualities of the work speak with unbridled force about another world than the historical universe of figures, letting sensibility grow and sensation take over, despite the recognizable elements. Then we are back at a familiar chapter of art history, where conventional subjects freed the painter, and the viewer, to concentrate on painting itself. Cézanne's apples on an angular cloth on a tabletop – anyone can tell they are apples. Once that is done, the painting can begin.

Therein lies the great liberation, which is also the true abyss. Sensation *is* an abyss, a statement about other spaces than that of description and the described, spaces beyond our media of orientation. Such spaces lie like a shadow, or a light, across Kirkeby's work, in places where we seem to momentarily lose our footing. Describing that experience, in his brief book on Bellini, another volume in his series on the classics, the artist notes that the power of the pictures comes from all the things that do not belong to the Christological inventory – the portrait of the crucified Jesus – and from the way in which the rocks, landscape and sky are painted. Colour. Empty areas that have fullness, the fullness of colour. As in the work of Fra Angelico. That is what speaks to the viewer, beyond the narrative. There, and here, Kirkeby's art is for everyone, not just the initiated.

Poul Erik Tøjner, Louisiana director. Curator of exhibitions of the work of Per Kirkeby, in 2002 and 2008, and author of books on Kirkeby's paintings and sculptures.

13

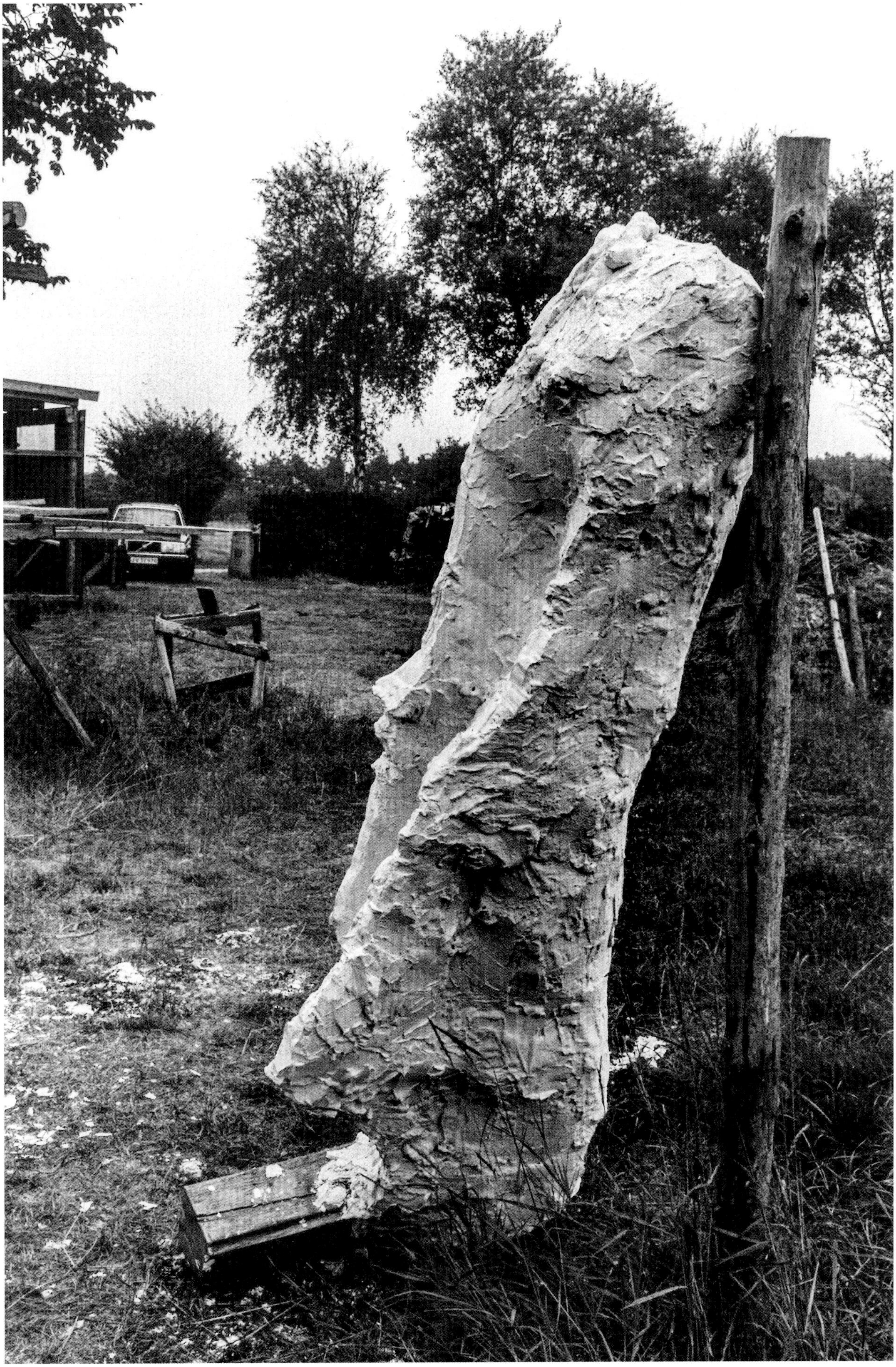

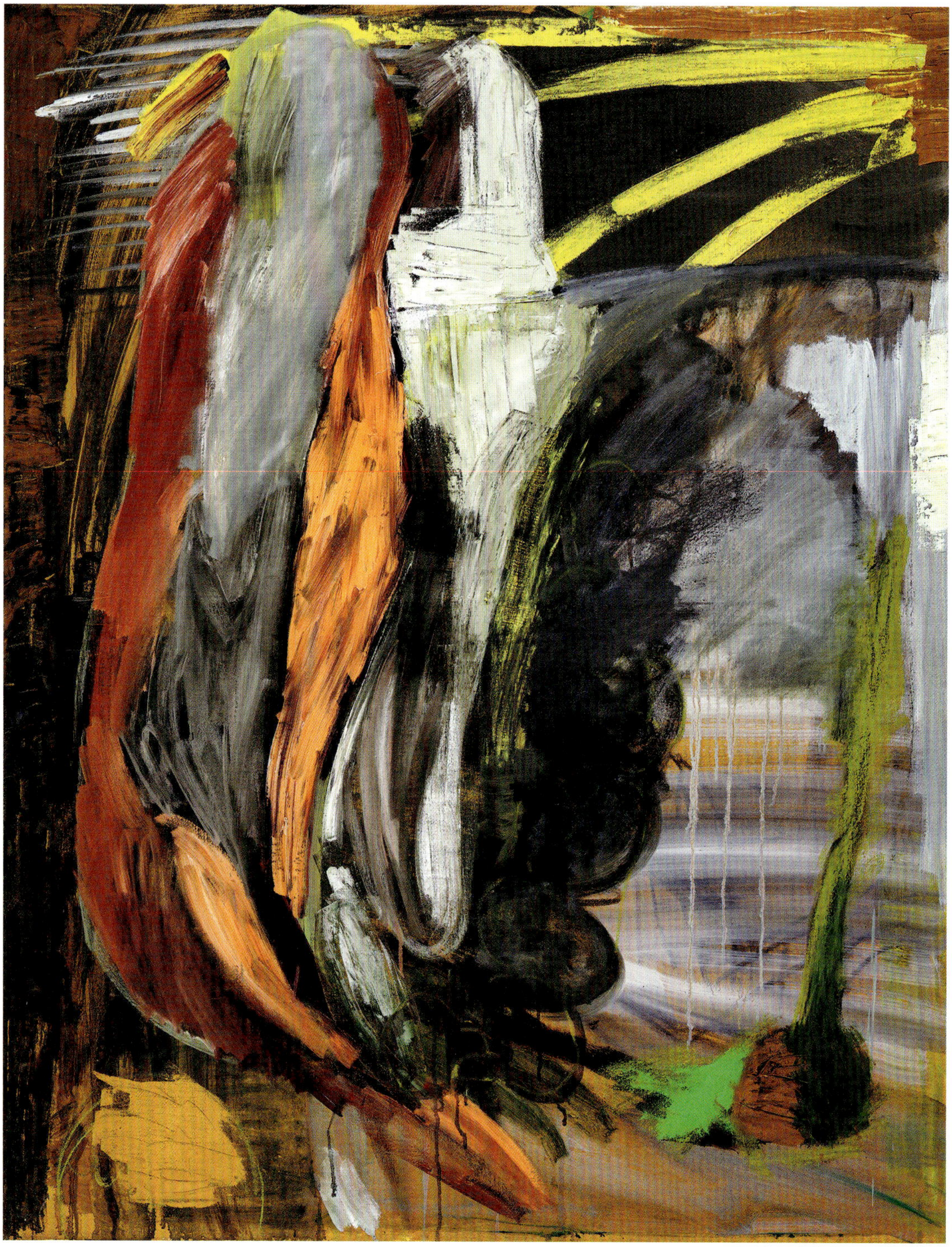

Vibeke (Naples Yellow), 1982 / 130 × 100 cm
→
Large Head with Arm, 1983 / 199 × 82 × 40 cm

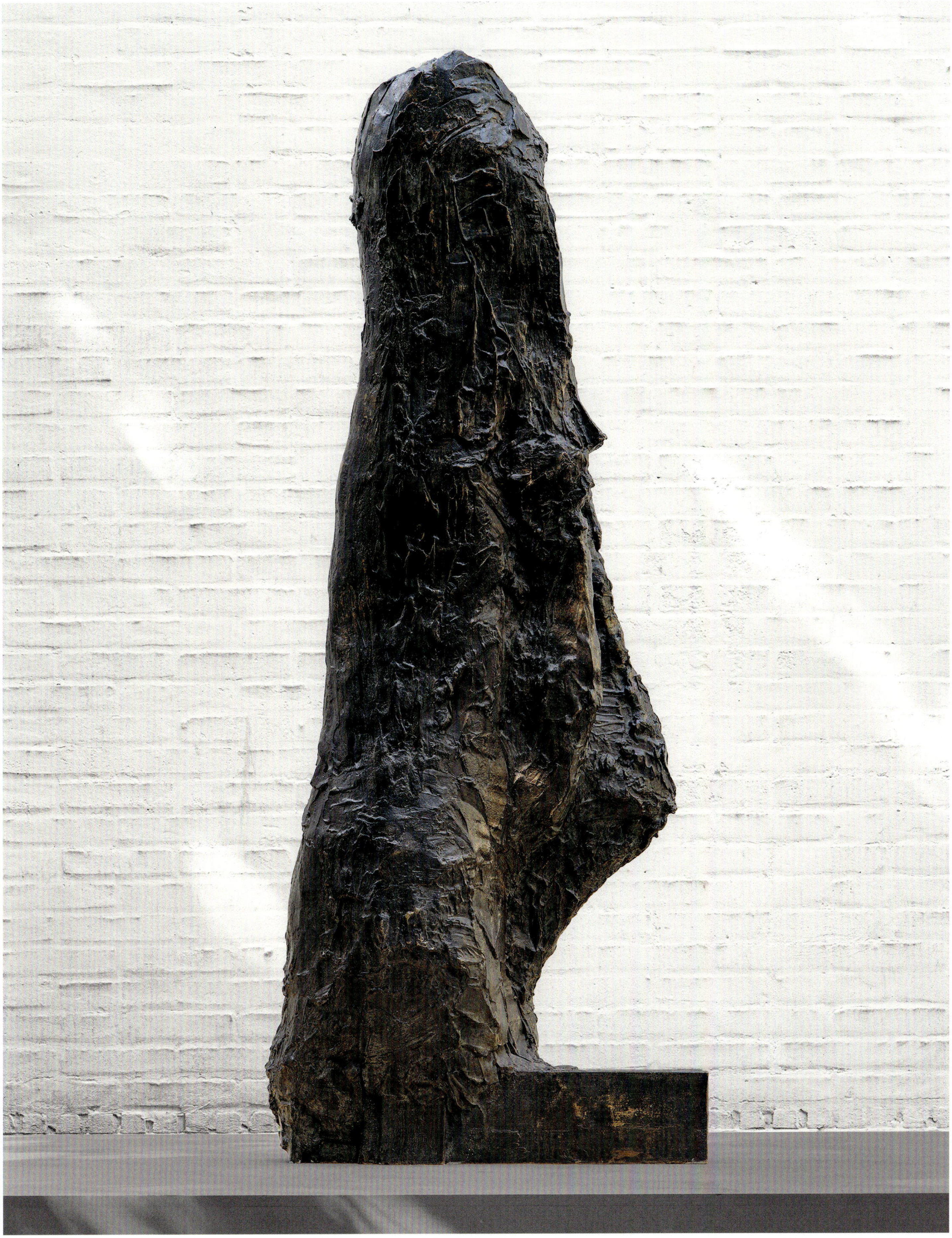

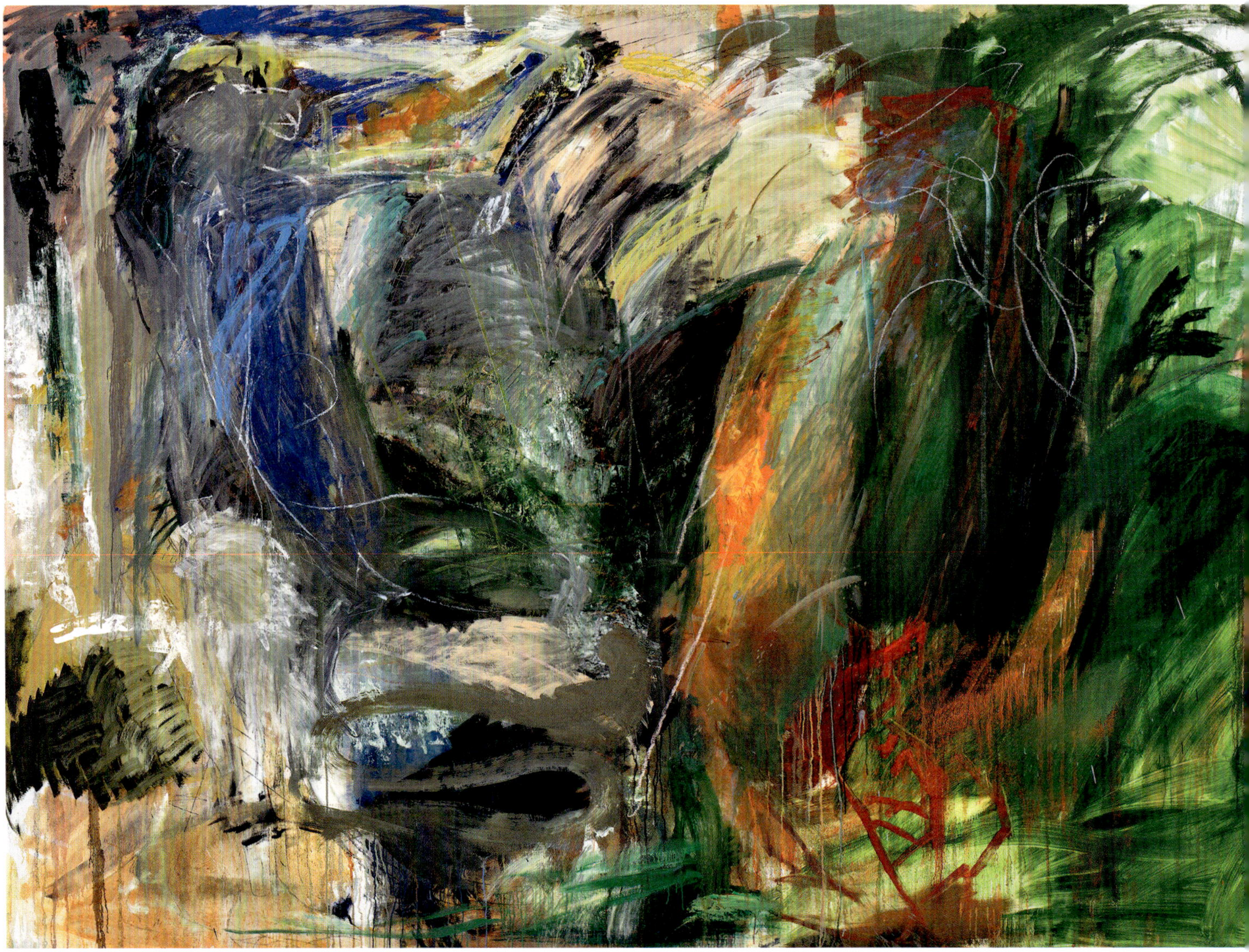

Untitled, 1979 / 208 × 278 cm

→

Untitled (Karlsruhe), 1983 / 48 × 36 cm

Untitled (Karlsruhe), 1983 / 48 × 36 cm

Untitled (Karlsruhe), 1983 / 48 × 36 cm

Prototype 29, 1982 / 47 × 34 cm

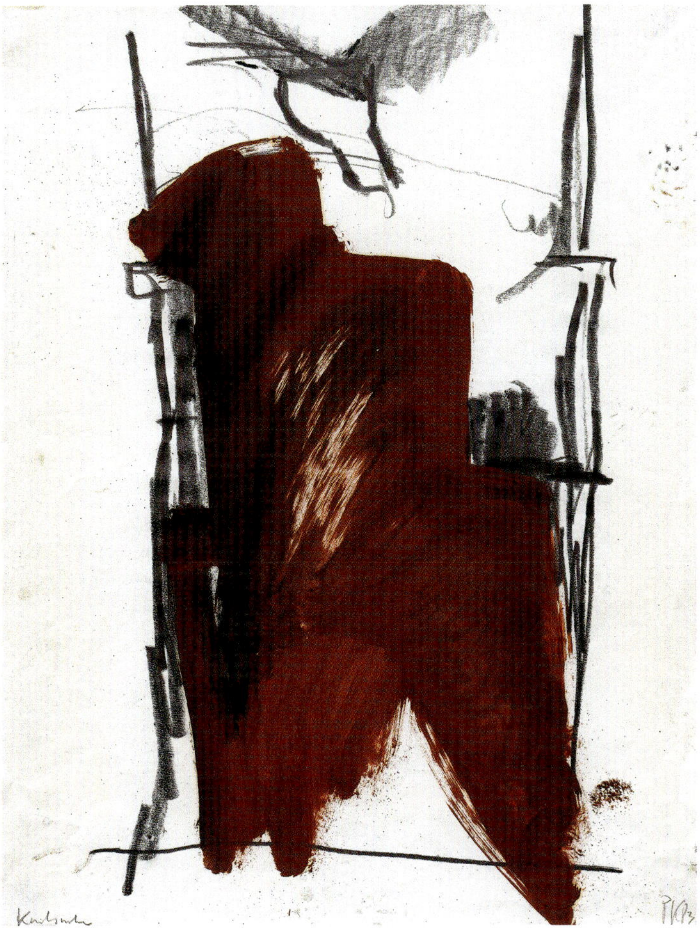

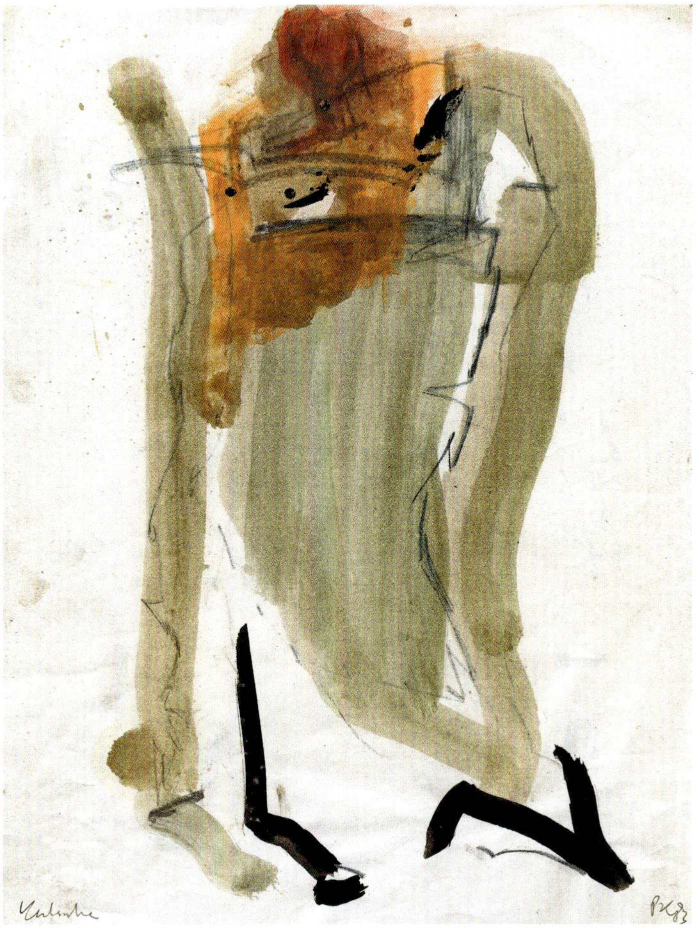

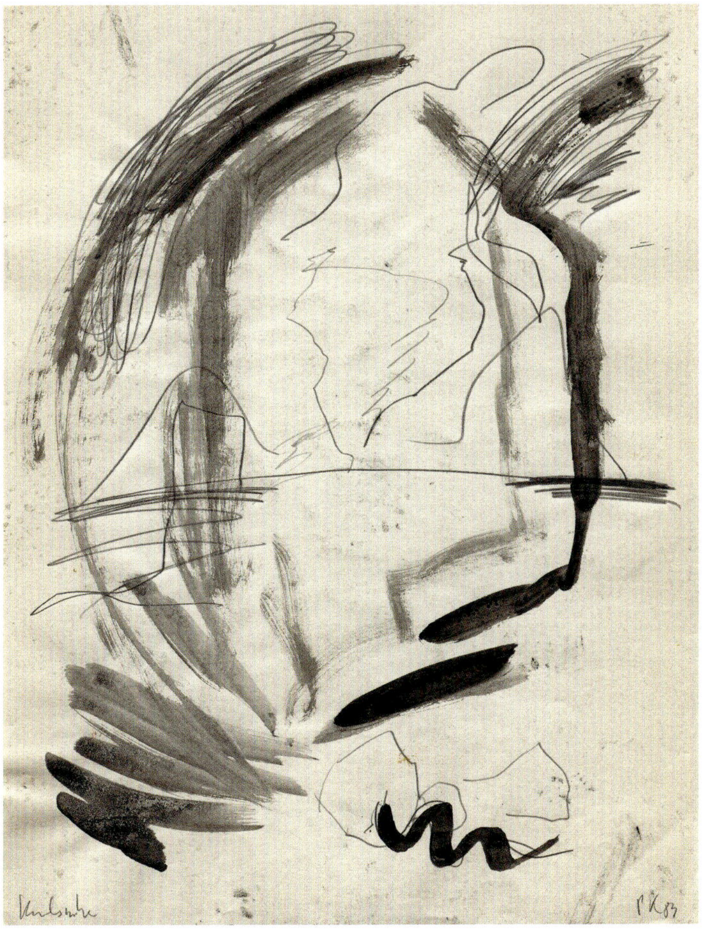

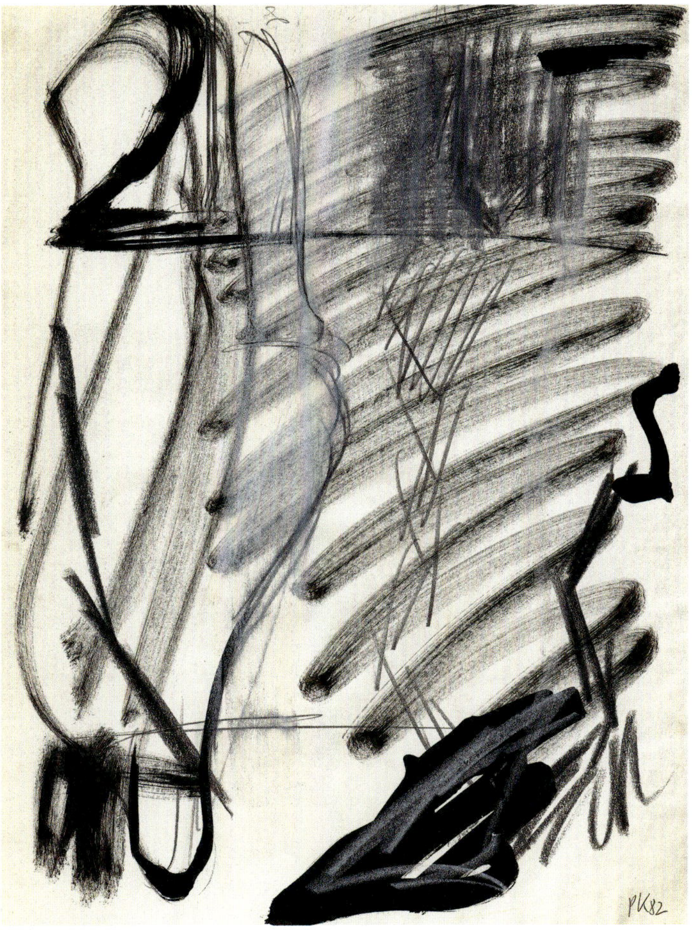

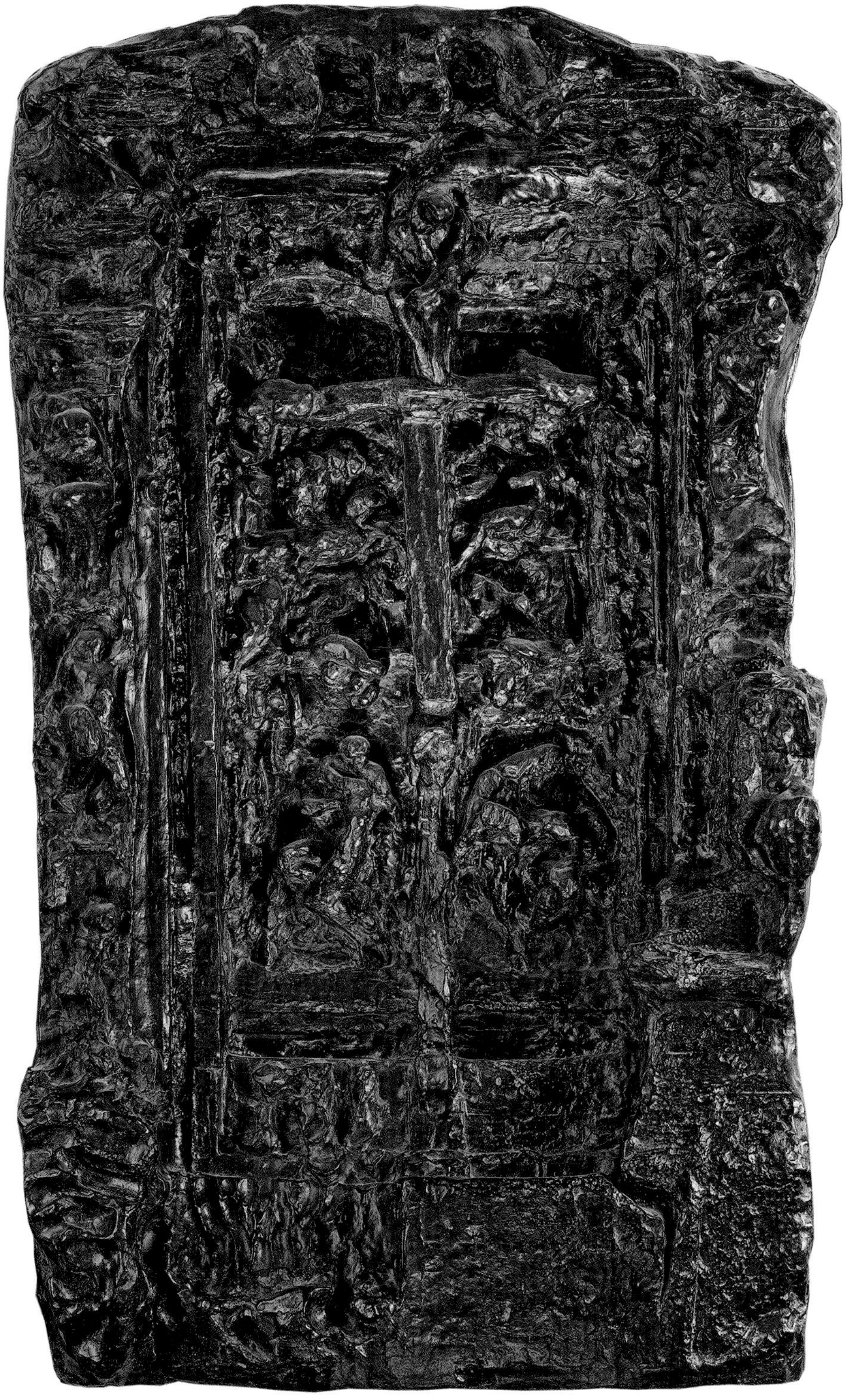

Model: Gate, 1981 / 30 × 29 × 16 cm
Gate, 1981 / 36 × 24 × 15 cm
←
Auguste Rodin
Troisième maquette pour la Porte de l'Enfer
c. 1881-82 / 110 × 74 × 28 cm

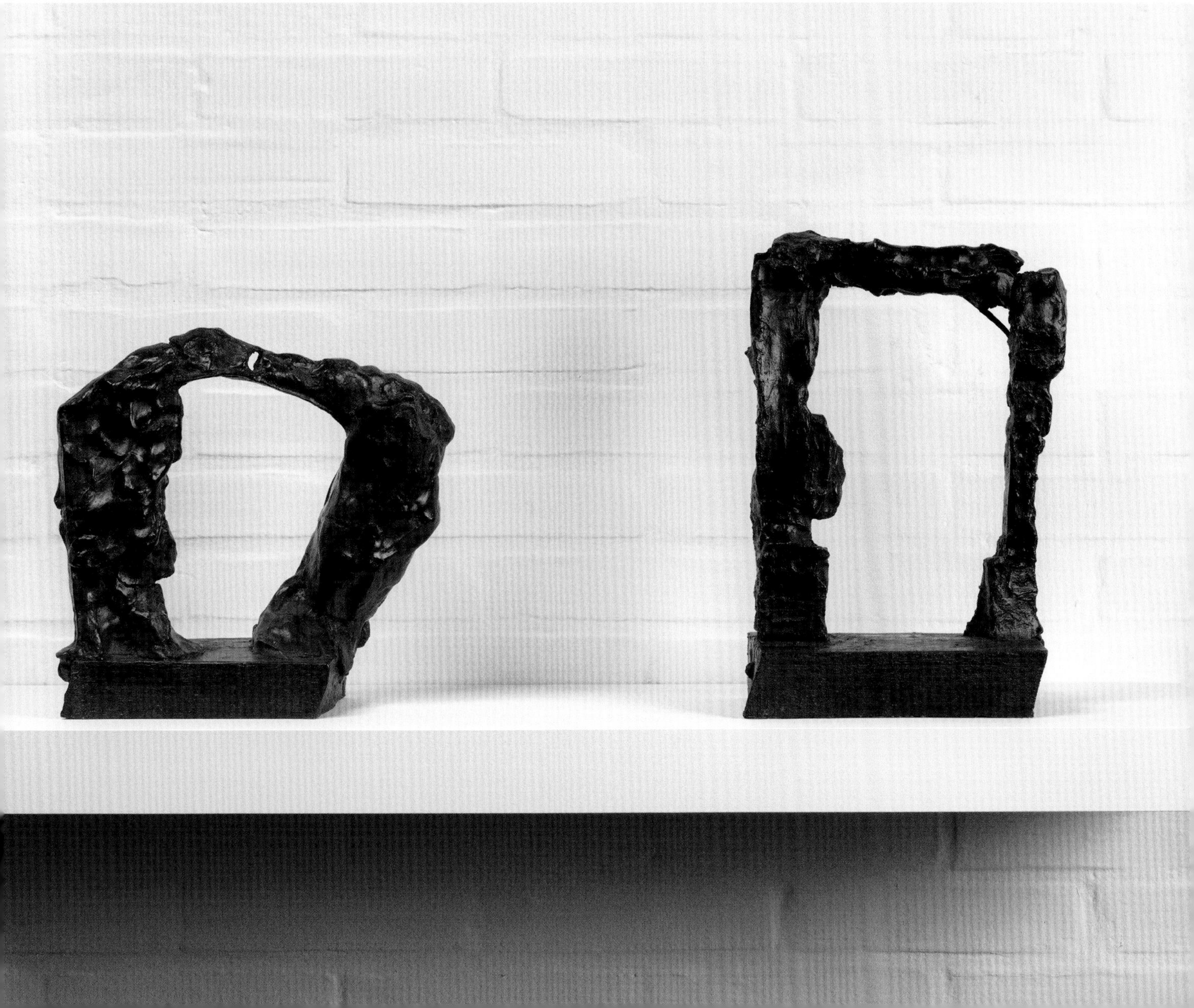

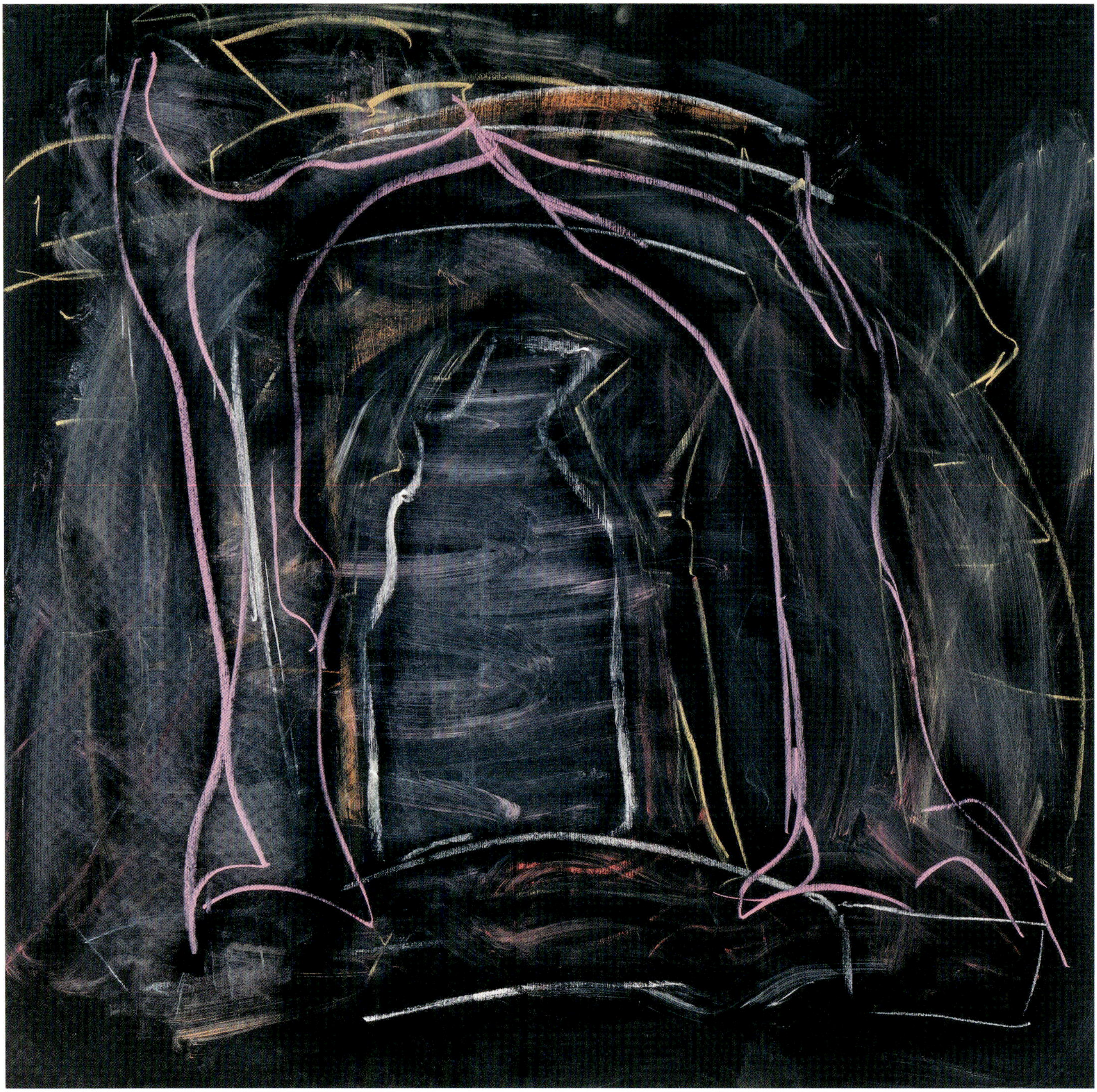

Untitled, 1985 / 122 × 122 cm
→
Head and Arm: Gate, 1984 / 85 × 83 × 68 cm

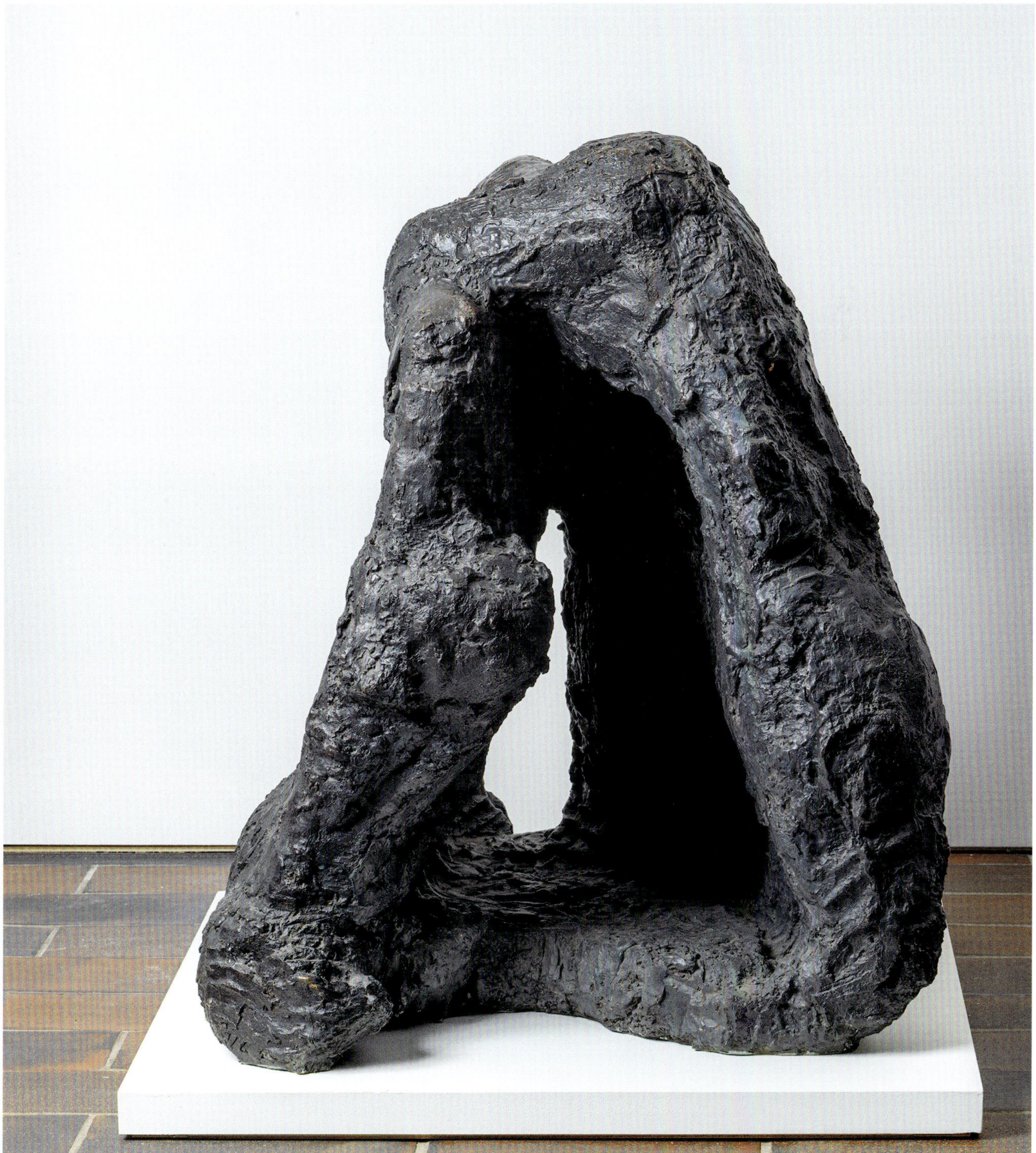

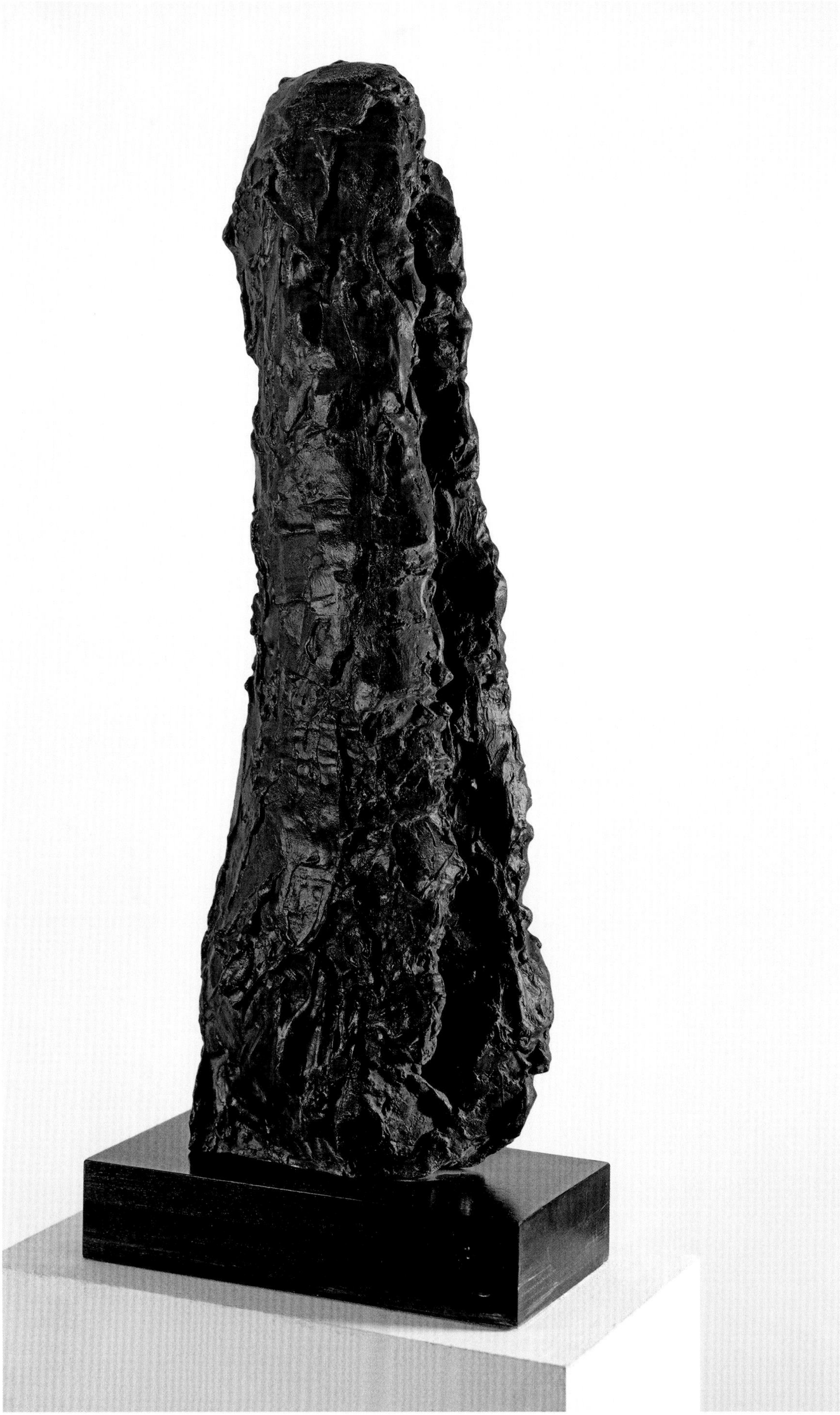

Model: Two Arms I, 1981 / 28 × 36 × 19 cm
Arm and Head no. XIII, 1984 / 56 × 28 × 16 cm
←
Arm, 1983 / 88 × 16 × 31 cm

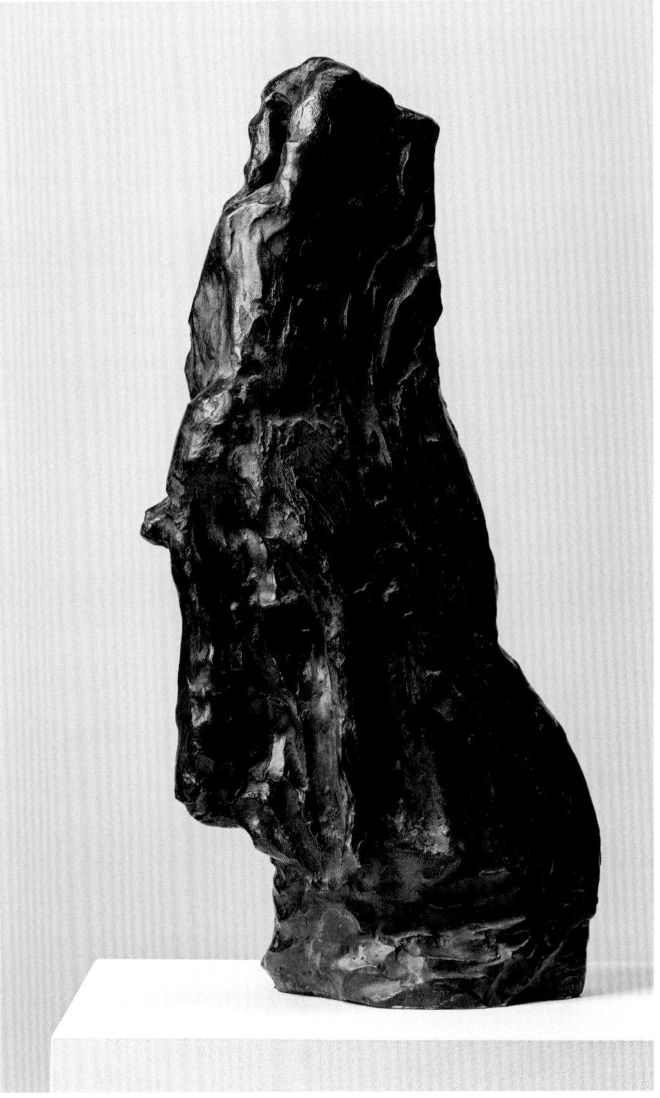

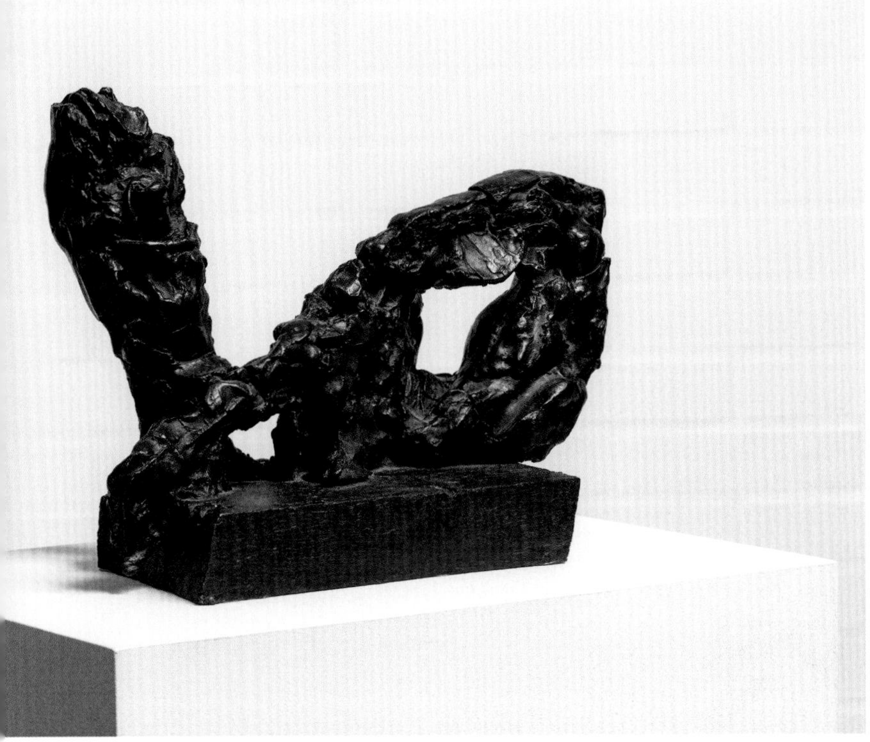

Mother and Child, 1983 / 201 × 201 cm

→

Torso II, 1983 / 196 × 122 × 48 cm

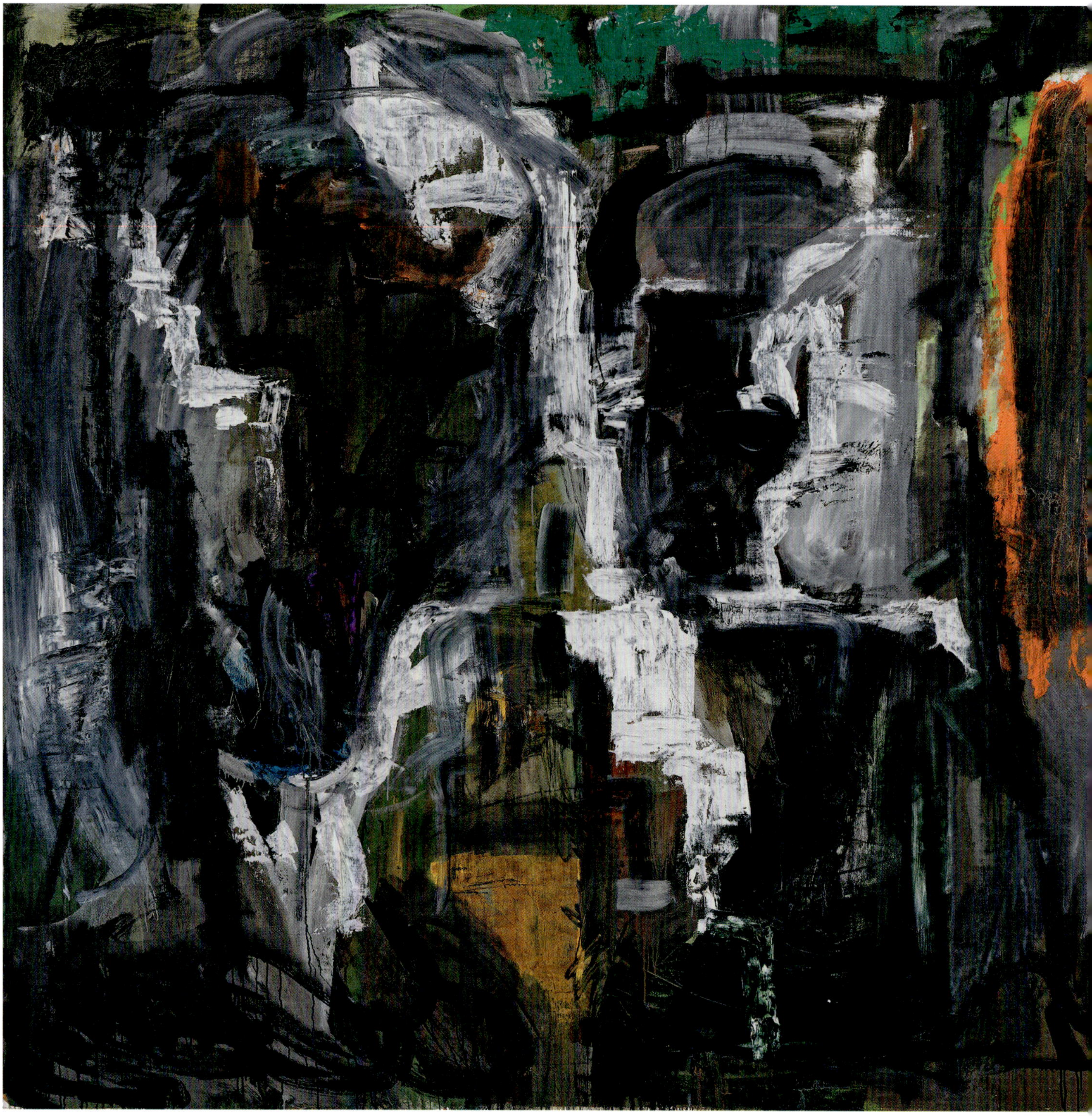

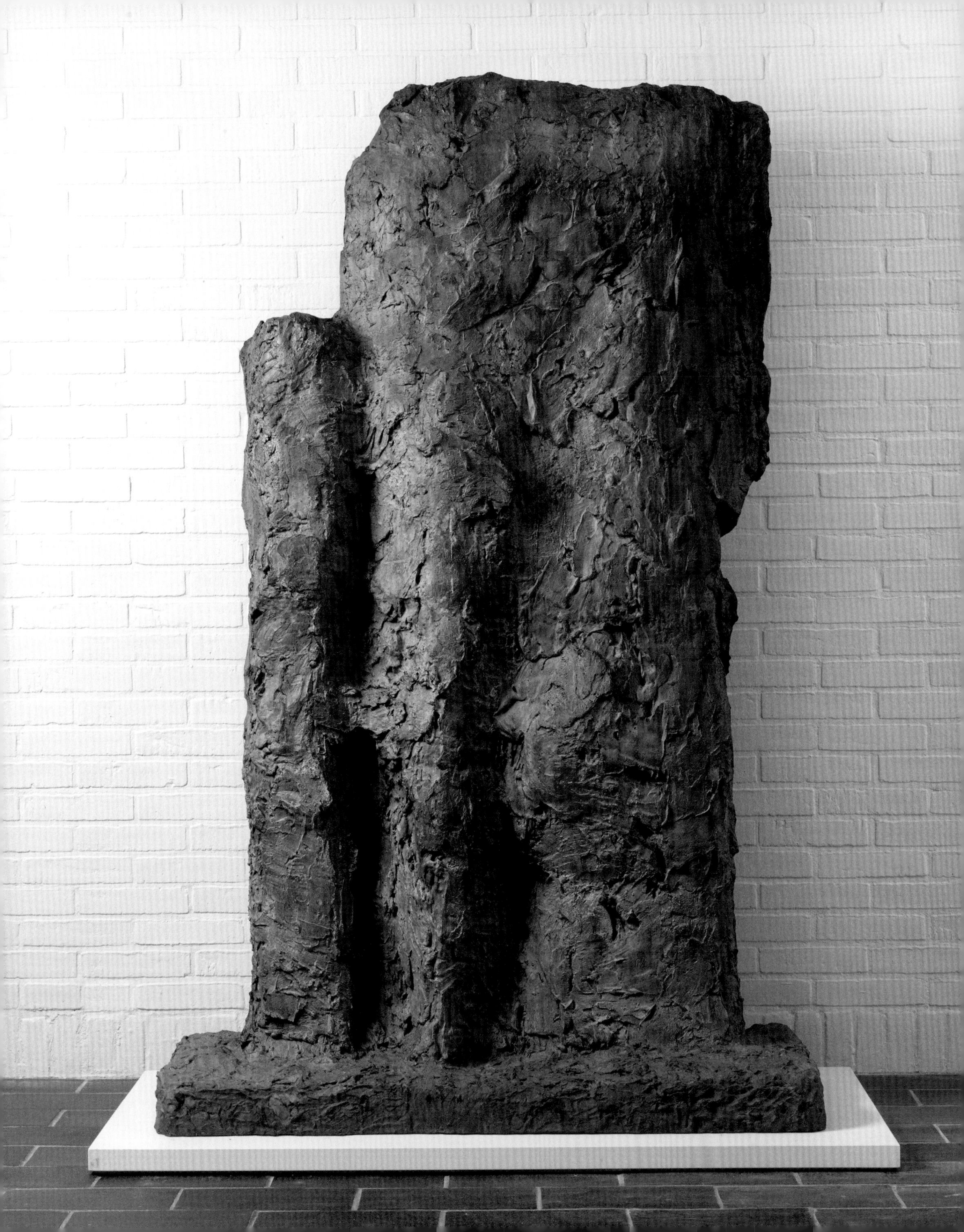

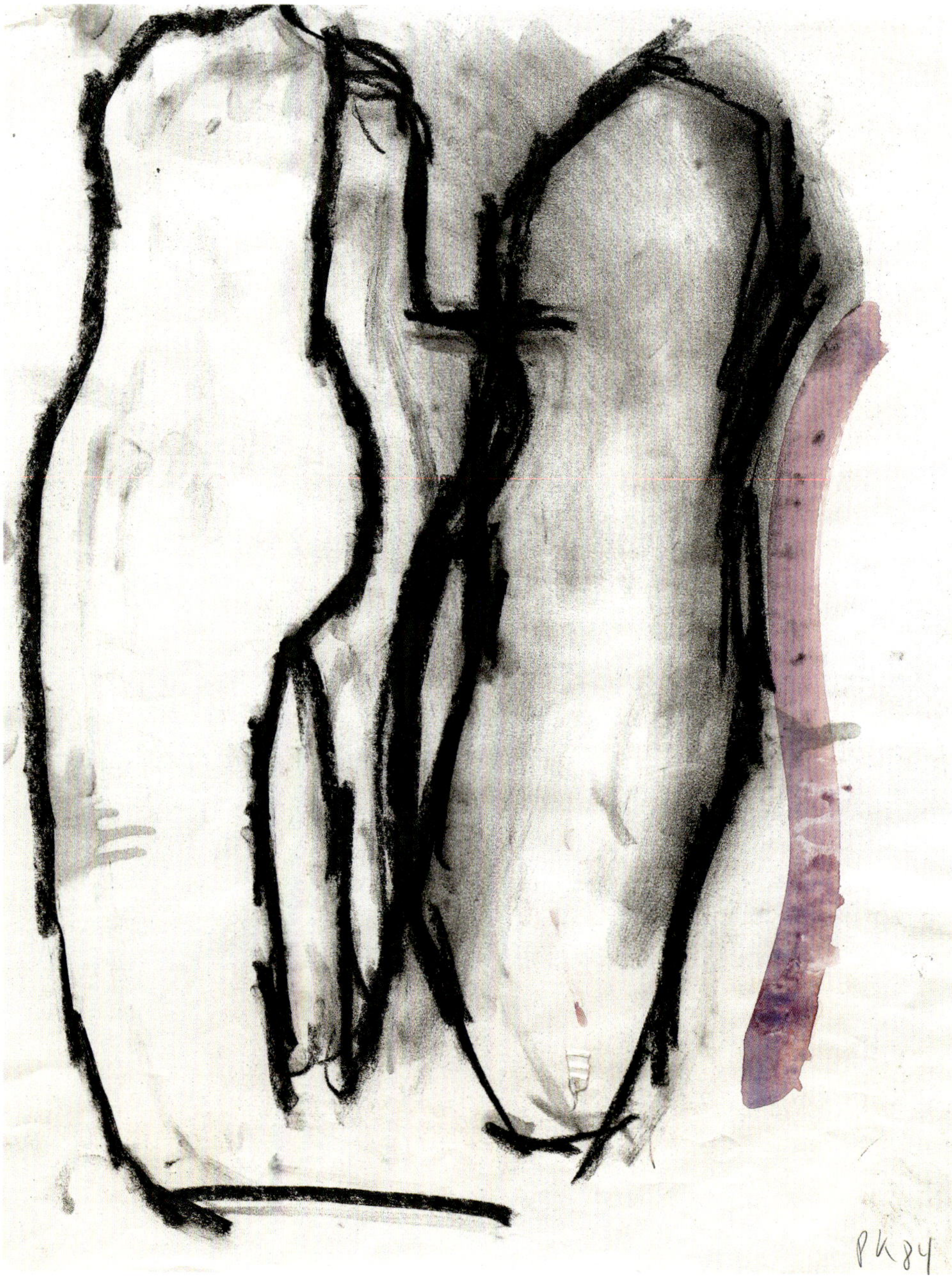

Untitled, 1984 / 47.7 × 36.1 cm
→
Figure, 1983 / 211 × 49 × 68 cm

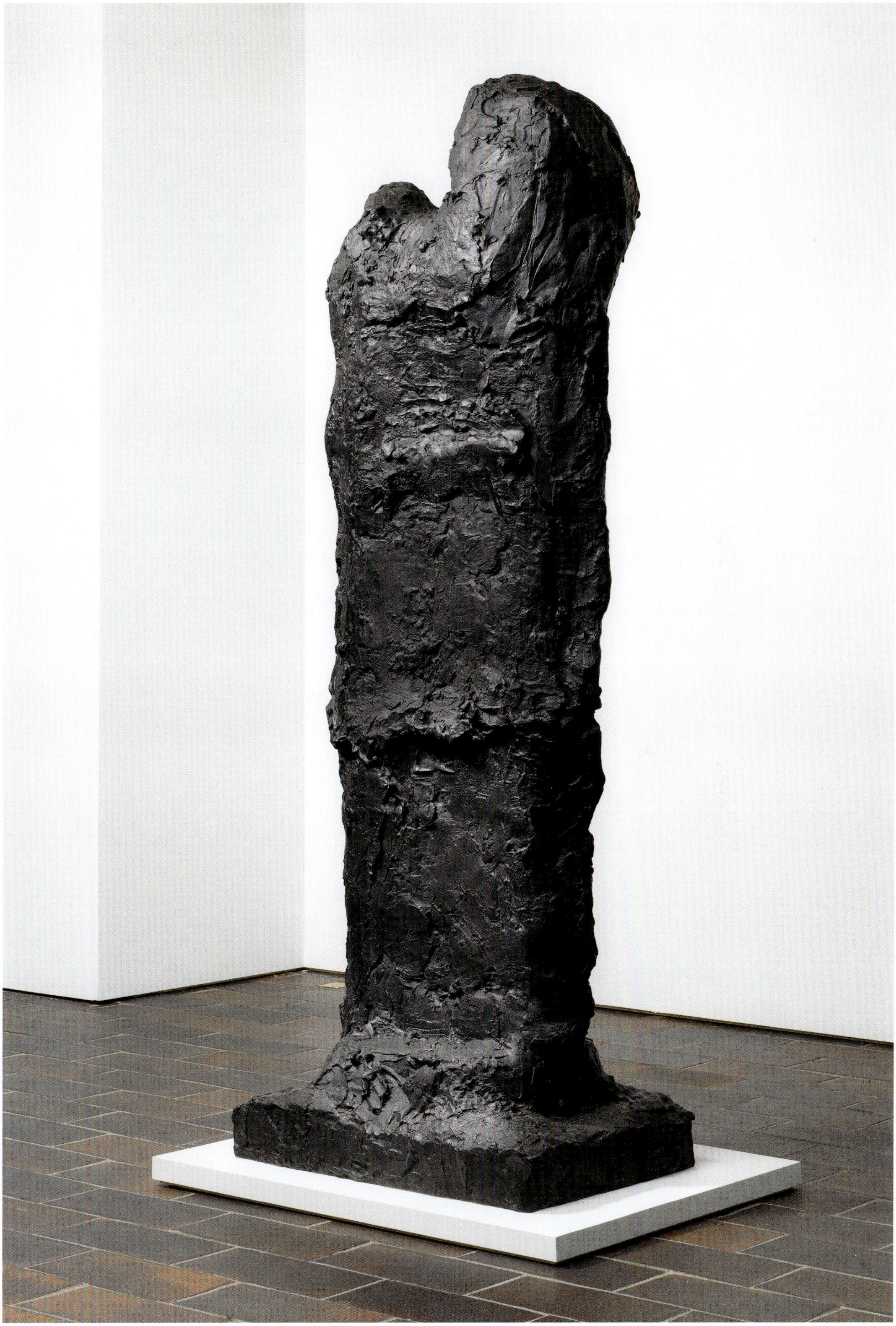

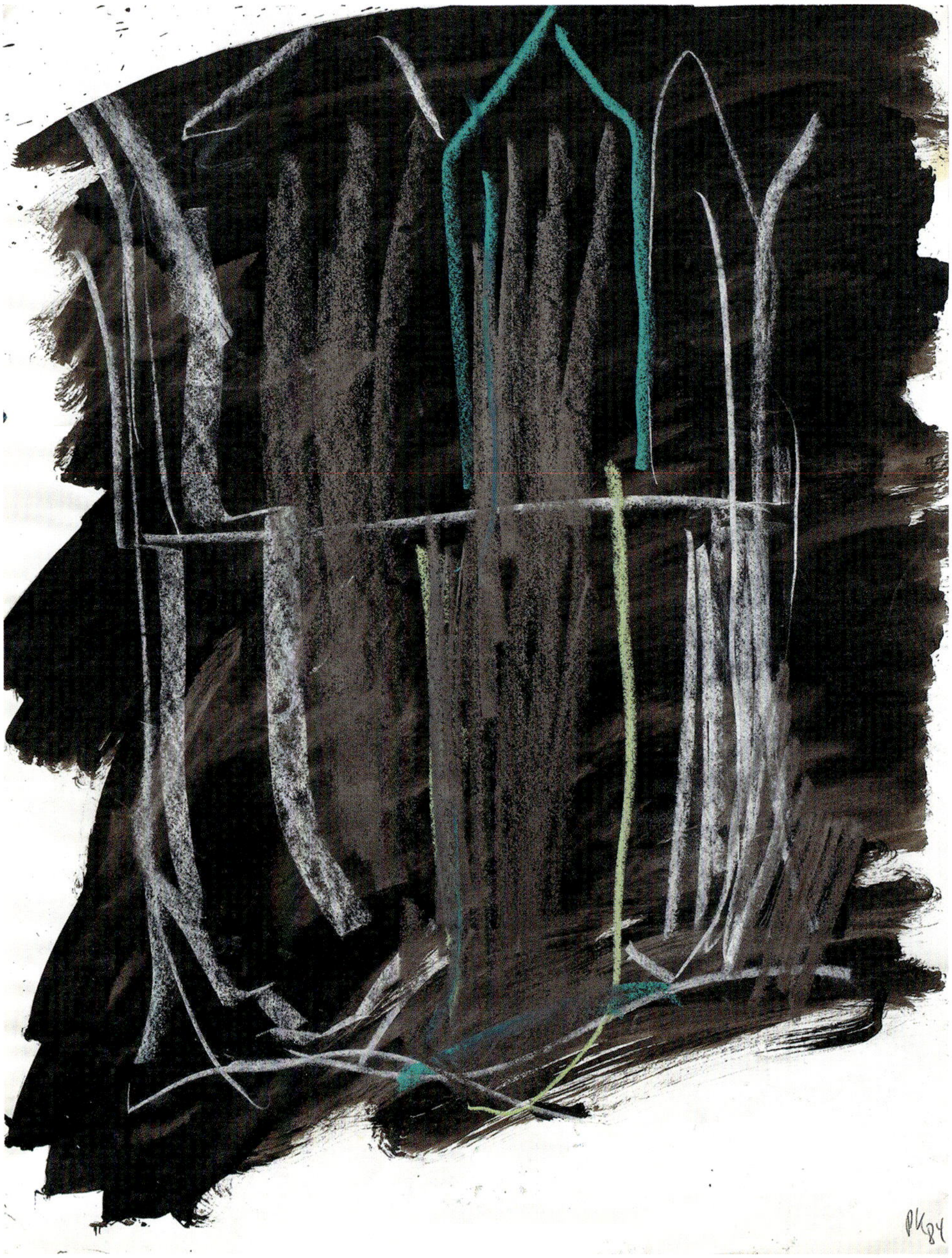

Untitled, 1984 / 56 × 42 cm
→
Torso Branch, 1988 / 208 × 158 × 78 cm
→→
Installation view, *Per Kirkeby – Bronze*, Louisiana

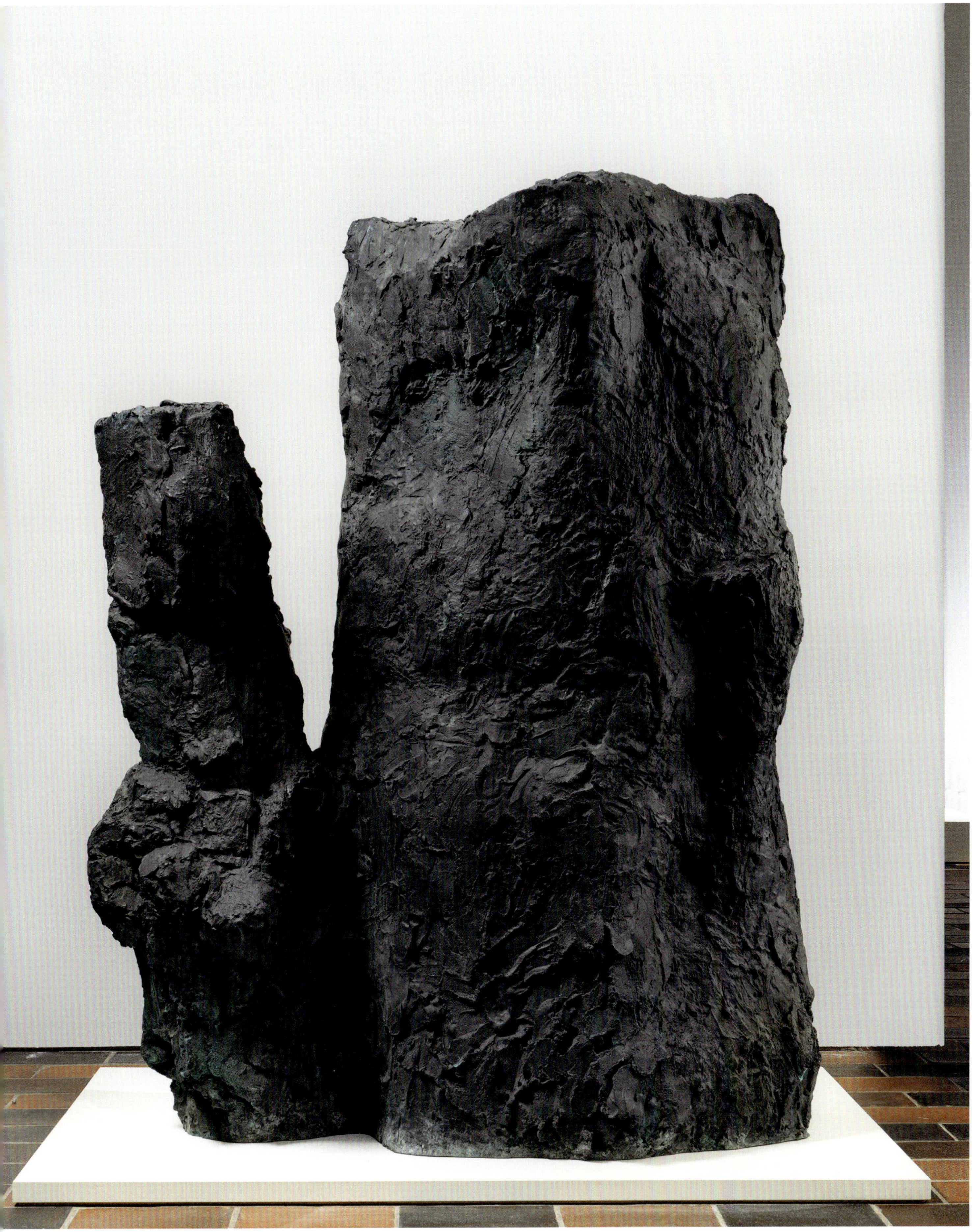

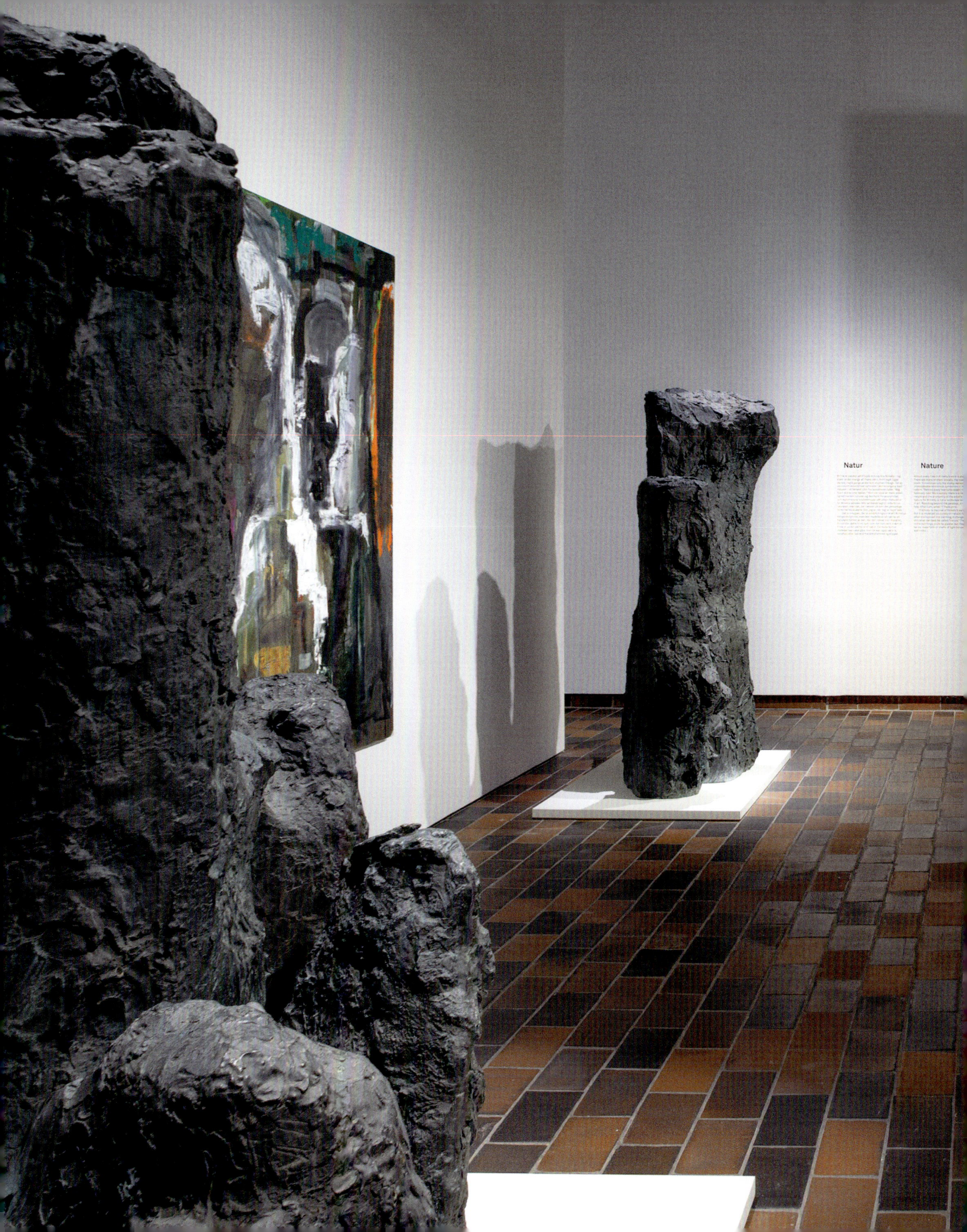
Natur
Nature

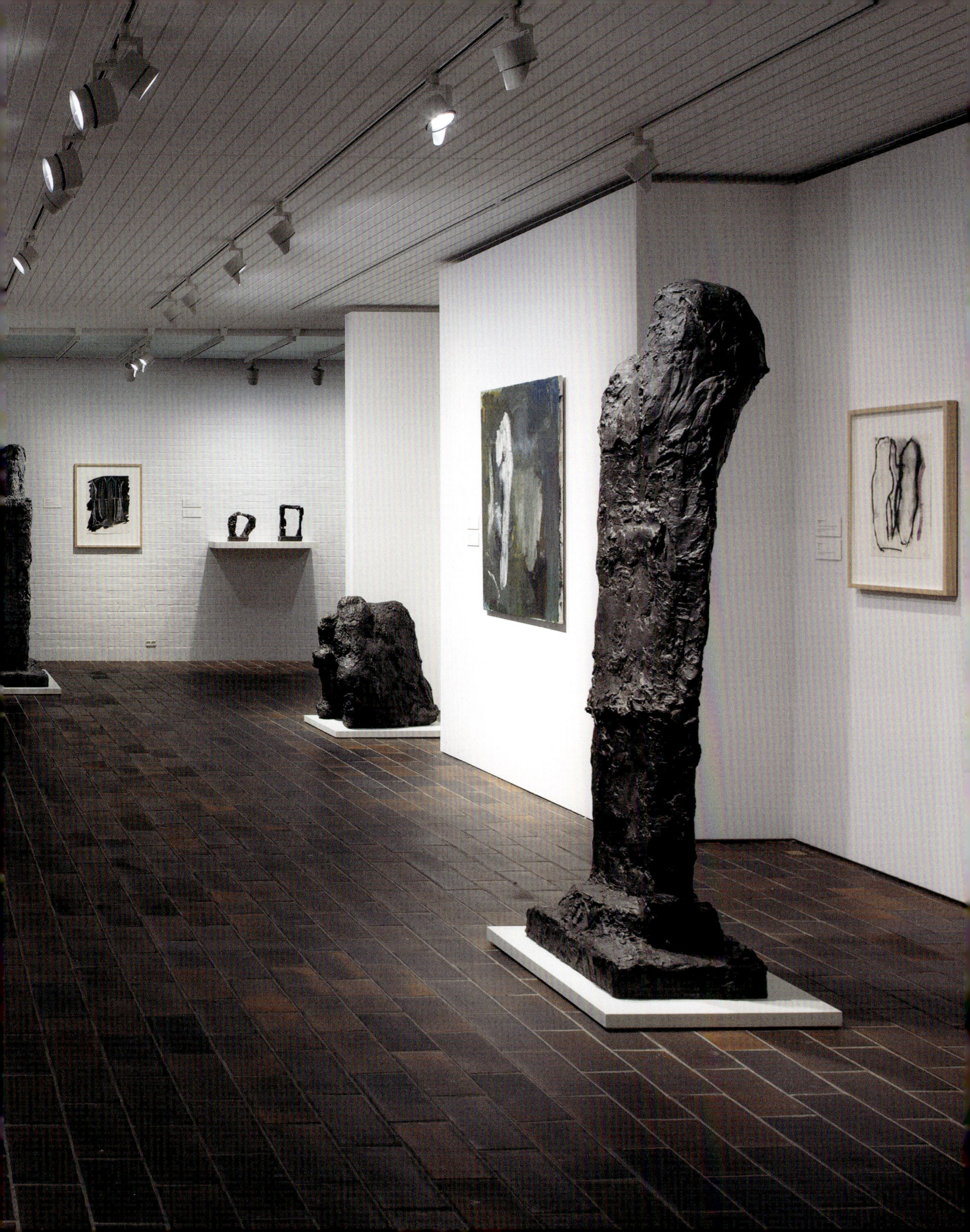

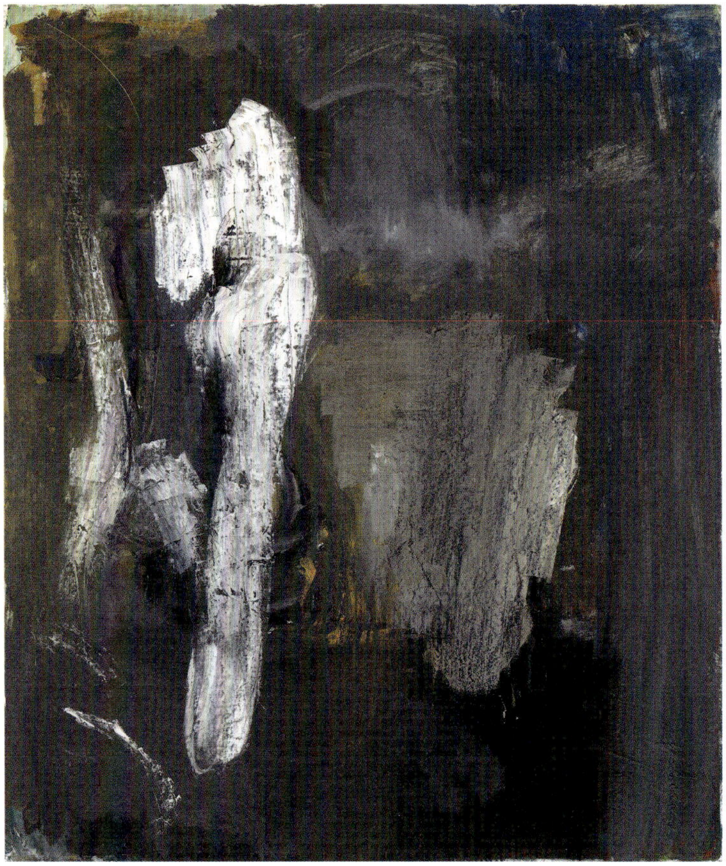

Untitled, 1983 / 120 × 101 cm
→
Landscape, 1983 / 200 × 200 cm

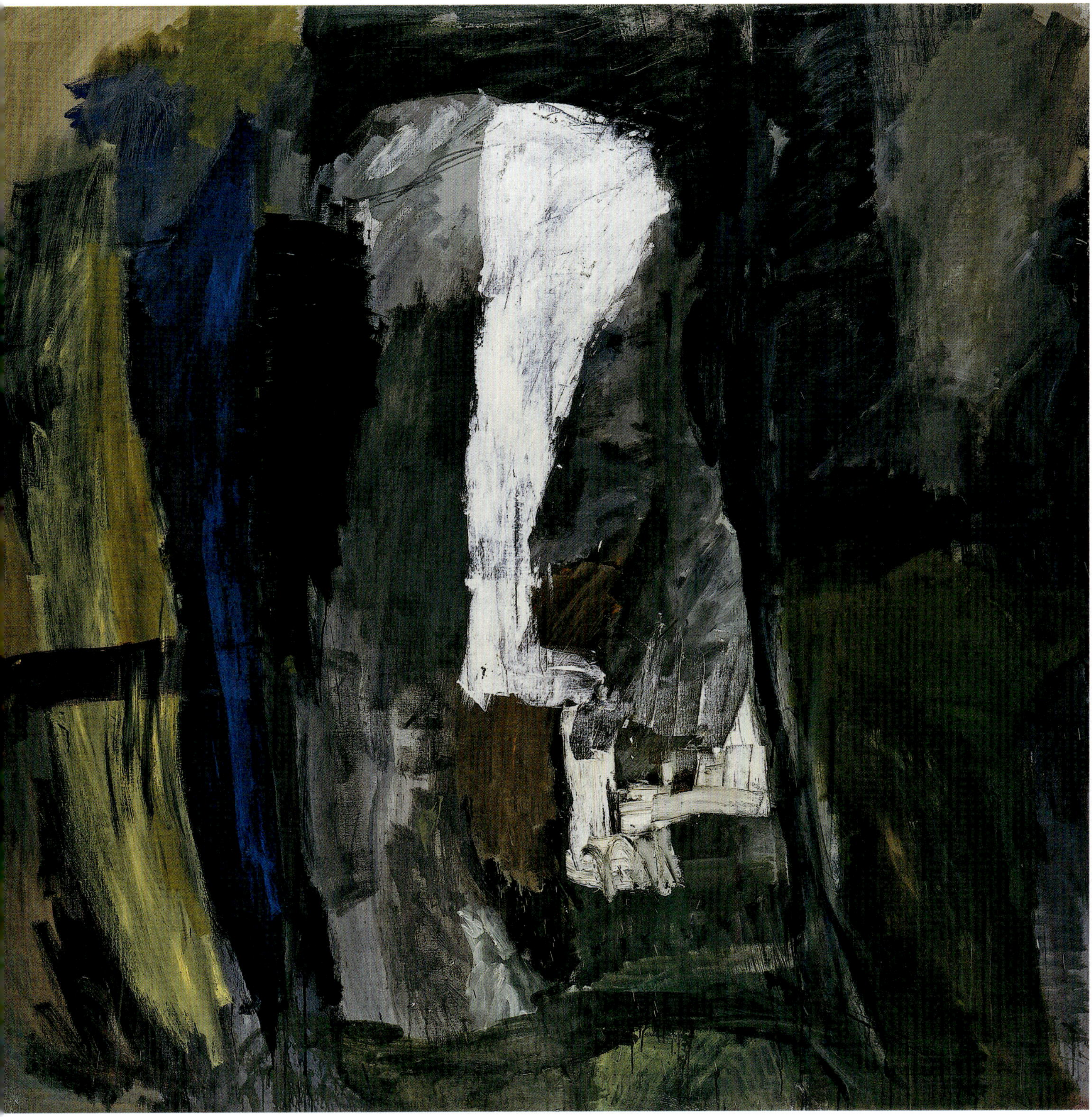

Battling Giants

Erik Steffensen

Working with sculpture almost cost Per Kirkeby his life. Because his nature, or perhaps some kind of male obsession, drove him to make his sculptures larger and larger, to the very the limit of the impossible. In keeping with which, at the turn of the millennium he left his distinctive mark on a rooftop in Berlin, where eight sculptures by the artist were installed. Sculptures that imply the ambition of imagining even greater feats, as seen in the nose and heads visible in over(human)size on the roof of the Bundesrat building. If we imagine who the bronze nose might belong to, the figure would be as tall as the building in the centre of the German capital. In this sense, the sculptures are a heroic fairy tale in which death is a constant companion, even more so than in Per Kirkeby's paintings where "death lurks behind every tree," as the artist once put it. What is it that makes some men's need to be seen so strong that they are willing to risk their life – or part of it? To aim so high, to express themselves on such a monumental scale? Maybe this is the only place where they reach a limit, where they feel alive? The artist wanting to be immortalised through his métier. And as in any grand gesture, with the ever-present danger that it could all go dreadfully wrong.

"The artist checked out before the grand finale during the summer the Bundesrat sculptures were installed on the roof to reign over the city for all eternity. Six bronze heads and two portal walls in relief. The entire length of Leipziger Strasse was cordoned off so the cranes could lift the heavyweight monuments into place. Per had his usual henchmen with him. And his father Alfred, who watched it all, presumably pleased at the achievement in his quiet engineer's mind. It was an embellishment and coronation, a symbol of the dignified rise of the German capital after years of decline and the divide between east and west. Per felt the joy of achieving something Alfred would also appreciate … Berlin was a father-and-son trip, many years after their bike trips to Western Jutland. There were so many layers of life experience here, that it started to look like a cycle of repetition."

The quote is from my Kirkeby biography *At trække en streg* (Drawing the Line), published in 2017, when Per Kirkeby was still alive. He was particularly pleased to have made a monument to the memory of his parents, something he saw as completing the cycle of a life lived to the full. During the 70 conversations we had, accompanied by reading his countless diaries, we often returned to "the catastrophe" – the first brain haemorrhage he had on his way home from installing the sculptures in Berlin. He collapsed on the ferry to the Danish island of Læsø just after it left shore. The ferry immediately turned back, saving Per Kirkeby's life. The artist talked most about what that meant for his life as a human being, for his marriage, for his situation. About his pain. And was frustrated that he could no longer work at full speed.

He started to approach his work in a new way, often with a religious slant. The beams of the cross and other Biblical themes. After a while I drew his attention to the work he was involved in prior to the brain haemorrhage, and asked who had been with him in Berlin. Only then did his father come up. "He must have been proud and happy to see his son occupy the city in such a distinguished place. And with such a feat of engineering," I said. "Yes," Per replied, apparently surprised that I would attach any importance to the fact. Some pieces of the puzzle started to fall into place. His father accompanied him to Berlin, quietly following his son as in a classical legend. The old life connected to the new, mental scaffolding ensuring stability. Father and son. But Per Kirkeby's monumental sculptures of heroes and figures and fragments living in the darkness of bronze are more about his quest to reach the pinnacle of immortality than any family feeling or back-up. The two largest bronzes on the roof in Berlin are called *Jason – Clouds*, a reference to Bertel Thorvaldsen's breakthrough work *Jason with the Golden Fleece* (1803, p. 52) – and the divine. The sky is heavy, as if the beams of the cross at the top of the stele have replaced the clouds that should be there.

Throughout his life Per Kirkeby saw himself as lone figure battling giants. A boy and man who had been betrayed and abandoned. He wanted to be part of the equation, and grappled with Antiquity, Christianity and Nordic mythology. He wanted to be a hero, despite all the serpents that slither around the art world, serpents he literally had sculpted and cast in bronze, just like Jason on his quest to find the golden fleece. With the help of his wife Medea, the hero Jason slays the sleepless dragon and overcomes other trials that win him the crown. Like Kirkeby, Jason had a dual nature with its dark sides. Instead of being grateful for Medea's help, he took a new wife. Then Medea took revenge by killing their own children and the new wife. Per Kirkeby's sculptures are full of high and often menacing drama. The battle between life and death that takes more than blood, sweat and tears to create. The work of an intellectual artist. If you are born in a small country, the world is a vast arena for a conqueror who wants to be the best in their field. Which is what Per Kirkeby wanted. That he identified with the legend is beyond doubt. Jason lives on after the loss of his family before meeting his fate in old age. His ship Argo, which had protected him and the Argonauts, was to be the death of him: Jason was asleep under the stern of the rotting vessel when it collapsed and killed him.

Jason Balken I+II, 1999
Bronze, 2 × 400 × 200 × 80 cm
Bundesrat, Berlin

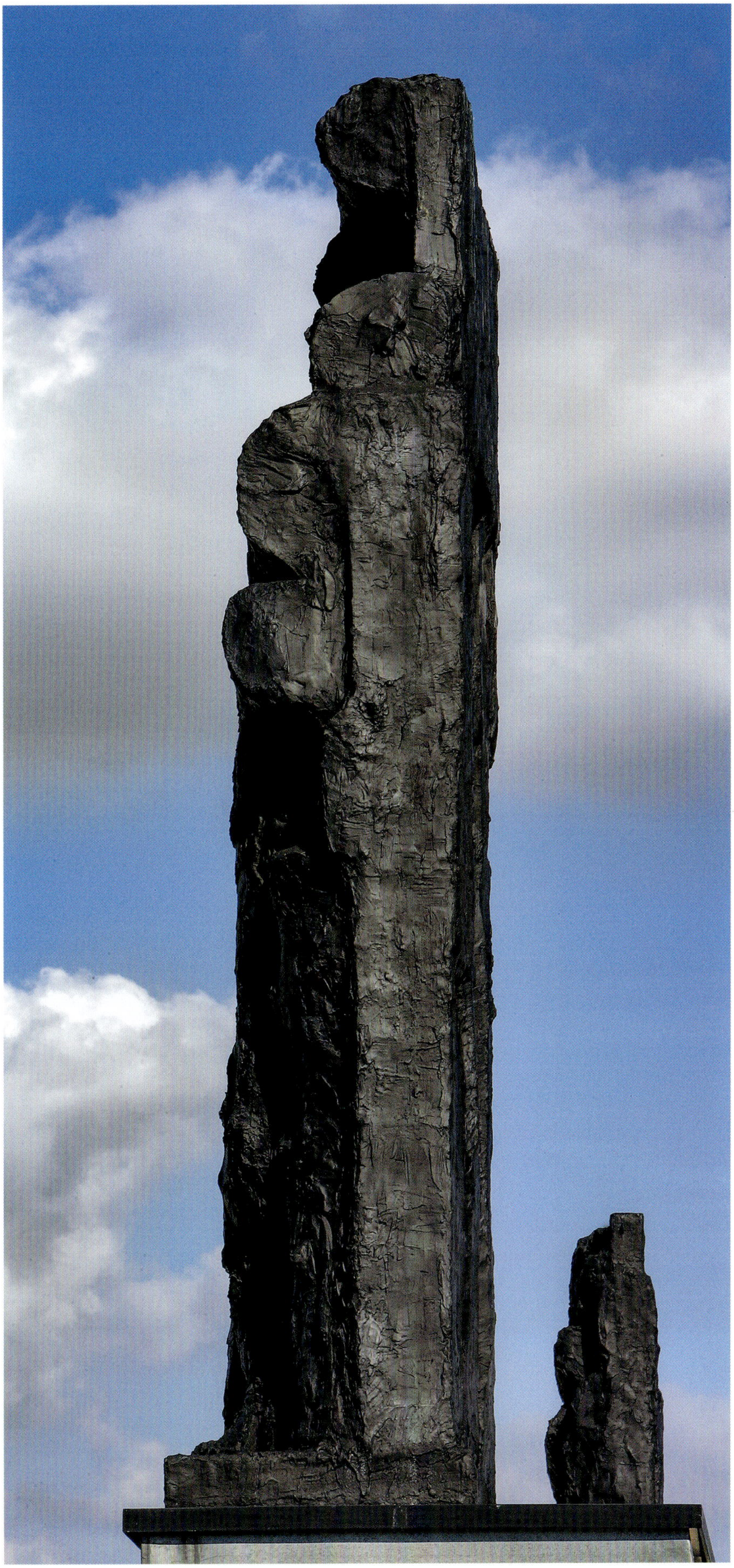

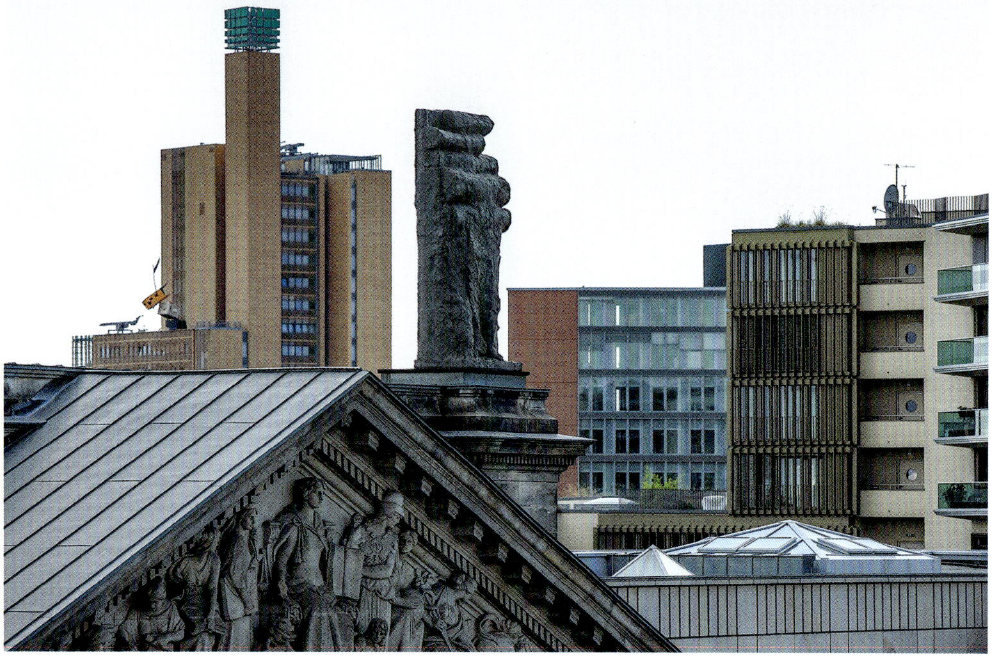

Jason Balken I+II, 1999
Bronze, 2 × 400 × 200 × 80 cm
Nasen I-VI, 1999
Bronze, 6 × 150 × 100 × 100 cm
Bundesrat, Berlin

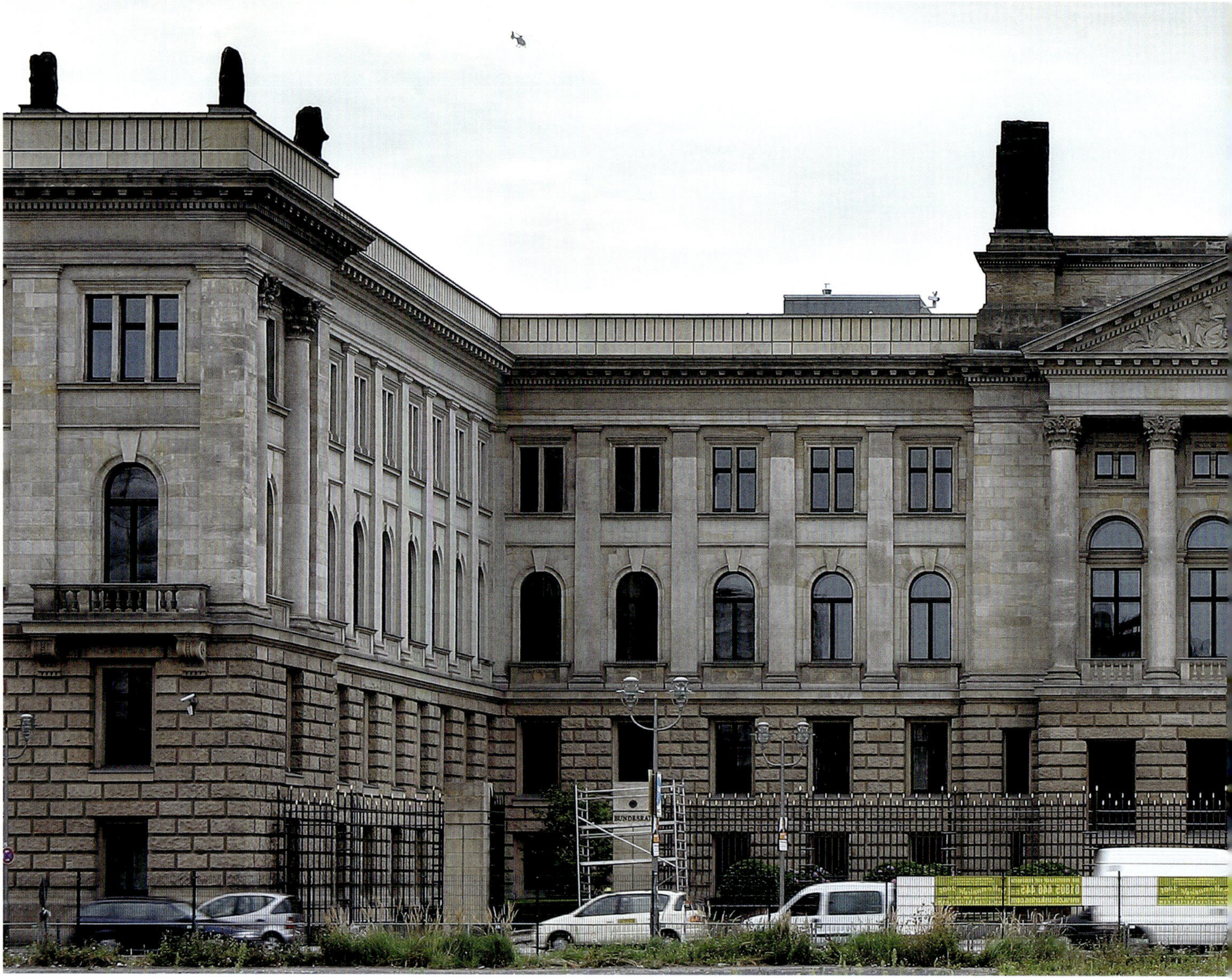

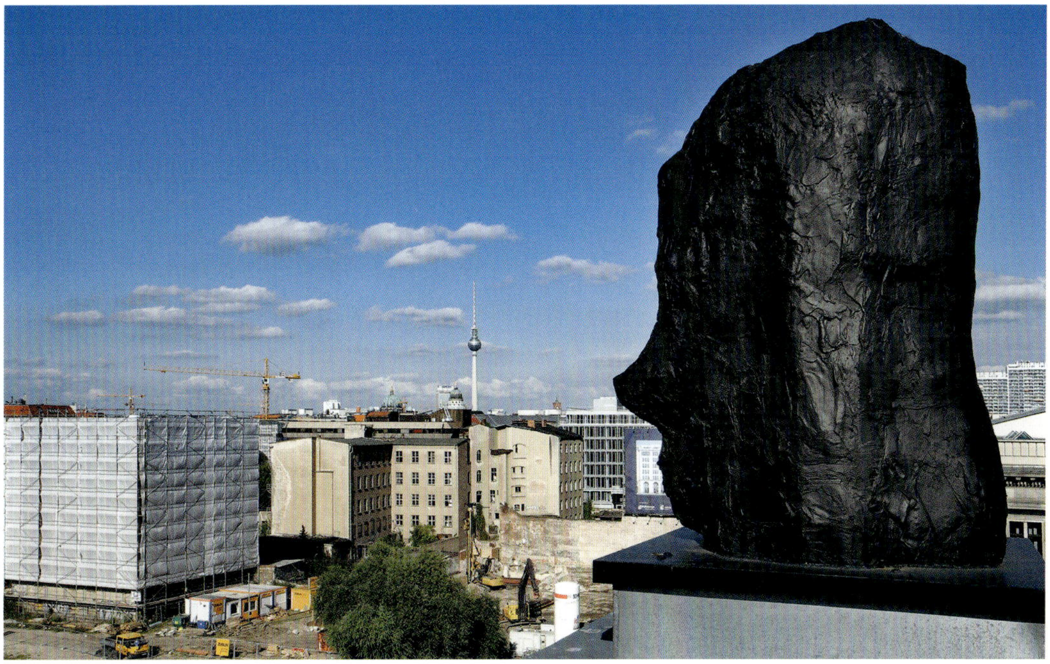

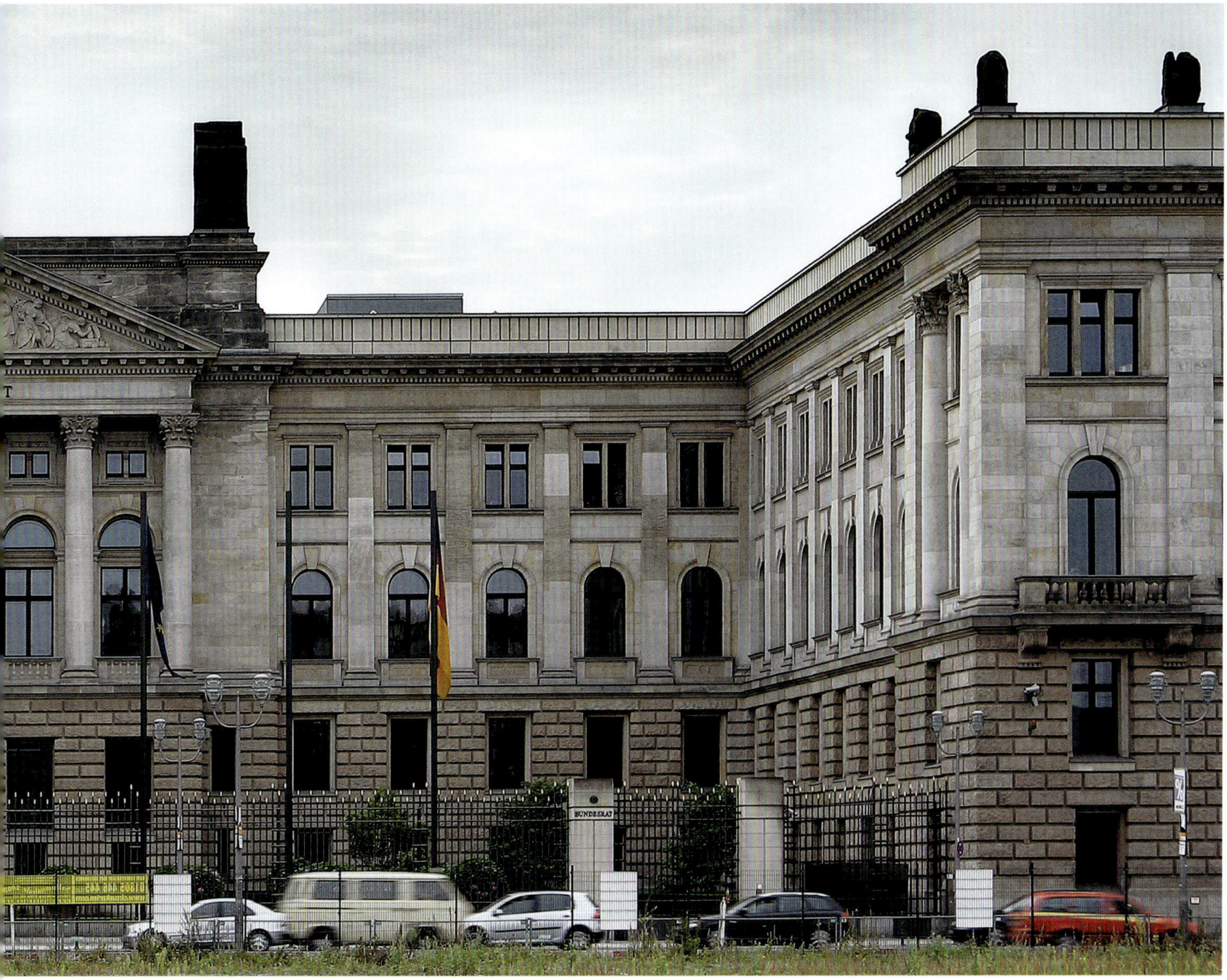
BUNDESRAT

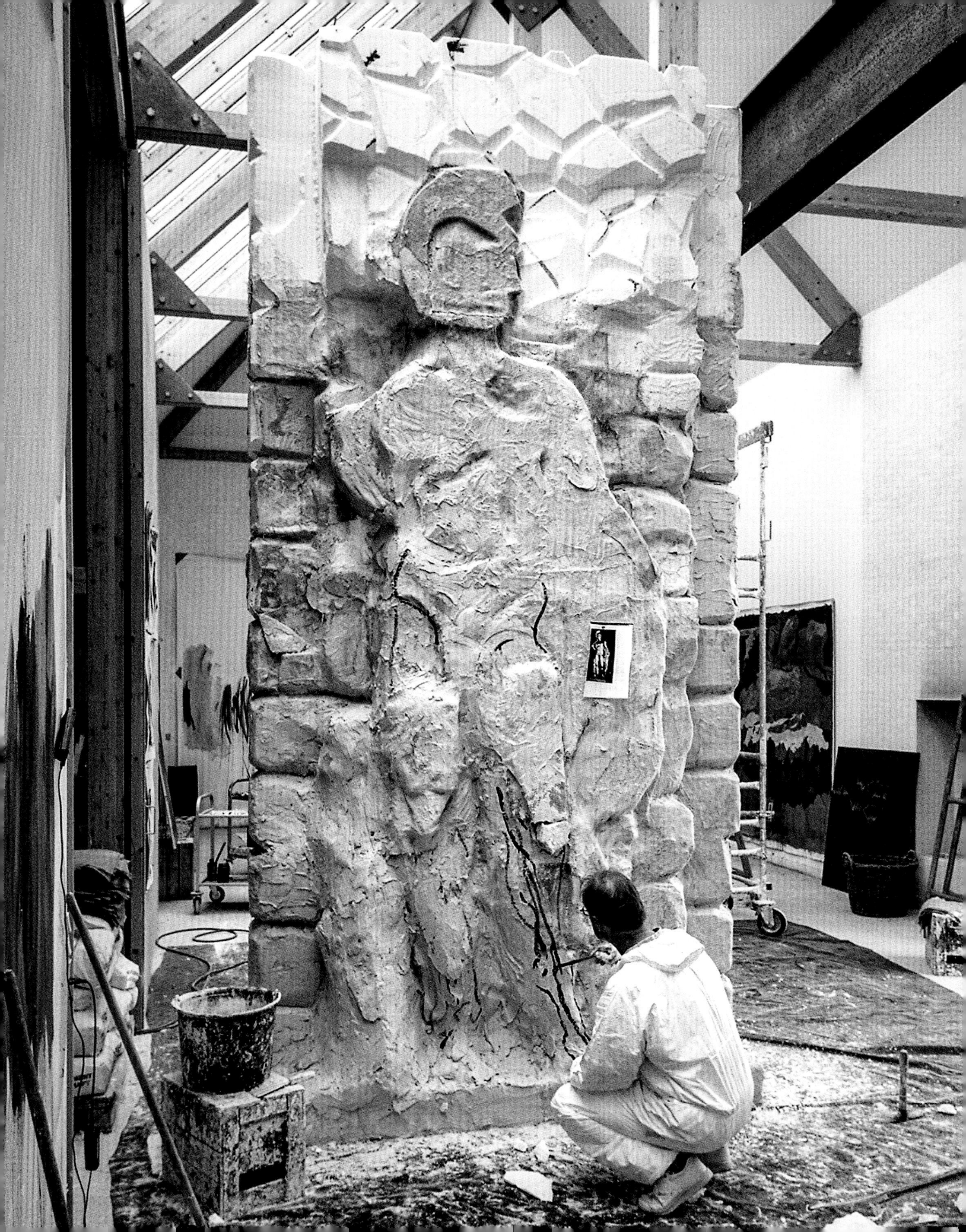

As a child Per Kirkeby's idol was the comic strip hero Prince Valiant. Another hero Per Kirkeby identified with way beyond the innocent fascination of childhood. In middle age he would sometimes say it had been his fate to meet and marry a blond. That he had been married to a brunette before had merely been a bump on the invisible path of destiny he shared with Prince Valiant. The artist used comics and other printed matter that was at hand to create new images. We can follow the artist's path to maturation through Pop Art pictures of heroes and romantic imaginings on Masonite boards in the 1960s, to more tentative attempts at gestural abstraction in the 1970s, before finally finding his feet with a 1978 oil painting at the end of the decade he celebrated his 40th birthday.

Untitled, c. 1963
Oil on masonite, 122 × 202 cm
Fonden til udsmykning af Herning Handelsskole
←
Per Kirkeby in his studio on Læsø, 1998

As he started to mature as an artist, the first large oil paintings on canvas were marked by intellectual attempts to paint in the grand style: indistinct figure com positions based on pictures in the books in his expanding library. Old-fashioned, handmade art far removed from the collages that had dominated his work to date. In the early 1980s there was a further shift in his painting. Per Kirkeby had bought a farm on the island of Læsø, where his contact with nature was more direct than could be found in books. The colours he used changed, and figurative elements became more apparent. Between the layers of the painting there was a fleeting glimpse of a red lobster on a table or a horse in the landscape. It was obvious that the world became more tangible and less ethereal during the years he grappled with the transition.

At the same time, international interest in his work was growing, increasing the pressure and workload and raising new questions. International mainstream painting had taken a figurative turn, and Per Kirkeby did attempt to squeeze some sharp-nosed figures and other incongruities into his paintings. The new "wild" painting at the time was neo-expressionist and dramatic, and even though Per Kirkeby was in a lyrical, abstract phase he hung on as best he could, "moving into oils" as his German gallerist put it. Per Kirkeby managed to take his painting in another direction drawing on everything he knew, from the early Pop Art paintings of the face of Brigitte Bardot or Tintin covers, to strange, isolated nomad tents, caves and cowboy shacks in mountainous landscapes.

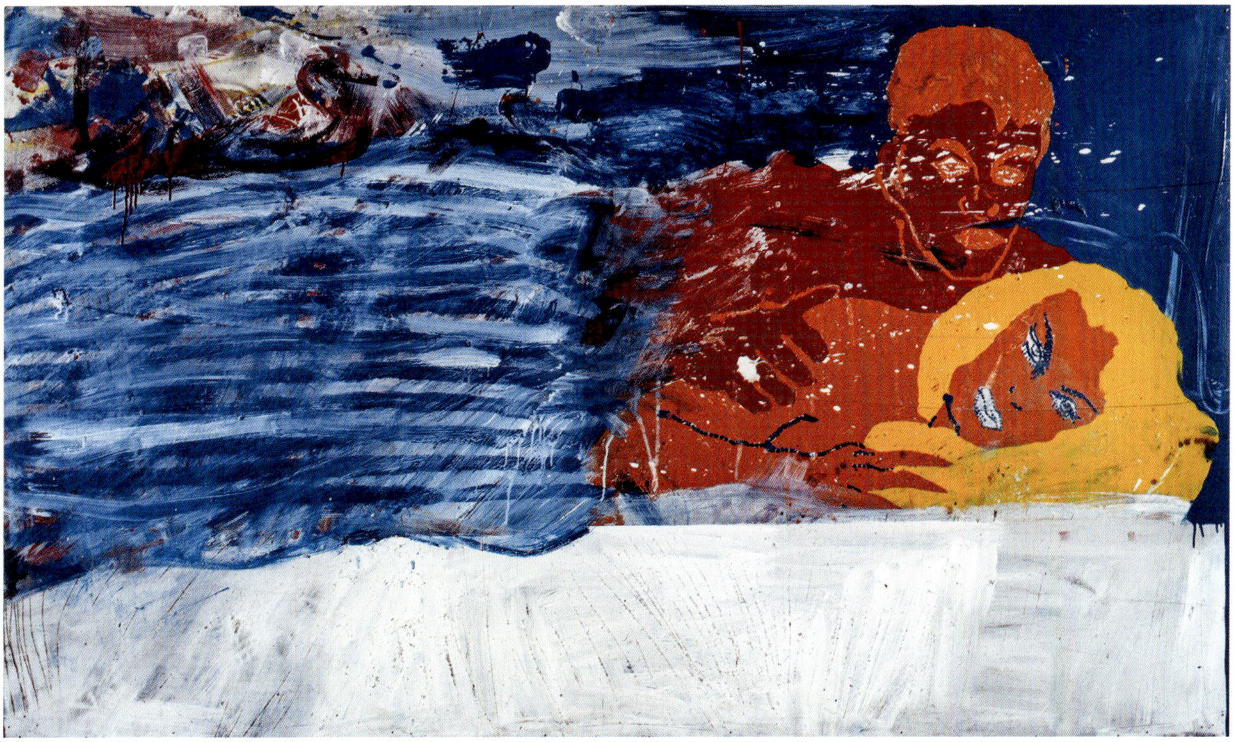

Visually and artistically Per Kirkeby returned to the geology he studied parallel to becoming an artist in the 1960s. He had specialised in Greenland and the Arctic, and geological motifs started to appear more and more. It was during this period, when everything seemed up in the air and an international career looked possible, that plaster sculptures also made their entrance. Per Kirkeby had started to look at nature both more directly and with the eye of a researcher. He started using local colours in his painting, and also started to explore the nature of woman. Which for Per Kirkeby meant his wife, Vibeke Windeløv, the model for ideas that were far removed from the glossy surface of Pop Art. His intimacy with his subject could be felt: many of the work titles from this artistically productive and profitable period in the mid-1980s include the name "Vibeke" in one form or another.

Per Kirkeby idolised his female subject, and started to prioritise intimacy above grand narratives. Although the latter continued to be an underlying presence. He had discovered a deeper connection between mythological narratives and his home life in Hellerup, on Læsø and in Germany, where he had been appointed professor and lived, taught and painted for long, stable stretches of time. Peace to work and produce, the chance to inhabit his work. Which encompassed it all: his marital conflicts, his dream of a lonely mountain hut and naked cliffs of desolation, plus anything else in the biological and geographical baggage he carried within, constantly available for exposure and further use.

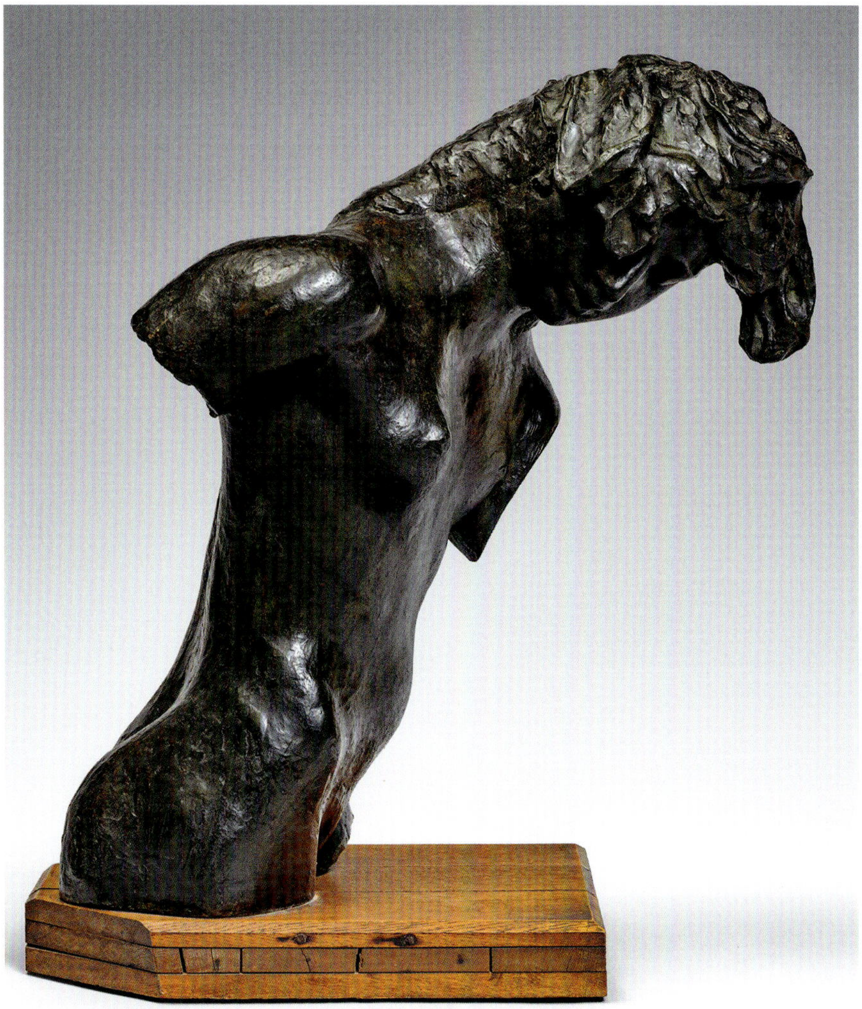

In 1980 Per Kirkeby and Vibeke Windeløv's honeymoon took them to Paris, where they visited the studio of artists Sonja Ferlov and Ernest Mancoba. "They lived in plaster," as Kirkeby recalled. Everything was covered in white, with Ferlov's sculptures standing on the floor. Not long after Kirkeby himself started to make plaster sculptures on Læsø, sculptures based on Vibeke's body – its details and fragments of her features. An arm and head, for example. He found another source of inspiration in the masterly, passionate sculptures of Auguste Rodin (1840-1917). The French artist had brought the sensitivity of the figure to life. His work was based on the sculptures of Antiquity, but was so alive that it brought history and tradition within reach. Rodin's bronze figures are sexy. And how many statues and figures is that true of? Per Kirkeby's interest in sculpture was erotically charged. He was turned on by the physicality of sculpture, could use it to prove something: valour and glory. He was also turned on by the idea of the woman, his model. But she was gradually released from the figure, forming, via sculpture, a contrasting element in his painting. Throughout most of the 1980s Per Kirkeby painted his figures and models not in skin tones, but in the black of bronze and white light of plaster. The 1990s marked the entry of colour alongside grand narratives, often in the form of legends or Biblical tales. The artist grew older. Living life to the full, until it lay in ruins. On the personal level divorce from Vibeke was on the cards, and on the physical level there was the brain haemorrhage with its ultimatum that he change his life or not live at all. The workload and pressure had to stop. The body of the artist had pushed the reset button.

Auguste Rodin
Figure de femme à mi-corps
c. 1910 / 73 × 41 × 64 cm
→
Per Kirkeby in his studio on Læsø, 1998

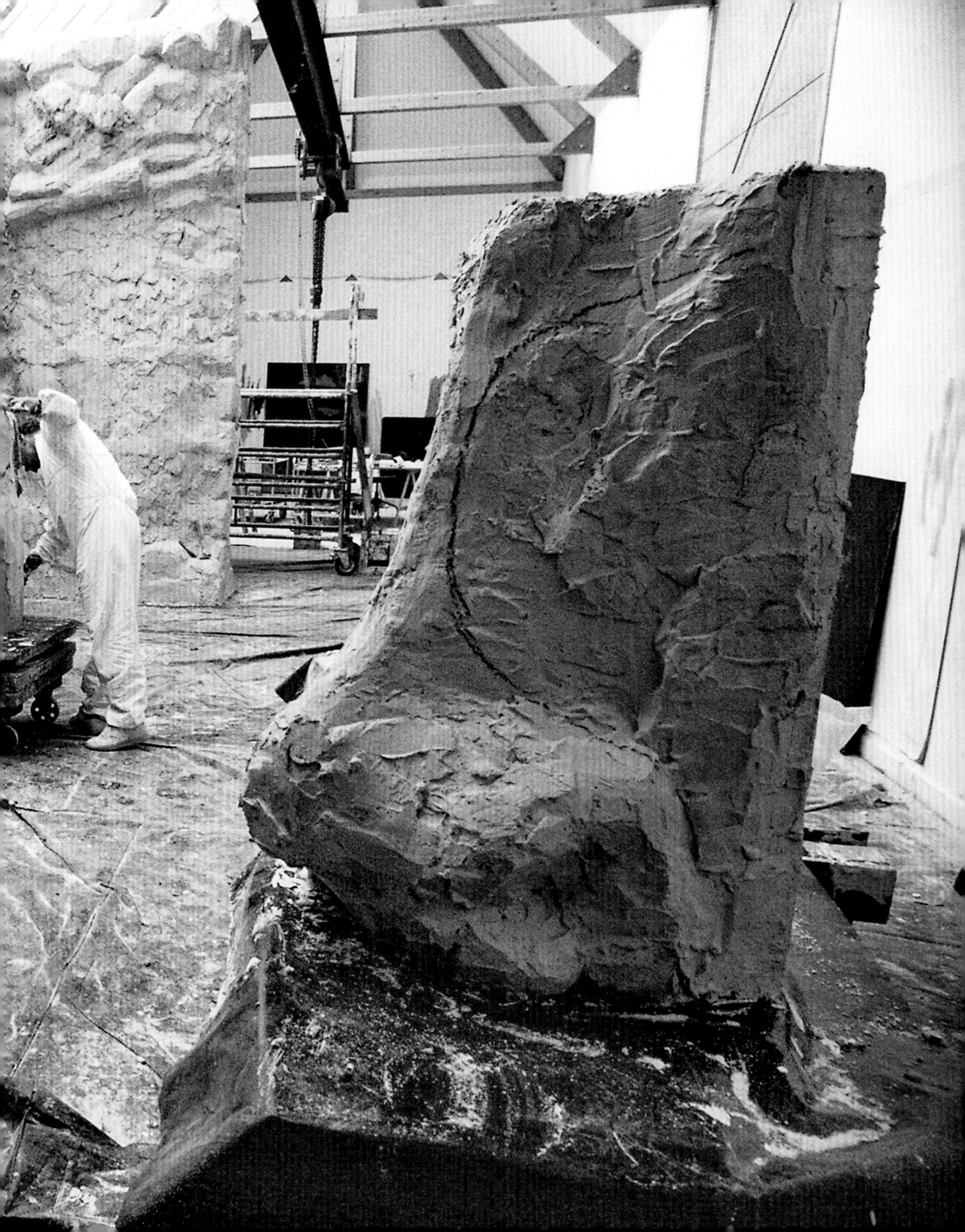

The masterpiece *Weltuntergang* (2001-02) was begun during this, the most difficult period of the artist's life. In many ways it can be seen as a synthesis of his sculptural works: a massive, brick-like presence in the world. When Per Kirkeby's bronzes gained monumental dimensions in the 1990s, history told us that we were dealing with Heracles slaying the hydra or the legend of Laocoön killed with his two sons by serpents, with the Resurrection of Christ or "the gates of hell," all of them with the same mythological undertone of the cosmos meeting the eye on the way to the end of the world. The painting is as flat as the surface of a rock wall, as are the monumental bronzes. And this, perhaps, is one of the laudable limitations of Per Kirkeby's talent: that he could only paint the surface, not depth. Depth lies in the many layers that comprise his paintings. There is no mastery of perspective, something we see in the flat world of comic strips on Masonite, the brilliant materiality of the beginning of his love affair with oils in the 1980s, and his masculine yet feminine approach to later works.

Bronze sculpture was an attempt to get around the figure. We are constantly confronted by challenges, collapse, the threat of meltdown, just like the symbols Per Kirkeby paints in his best works, such as *Viel Später* (1992) with its talus cone from the field reports of the geologist. With his bronze figures Per Kirkeby creates an alphabet, a vocabulary. But not one of geometrical forms like those created by his fellow artist Poul Gernes in the 1960s, when the two of them met and set out to conquer the art world with maximum impact and monumentality.

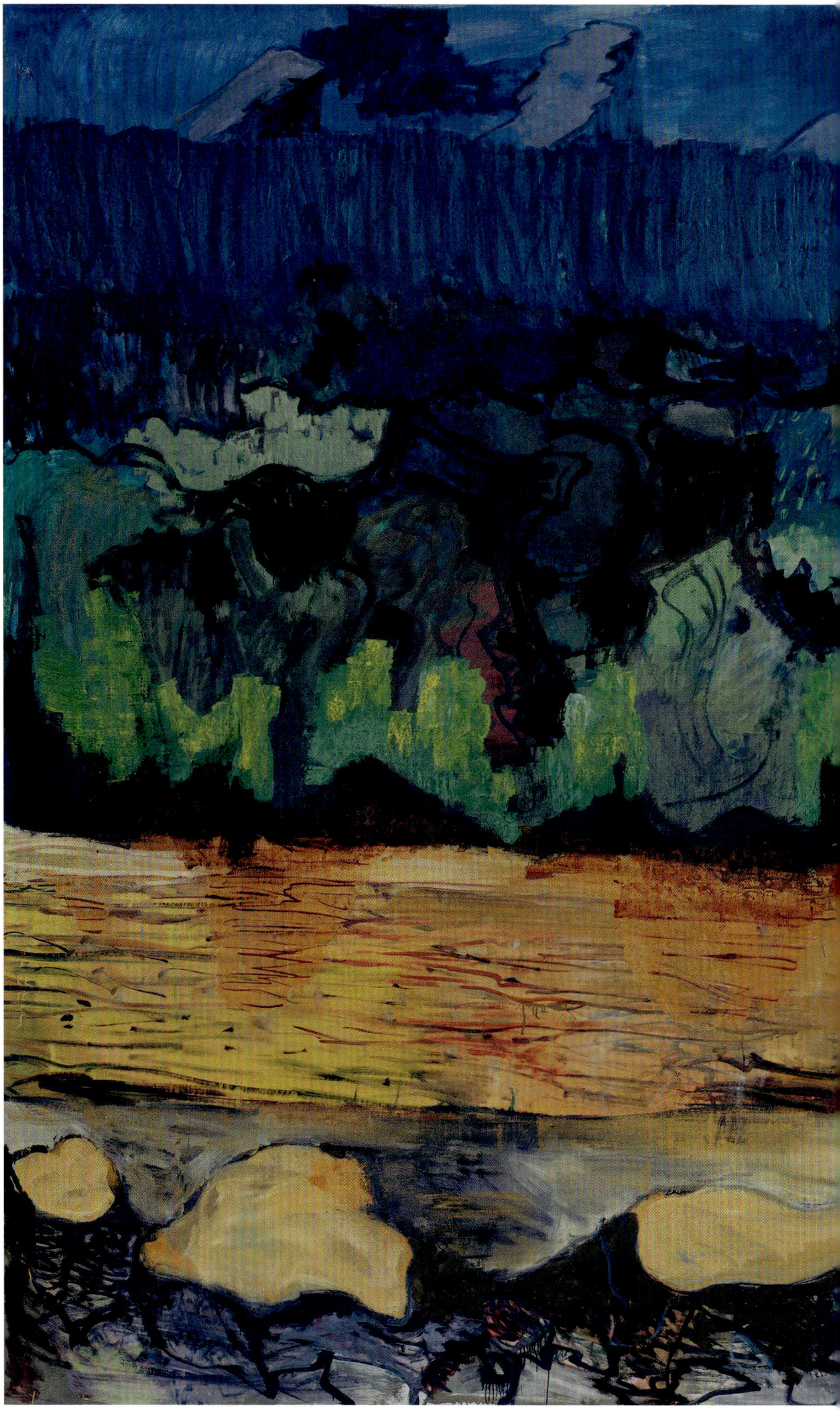

Weltuntergang, 2001-02
Oil on canvas, 300 × 500 cm
Louisiana Museum of Modern Art
Acquired with funding from Ny Carlsbergfondet

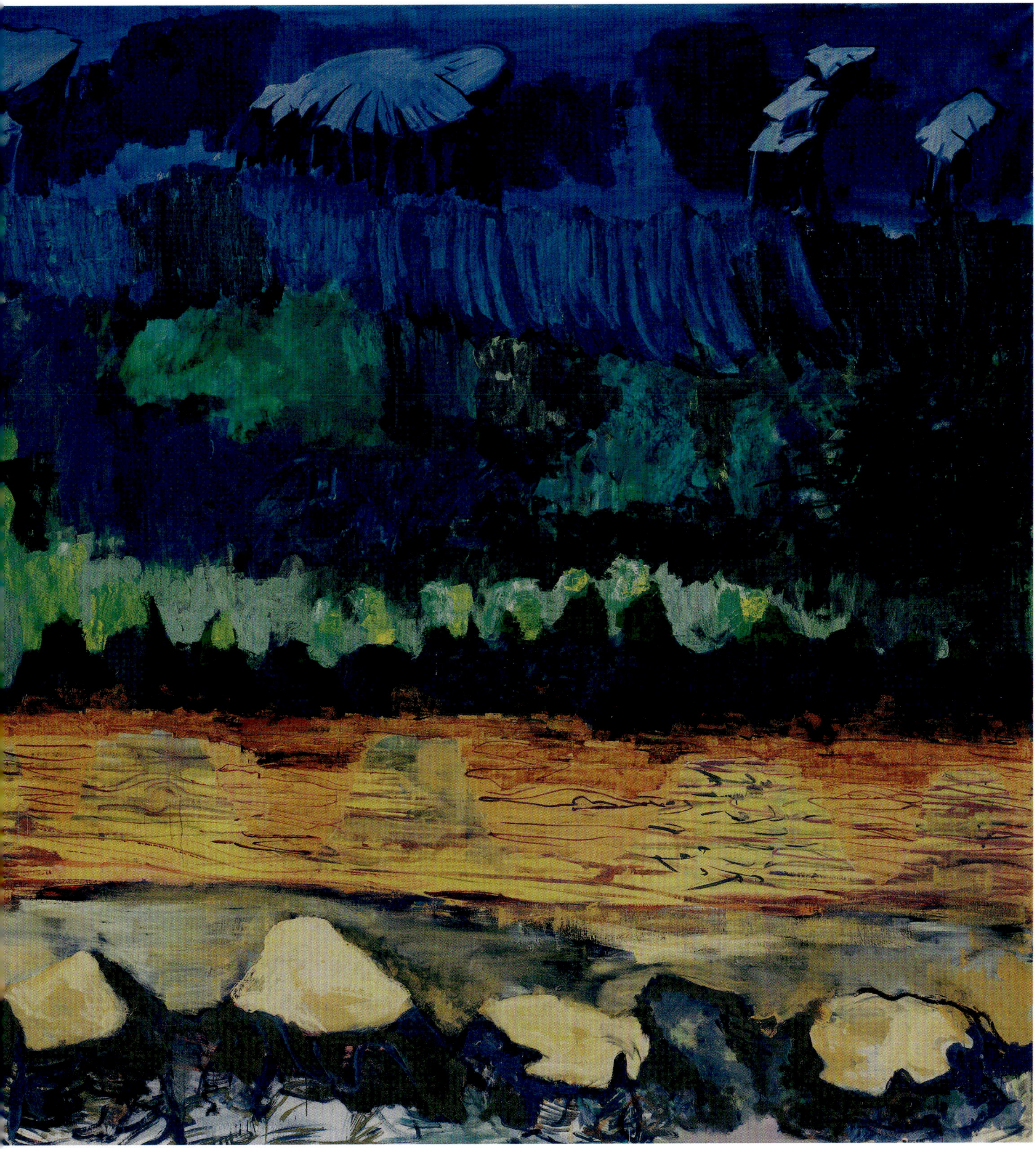

Per Kirkeby arrived at perspective and spatiality via his brick sculptures. These also exist as small, often square bronze models, whereas the larger works, gateways and walls, be they in bronze or oils, remain flat. Which is maybe what makes it difficult to redeem the space in between represented by the bronze reliefs. These, until now, have been a neglected chapter in art history, and not without reason. They do not really break away from the surface of the painting, remaining somewhat formless like objects in limbo. The existence of a stele or statue can be felt. A door or gateway mounted directly onto a wall is more of a challenge, as we can see at the Royal Opera House in Copenhagen, where four of Kirkeby's reliefs are permanently in place.

The paintings that represent studies for or the thinking behind these reliefs are probably among the most thwarted of the artist's works. A visible and new resistance can be felt. The beams are less monumental as beams than they would be in a painted universe, where they would be in the midst of something else, in the midst of other visual narratives. And it is perhaps here that we reach the sculptor Per Kirkeby's greatest endeavour: to unify and epitomise what Auguste Rodin started when he made his formidable work *The Gates of Hell* six metres high. Rodin's gates have no fewer than 180 figures and took the sculptor 37 years – or the rest of his life after being commissioned by the state of France to make the work – to complete. This kind of endeavour was in Per Kirkeby's blood when he started to embrace bronzes in the mid-1980s. His first series of works were figures and the bronze sculpture *Gate*, which he created in several versions on a smaller scale before it grew to monumental dimensions. Reliefs remain doors, walls remain walls, and figures remain figures in the work of Per Kirkeby. And that is more than enough, and took almost 37 years to unfold. Monumental with a dark human touch that absorbs the light.

Erik Steffensen is a photographer, painter and writer. He is the author of the Per Kirkeby biography *At trække en streg* (Drawing the Line, 2017).

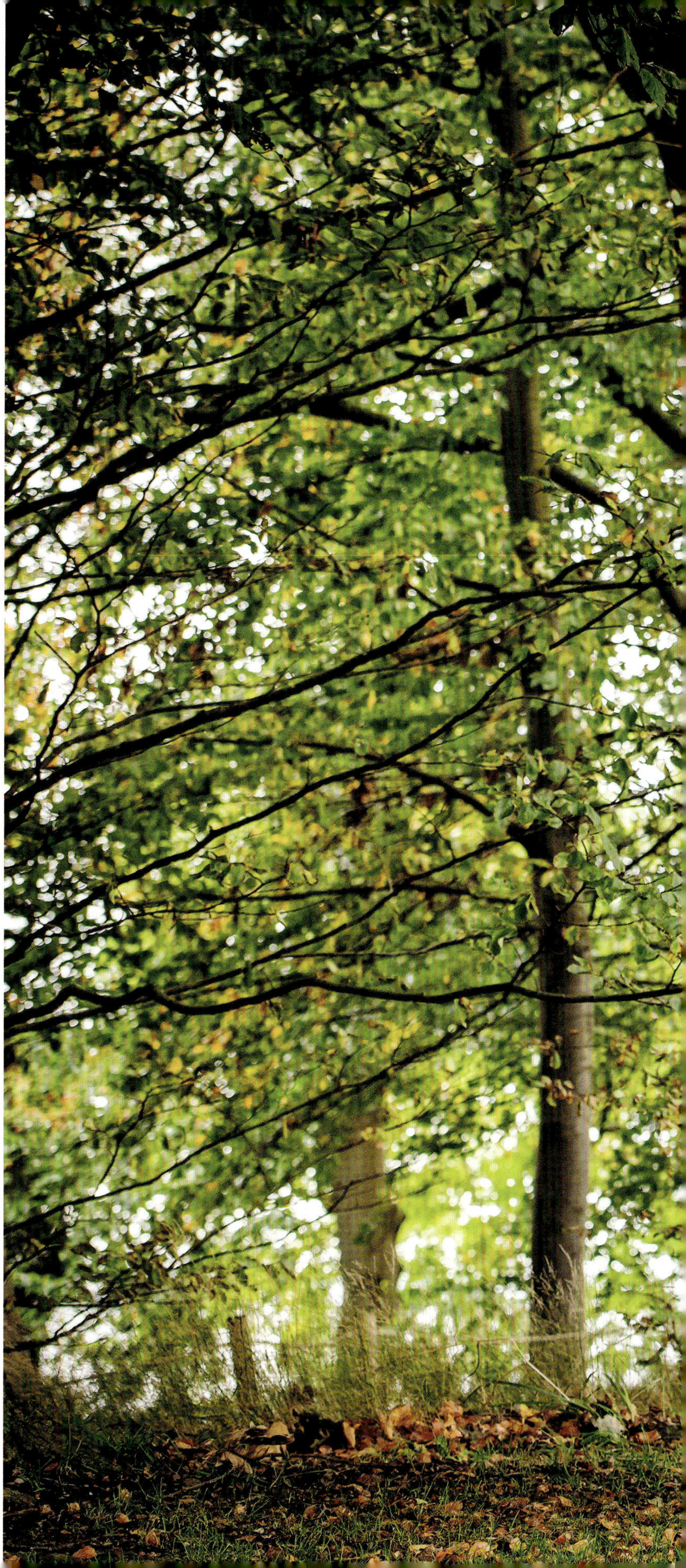

Gate II, 1987 / 256 × 178 × 82 cm

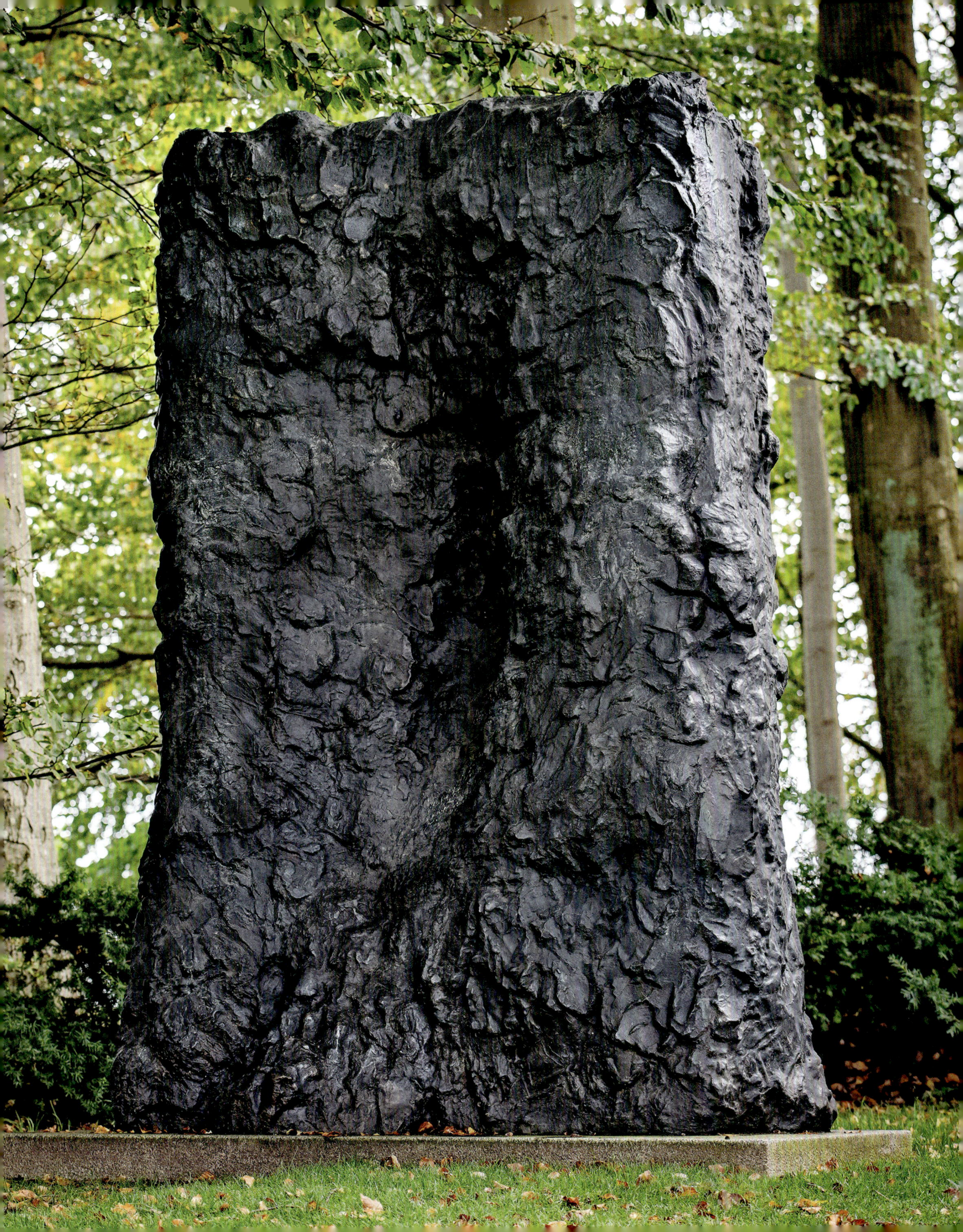

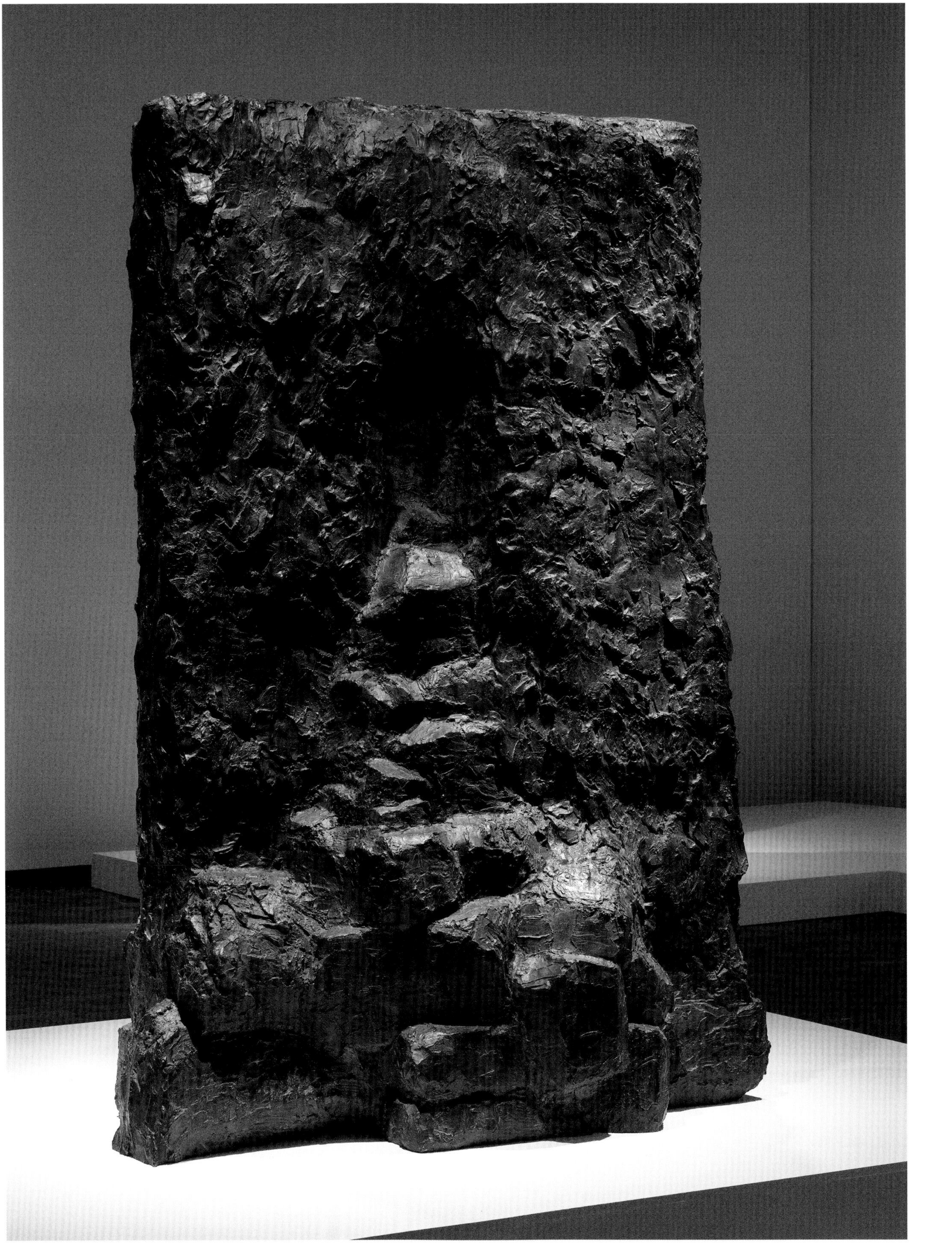

Gate I, 1987 / 220 × 150 × 75 cm
←
Resurrection, 1999 / 290 × 198 × 111 cm
→→
Installation view, *Per Kirkeby – Bronze*, Louisiana
→→→
Installation view, *Per Kirkeby – Bronze*, Louisiana
Left: J.F. Willumsen: **Titian Dying**, 1935

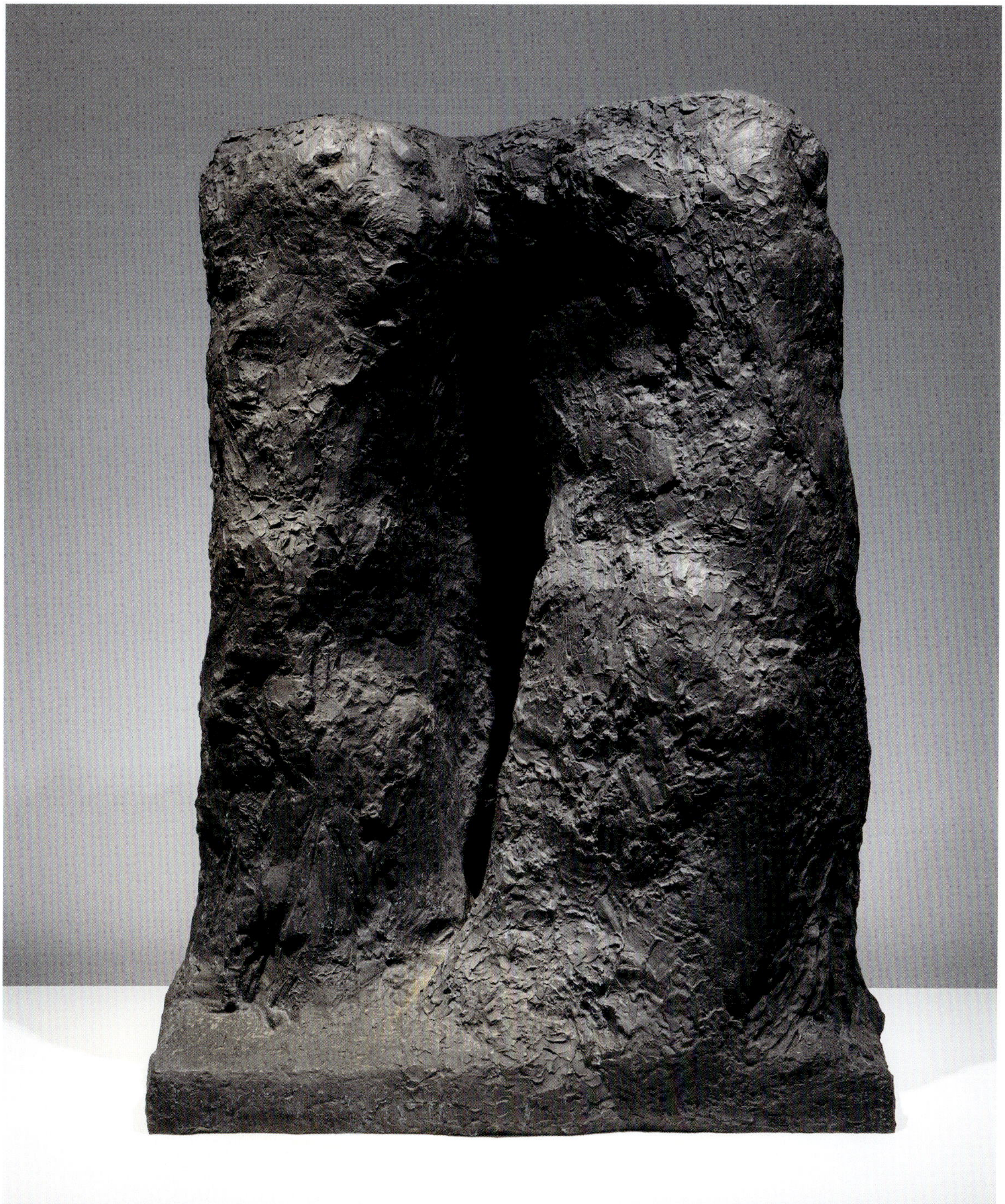

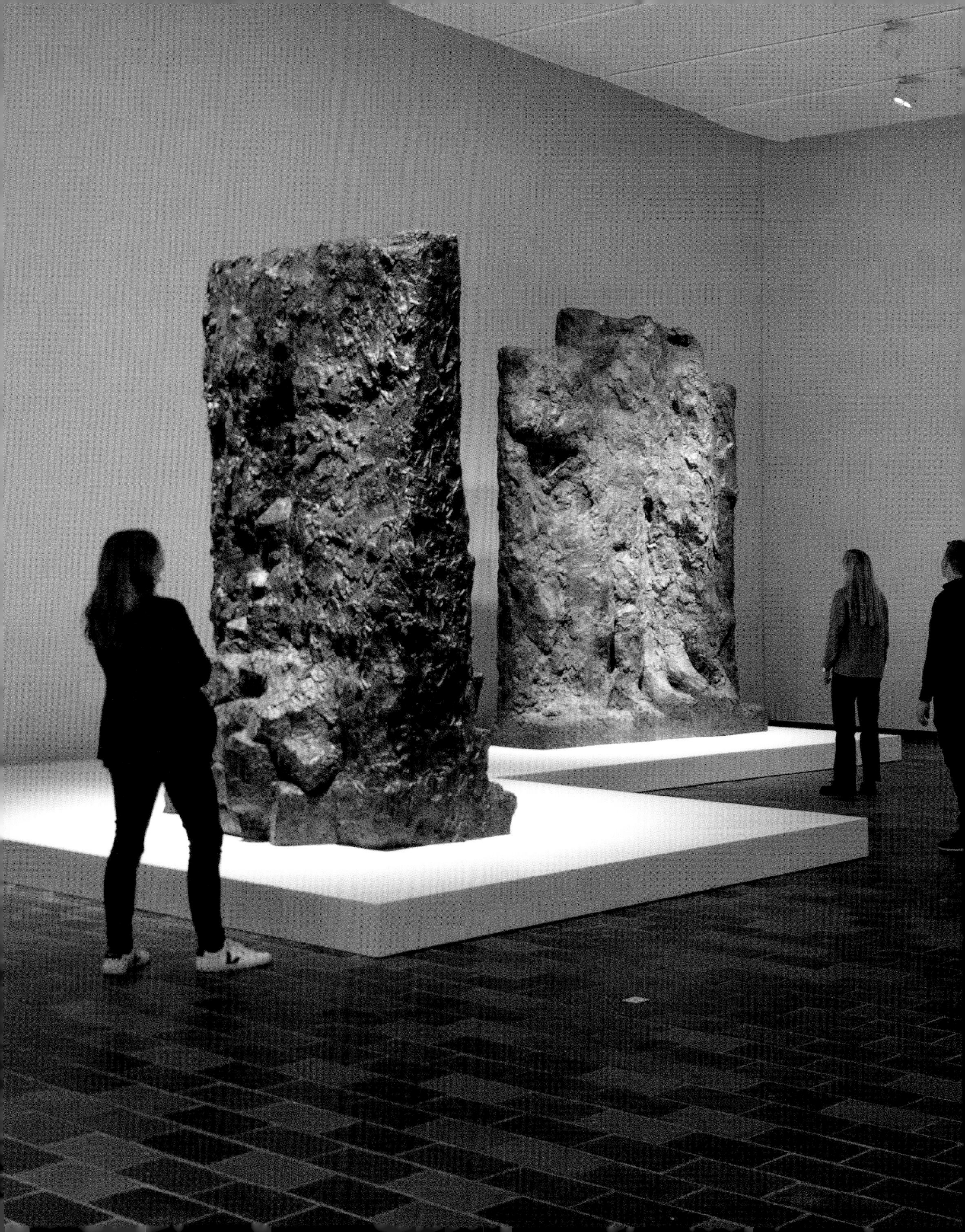

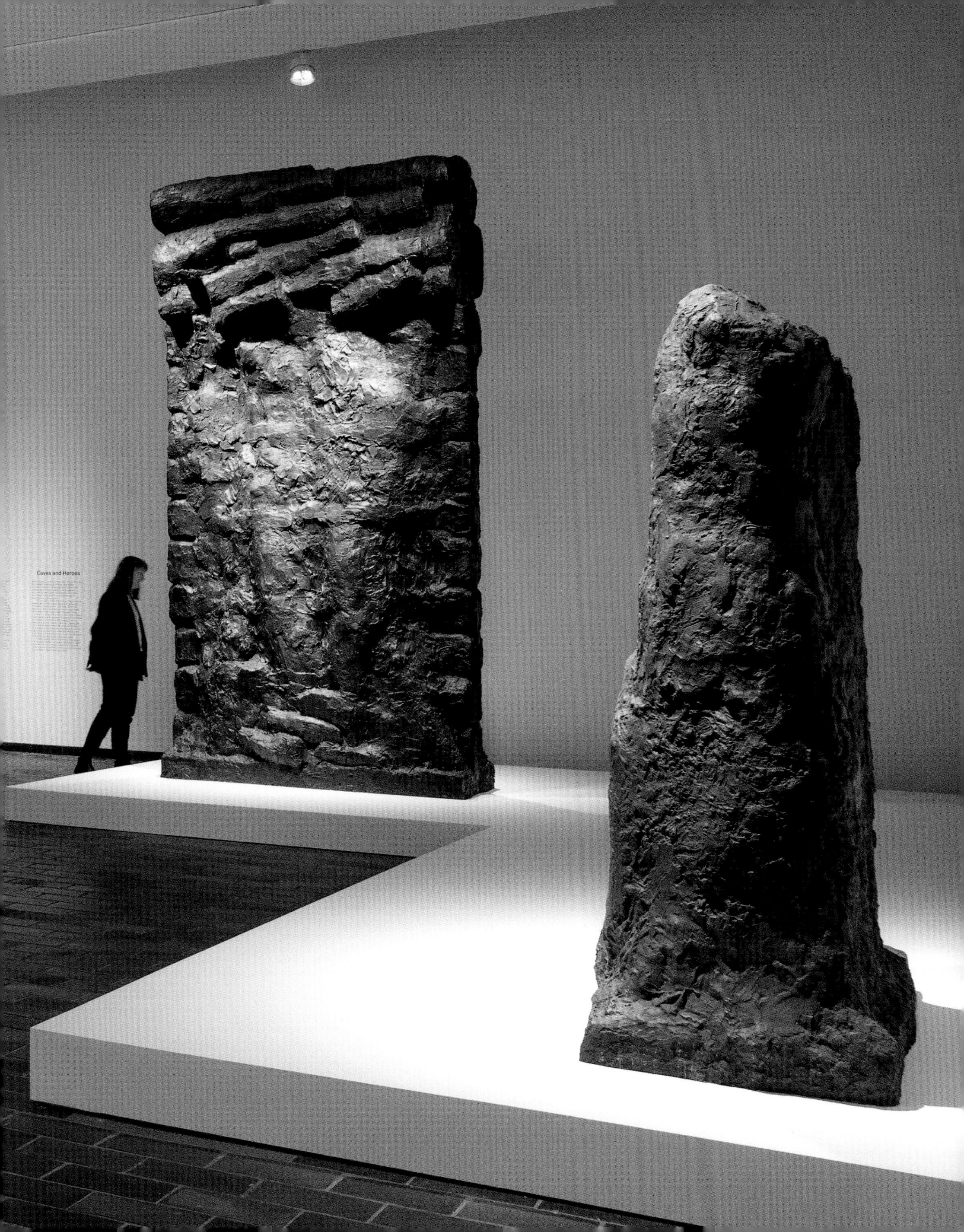
Caves and Heroes

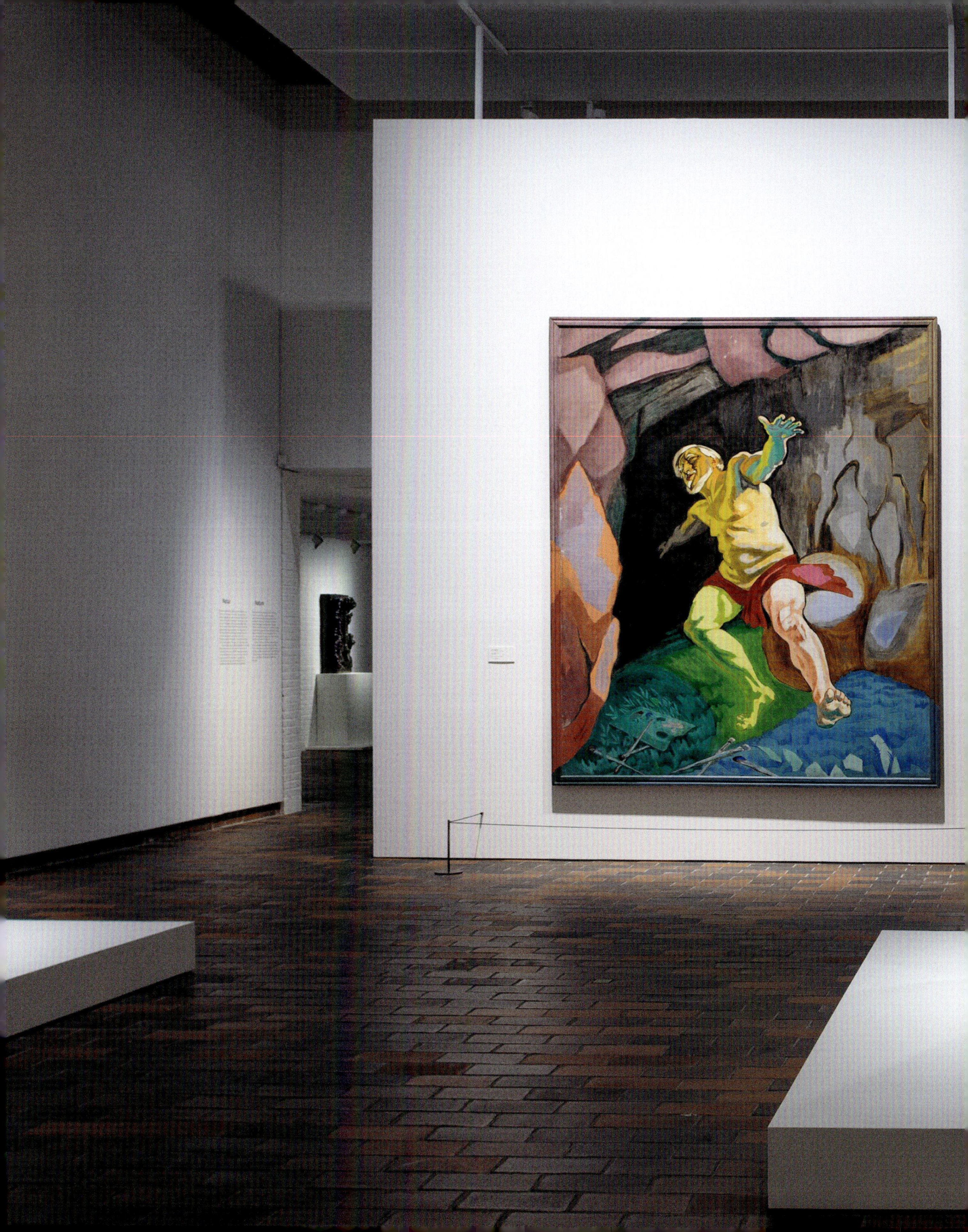

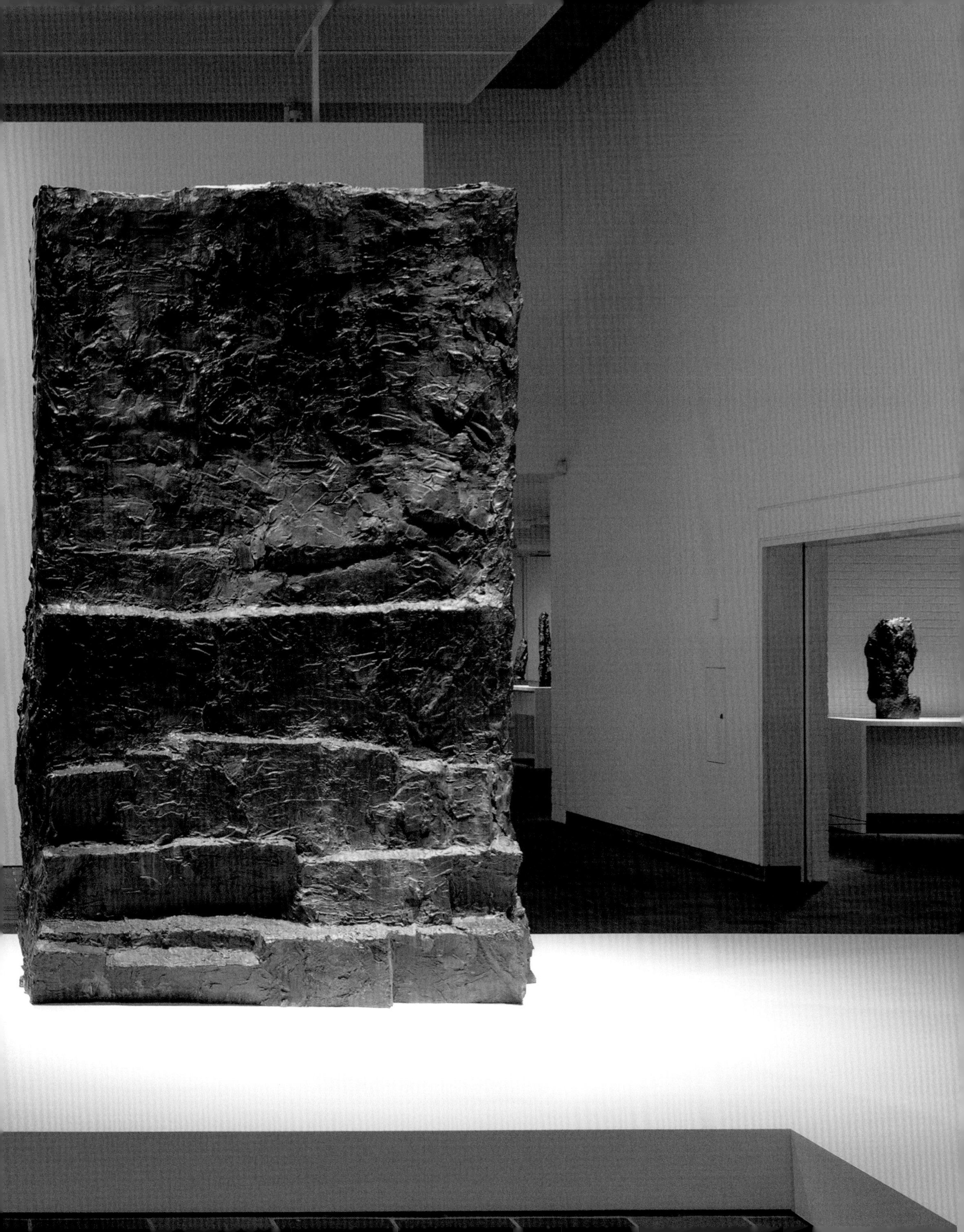

Jason

Jason and the Golden Fleece is a story of power, marriage and love. Jason's uncle, Pelias, has usurped the throne of Thessaly from Jason's father. But Jason can win it back if he brings Pelias the Golden Fleece, the magical fleece of a legendary ram. Helped by Athena, Jason equips his ship, the Argo, manning it with the greatest heroes of his day, the so-called Argonauts. Heracles even joins them for a spell. The task, of course, is near impossible and riddled with trials worthy of an Odysseus (the Odyssey may be partly modelled on Jason's mythical quest), but they finally succeed with the aid of Medea. Jason marries Medea and returns home, where Medea kills Pelias. Banished by Pelias's son, they seek refuge with King Creon. Jason later leaves Medea, who kills Jason's new bride and finally her own children to avenge herself on him. Jason dies on the Argo – crushed beneath the rotten prow, according to one version; by the ship's wheel, according to another. An ironic ending for a great navigator. For Kirkeby, Jason comes by way of Bertel Thorvaldsen. In several of his many books, Kirkeby discusses Thorvaldsen and how to interpret the famous Danish sculptor's classicism. When he was working on *Large Stele*, which is about Jason, Kirkeby had a photocopy of Thorvaldsen's *Jason* at hand to maintain his orientation. Kirkeby's Jason, however, is completely different from Thorvaldsen's, whose hero is still in balance. In Kirkeby's work, the body is a barely visible, load-bearing skeleton, while beams hover at the top. The image has been inverted, insofar as being a hero means shouldering a great burden.

Poul Erik Tøjner

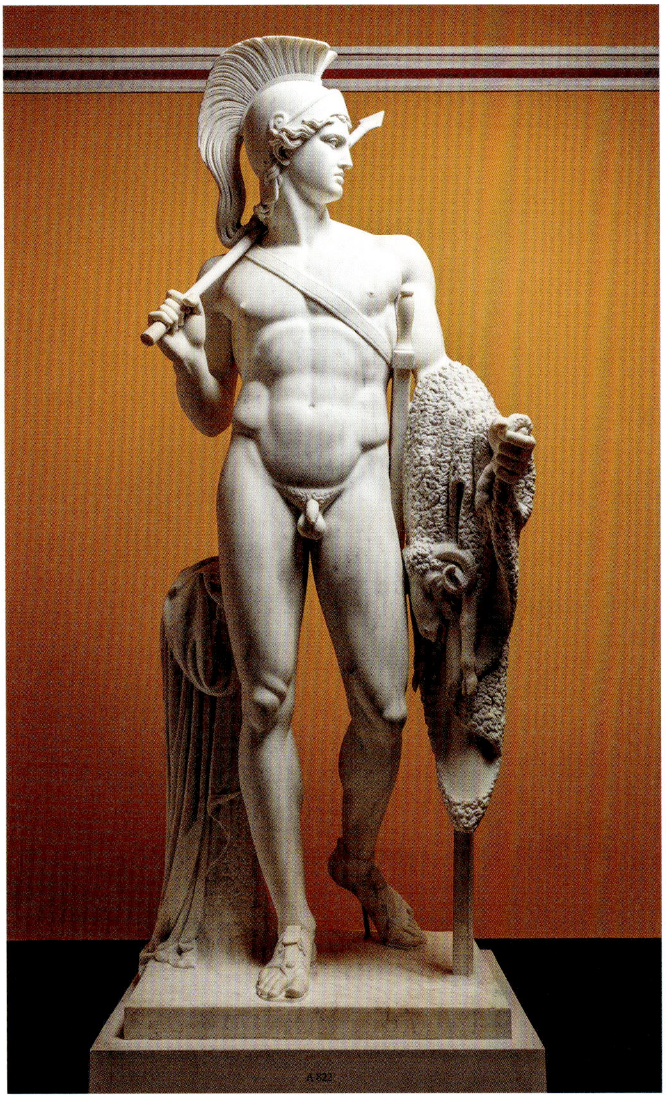

Bertel Thorvaldsen
Jason with the Golden Fleece, 1803
Marble, 242 cm
Thorvaldsens Museum

→
Large Stele, 2002 / 420 × 200 × 100 cm

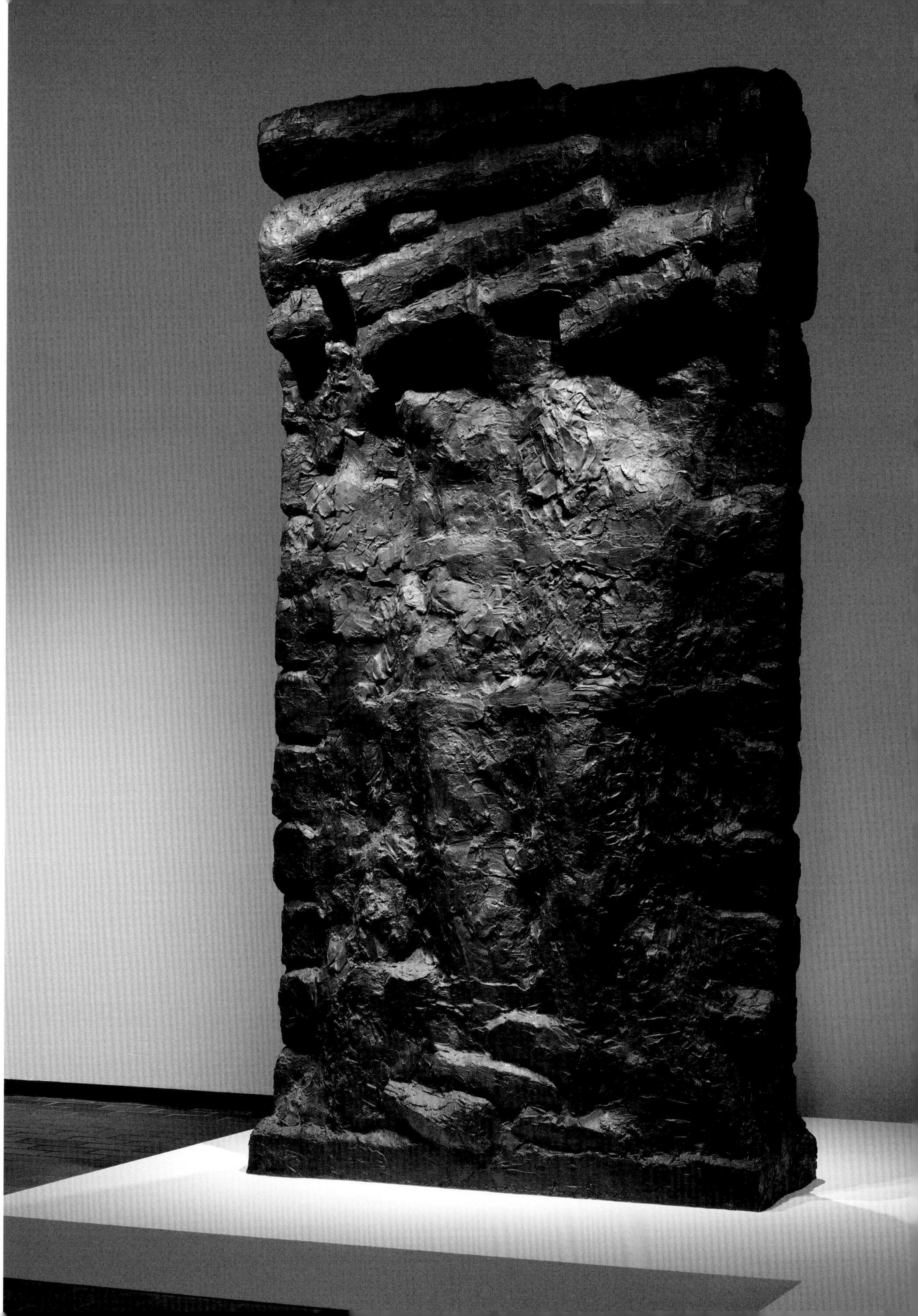

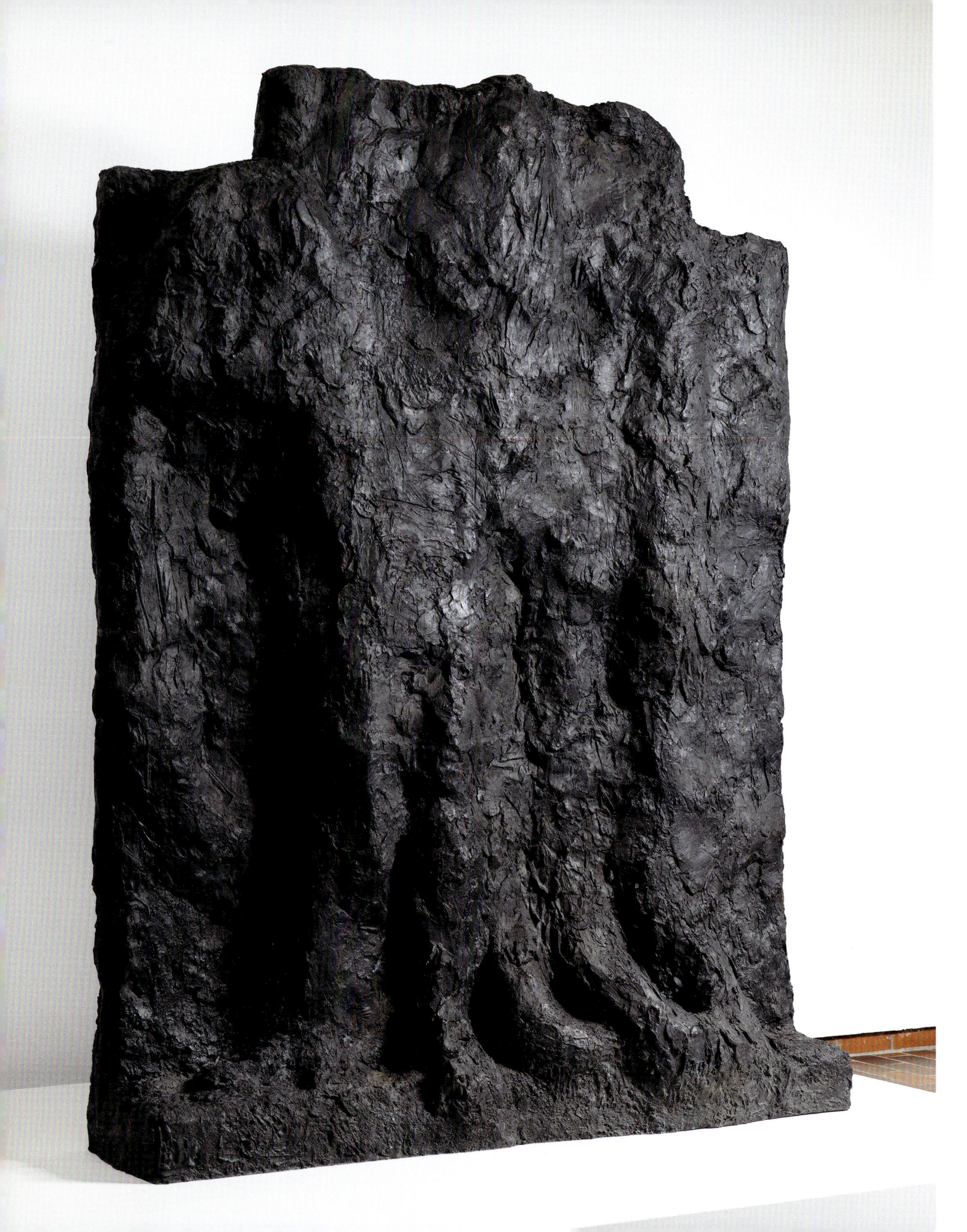

Heracles

Killing the Lernaean Hydra (Lerna was a region in classical Greece) is the second of the twelve labours of Heracles. The Hydra is a many-headed monster, whose breath alone is lethal. It has one immortal head, partly made of gold. Its other heads can be severed, but no sooner is one head lopped off than two other heads spring up in its place. The task is nothing short of a self-destructive nightmare for anyone who dares to take it on. Heracles performs his labours to achieve immortality, but he could not have slain the Hydra without a little help. His nephew Iolaus lit a fire around the Hydra and used a brand to cauterize the monster's necks before new heads could spring up. Striking the final blow, Heracles severs the Hydra's one immortal head, which he then buries. Not everyone approved of his deed. Some even thought Heracles had cheated by involving Iolaus.

For Kirkeby, Heracles is, of course, a great classical myth, one in which the artist can mirror himself, after a fashion. But above all, Heracles is a sculpture by Rudolph Tegner, the great Danish Symbolist, or Vitalist, who went his own way and was marginalized in his time. Such an existential watermark is hardly what Kirkeby is after as much as the way in which Tegner made his sculpture. One big wall is how Kirkeby describes it. He reads this gate-like sculpture into his own observations on Rodin's *The Gates of Hell*. This is the jumping-off point for Kirkeby's sculpture, which today stands in Aars. The labours of Heracles resemble the trials of Jason, another of Kirkeby's heroes, and the art-historical reference is no doubt not the only one informing his choice of subject. Such labours are also those of the artist.

Poul Erik Tøjner

Rudolph Tegner
Heracles and the Hydra, 1932
Fountain in bronze, 611 × 597 × 168 cm
Elsinore
←
Heracles, 1991-92 / 345 × 254 × 75 cm

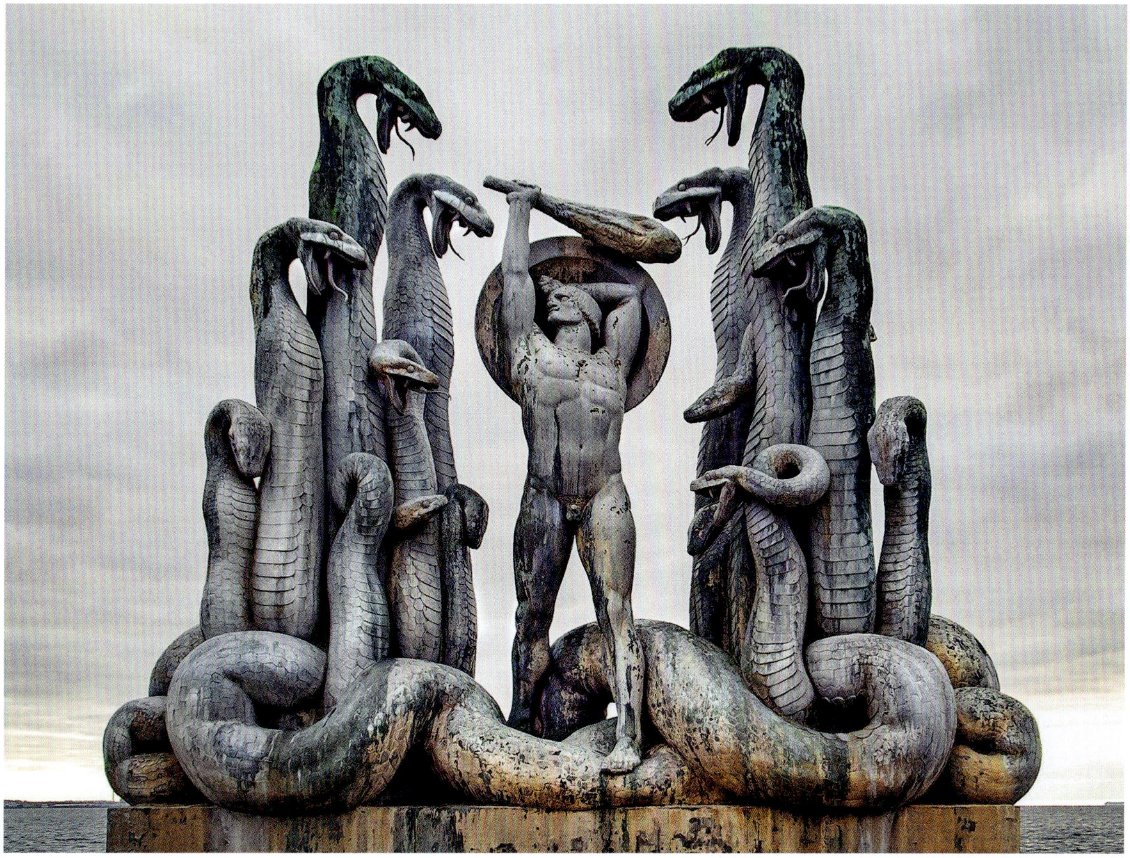

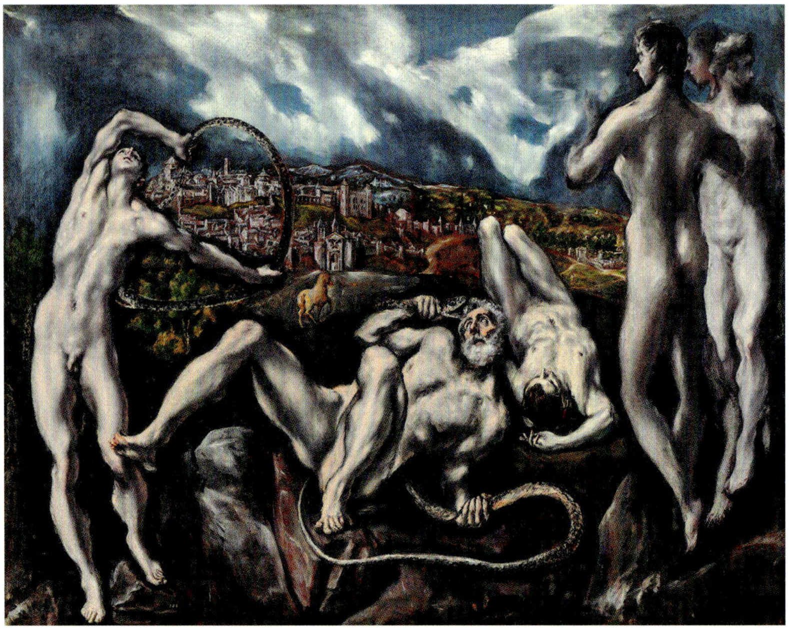

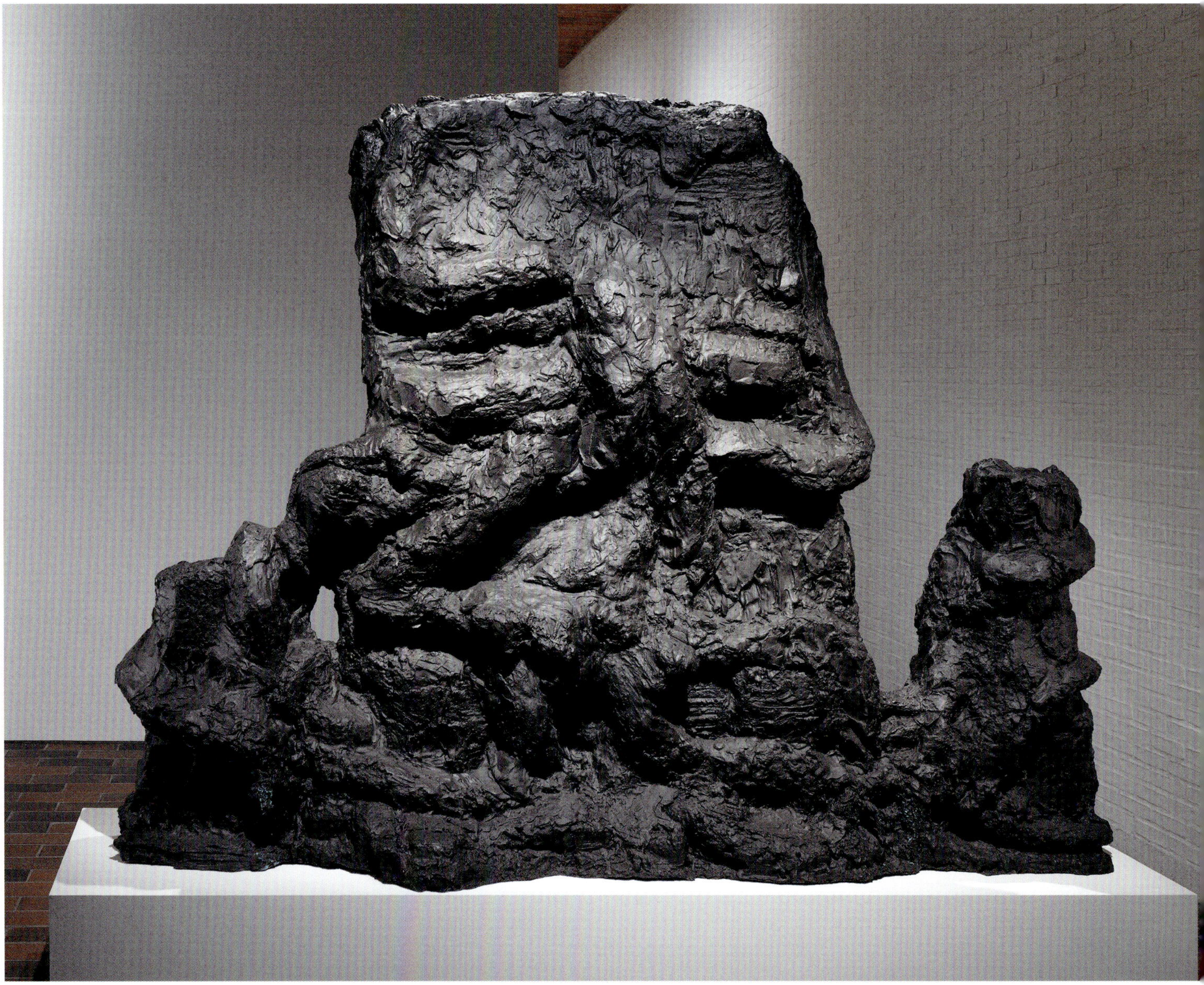

Laocoön

While Heracles slew the many-headed Lernaean Hydra, Laocoön did not stand a chance against the two sea serpents sent by Apollo to punish him and his two sons. Laocoön's crimes were many: he did not stay celibate, as he had promised Apollo (he lay with his wife in a temple of Apollo), and he warned the Trojans of the strange wooden horse left behind by the Greeks that led to the fall of Troy. Antiquity had its own Laocoön sculpture – made by three sculptors in Rhodes, if Pliny is to be believed. The sculpture's real fame came after it was rediscovered in the Renaissance, when its delicate balance between drama and harmonious form became highly influential. Laocoön is portrayed at the moment when terror is expressed in a cry – a feature that the German philosopher Lessing later made a key point of his essay on the sculpture (today, the essay is almost as famous as the sculpture). Lessing examines what sculpture and visual art can do as compared to poetry. While poetry unfolds in temporal sequence, sculpture must realize a peak point, in this case the height of the character's suffering. El Greco, the Mannerist master who was the subject of a brief book by Kirkeby, painted his Laocoön as a protest against the Renaissance love of harmony and balance. Distorted, crooked, exuding doom, El Greco's work is radically different from the noble music of a classical monument. Kirkeby, in his version of the drama, likewise makes an ornament of pain.

Poul Erik Tøjner

Laocoön, 2011 / 400 × 200 cm

←

El Greco

Laocoön, c. 1610/1614

Oil on canvas, 137 × 172 cm

National Gallery of Art, Washington

Laocoön, 2012 / 220 × 260 × 60 cm

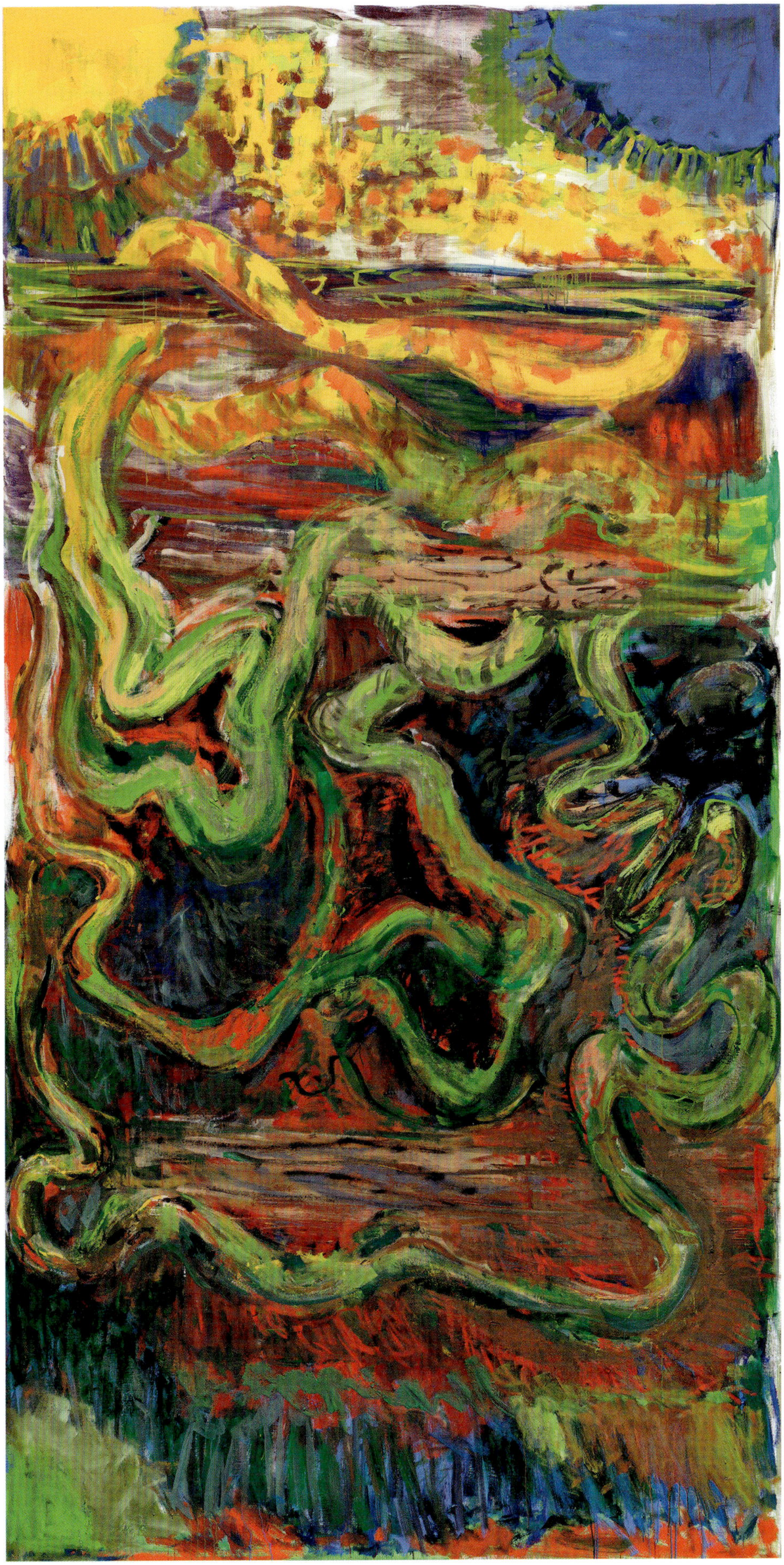

On the Erotic in the Work of Per Kirkeby

Ulrich Wilmes

In a critical comment on a text about the development of Per Kirkeby's bronze sculptures, the Danish cultural critic Lars Morell pointed out in 1998 that not a word had been said about the erotic theme.[1] But even though questions are asked about it in his own highly detailed conversations with the artist, the subject, which is indeed important in Kirkeby's work, is even there only discussed in passing. This justified criticism may thus be taken as a cue for a renewed examination of the works with a view to tracking down the erotic in their subjects and their execution. The work examples cited below only contribute to a sporadic approach to the complex.

Against the background of the oeuvre in general, the treatment of the erotic by Kirkeby becomes both difficult to penetrate and intriguing, because it is rarely a directly evident feature; it is more a subtly concealed undercurrent. Like most of his themes, erotic motifs are scattered on paths that lure the viewer on. The works seduce you into following the course of what you expect to be a narrative, and then leave you alone with objects that are decipherable, but whose meaning in the context is not revealed. As Poul Erik Tøjner has noted: "Contrary to the widespread notion whereby you are always expected to ask about the meaning of things when you cannot see what they represent, asking about the meaning of things when you *can* see what they represent is in fact even more crucial; that is, when the things that you can see they represent do not fall easily into a narrative that gives up its own meaning. In Kirkeby's case it does not – it is given meaning by Kirkeby. And is thus difficult to grasp – directly."[2] This means that the observation and identification of a narrative takes place only by way of projections in the observer.

All the same, the genesis of the bronze sculptures seems to have been stimulated by erotic motifs. With them, the artist created a new medium for himself at the beginning of the 1980s – a decision that was an understandable result of his then intensive preoccupation with the problems surrounding figuration, which can also be demonstrated in his paintings of the time, and which so to speak functioned as a trigger for a sculptural reworking of them. In Kirkeby's own words: "The connection is after all that they are almost already there when you look at my paintings from that period. They are prefigured in the paintings. They are just waiting to get out. It's fantastic when I see how sculpture lies waiting in those pictures to get out."[3]

With the bronzes Kirkeby at the same time further developed an original artistic will to translate biographical and image-creating material into "figures." As the artist explained: "If the figures, converted into metaphor, keep pursuing me, that's because I persist with something that was important right from the start of the 1960s: that art is *about* something, there must be a content."[4]

The bronzes present a tangible physicality along with an unconscious sensuality. They show no figures – but they are figurative. Their figurative elements are only in a certain sense perceptible. Their sensory nature does not consist of the revelation of the form, it arises from the process of producing them. The penetration of the formable material does not consciously aim at presentation, rather at the sometimes pleasurable exploitation of what Kirkeby called "idea = figure":

"The basis has been an anecdote that has broken down. A figure, the implementation of an idea, has collapsed, and in so doing has made manifest its own non-linguistic character."[5] A figure is created on the basis of a more or less specific biographical precondition with a fully premeditated unconsciousness. That is, Kirkeby elevates the sensory experience of the work above its linguistic description or decoding without abandoning the idea of content.

The synthetic structure which first and foremost characterizes the external appearance of the bronzes is evident in exemplary form in *Small Head and Arm* (1981). The small sculpture delineates a sharply profiled form where – in accordance with the title – head and arm have been fused together. The tangible modelling disguises the individual expression. Nevertheless the profile, with brow, eye socket, nose and cheek, is comprehensibly juxtaposed with a form which analogously appears as an arm laid behind a head. As corporeal stage scenery, head and arm involve narrative or "anecdotal" references. They are based on physiognomic features of Kirkeby's partner at the time, Vibeke; features that he felt attracted by. He regarded the characteristic facial features and the distinctive form of the arm as signs, out of whose collapse he produced the figure.

The facial features are enclosed in the upper arm. Accordingly, the arm and head, as elements of an organic fusion, seem in no way consciously chosen, as Kirkeby's description of the structure of the figure makes clear.

Small Head with Arm, 1981 / 35 × 23 × 16 cm

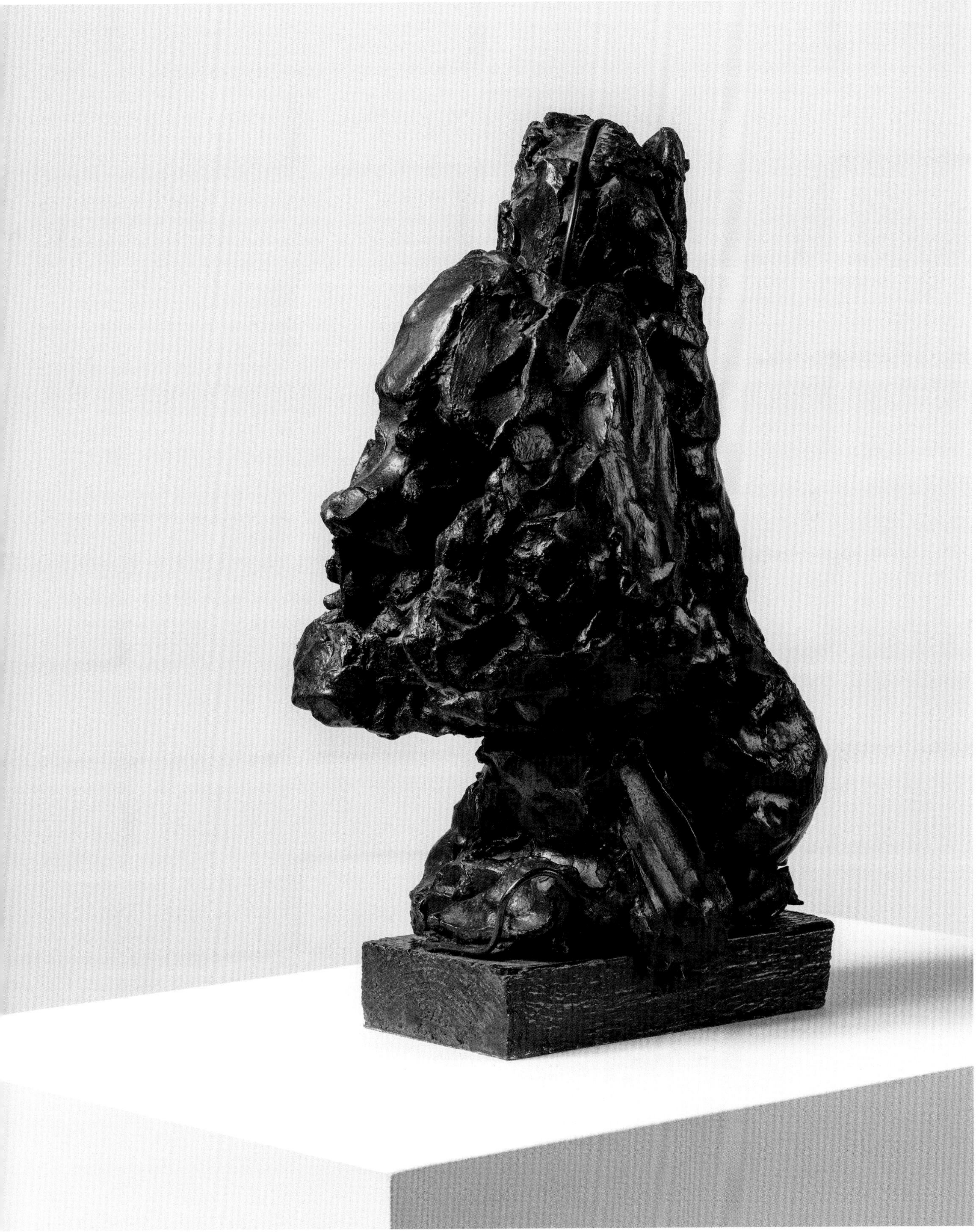

For example, he speaks frankly of the great delight these bodily features give him. He describes her "snub nose, high cheekbones and soft sensual lips" and "that fat – I mustn't say that – powerful, sensual upper arm", pointing at the excitement that can arise in the bodily relationship between two human beings.[6]

Two untitled drawings from 1979 are among the rare representations of recognizable full-length figures. The central motif is a nude female model. Here too Kirkeby stresses the facial profile – in a clearly Cubist manner – as well as arms and thighs as characteristic bodily features. Both exhibit a liveliness that comes from his use of various drawing and painting techniques. The contours of the figure are energetically emphasized by the assured placing of powerful crayon strokes that are coated and supplemented with a lightly inked wash. On one of the sheets the contour drawing ends in the depiction of jutting buttocks. The second sheet has more abstract brushwork which to a greater extent contextualizes the figure, such that it almost looks concealed. Nevertheless arm and thigh are clearly emphasized.

In the painting *Vibeke* from 1983, with similar precisely executed brushwork, Kirkeby marks out the back view of the woman. Minimal strokes of paint which draw the arm, shoulder and head are sufficient to define the figure. Only the green snake in the bottom corner, separated from the woman by an indeterminate, radiant white barrier, adds an attribute that symbolizes a narrative element of seduction and deception. The recognizable motifs emerge from abstract surroundings which cannot be decoded. On the other hand the indeterminacy leaves the viewer consigned to a state of doubt about what is visibly accessible.

In *Large Head with Arm* (1983) (p. 63) Kirkeby forms the figure from two body fragments, the anthropomorphic combination of which he expands symbolically. The sculpture, which is built up over a narrow base, has an agitated surface and a clearly demarcated form which intensifies the intended sensation produced by the specific bodily features. The external closure of the figure is breached by a formal penetration that splits it from head and arm. This gaping opening leaves both elements in a state of tension. The sculptural modelling brings about a shading of the profile side which determines our perception of the sculpture from both one side and the other. As Kirkeby explained: "In the final analysis .... [you distinguish] the figure and make the rest shadow – that is, the two things are separated."[7] Although perception of the form depends on the perspective of the given observer, this separation has an aggressive, telling effect – it is in a way the actual subject of the sculpture. In reality it functions as the shameless enlargement of a vulva which on the basis of the synthesis of profile and upper arm, stylized into erotic fetishes, copulates in a bizarre, peculiar portrait.

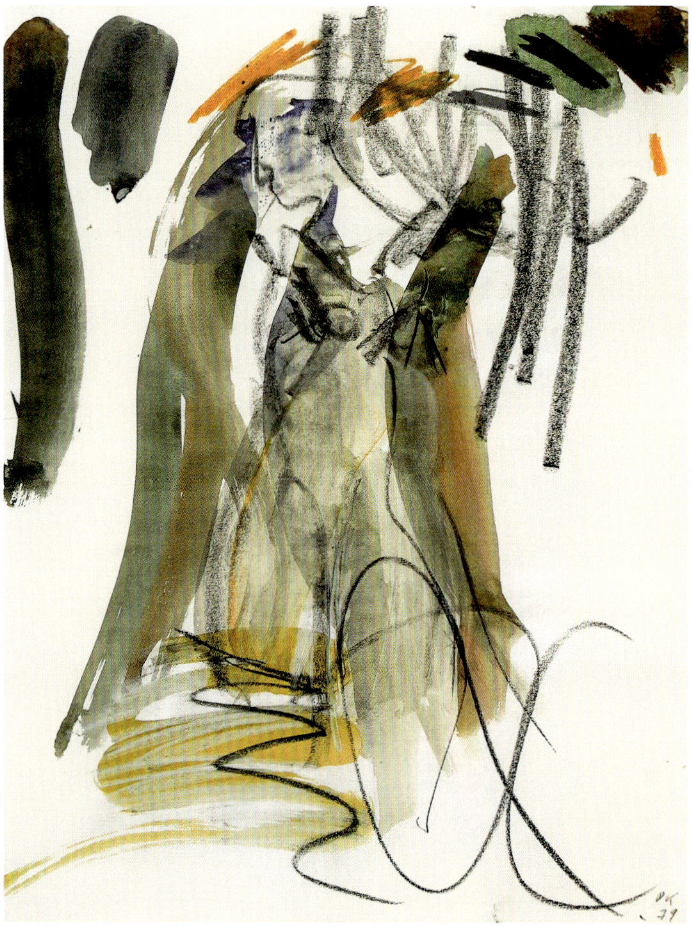

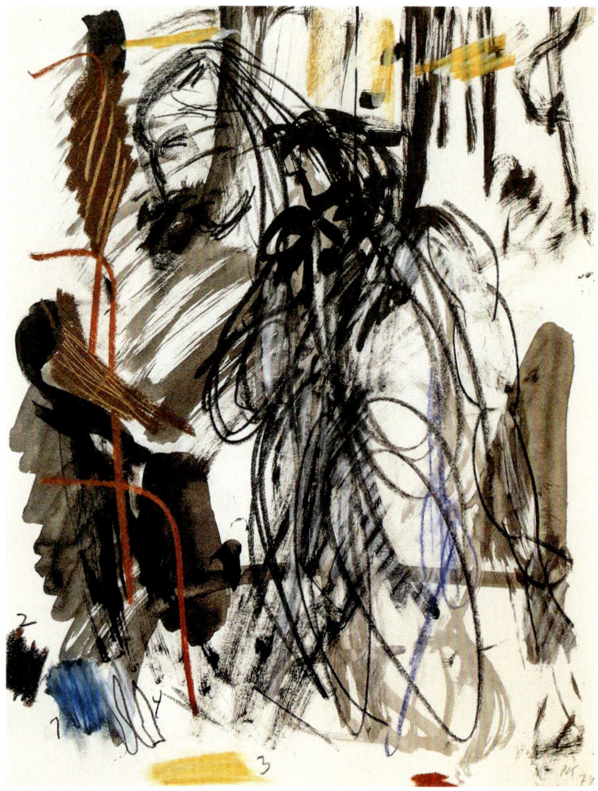

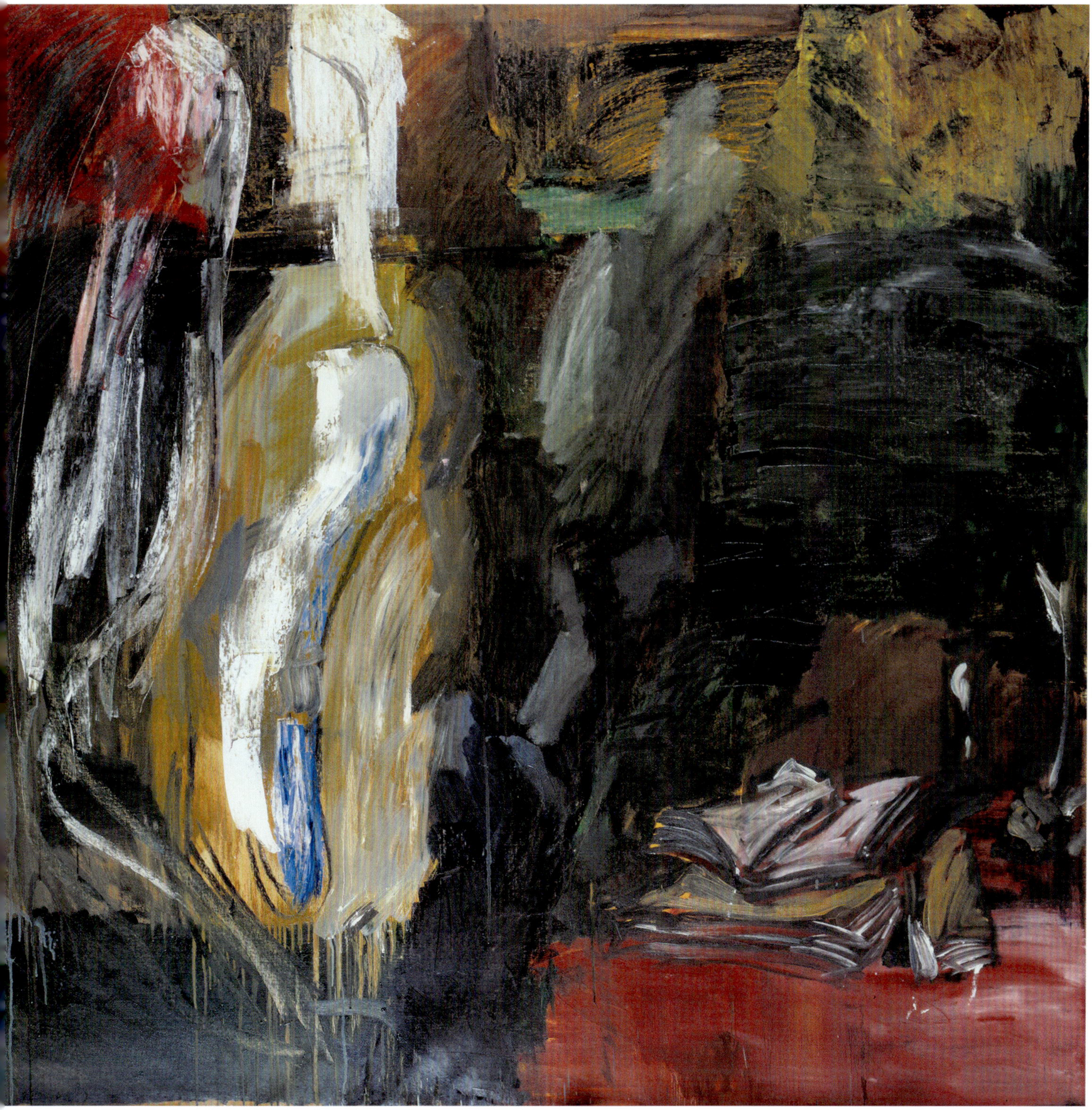

Vibeke, 1982
Oil on canvas, 200 × 200 cm
←
Untitled, 1979
Pastel, wax, crayon, gouache on paper
Untitled, 1979
Pastel, wax, crayon, gouache on paper

In this connection a remark that Kirkeby let fall in relation to the images to which Vibeke gave rise can be applied to the early bronzes: "It's all those layers, stories, frictions and unresolved problems – it's just that in my view they are in many ways unresolvable, and that is in fact what makes a painting ... If you have figure as idea, you can say that they cover the same thing. You can also be a little kinder to yourself and call it figuration. 'Figuration' is in other words very close to 'sign'. That's what happens with many of these Vibeke images."[8]

The execution of the figure is something Kirkeby does consciously and yet at the same time abandons to unconscious control. In its origin and course the transformation of the bodily sensation remains transparent and communicates the haptic appropriation of an emotional experience. The reception of the process is thereby consummated in the "non-linguistic" perception of a figure as a totality. Its form communicates Kirkeby's penetrative preoccupation with a specific bodily image which he develops from the real model, in the certainty that we do not have access to the objective nature of things, and that we remain dependent on the perception of external appearance. This bodily appropriation of the real, which for us can always only have the character of phenomenon, thus in the nature of things remains fragmentary for Kirkeby.

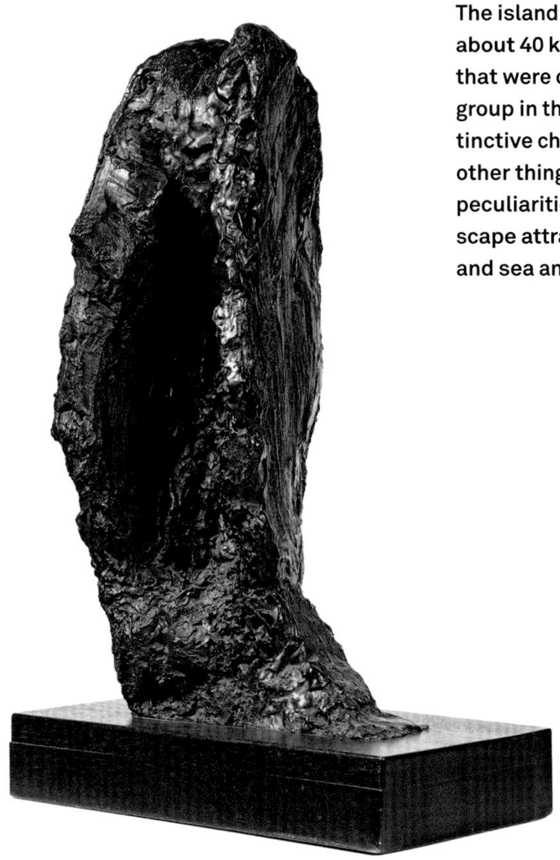

The early work group from the years between 1981 and 1986 with its variations on the theme "head with/and arm" depicts a spectrum of different figurations. Given that Kirkeby has spoken of how the "figures" almost "pursue" him, it would appear that they caught up with him in the bronze sculptures, or he let them catch up with him subject to the conditions of a specific place. *Læsø Head I* to *IV* (1983) links up with the same bodily fragments, which are partly given form in an unstinting, resolute fashion.

In 1980 Kirkeby had bought a former farm with the name "Hope" on the Danish island of Læsø, and established a studio for himself where the first bronzes were made. The island lies in the northern Kattegat, about 40 km from the mainland. The works that were created there make up a special group in the total oeuvre; they have a distinctive character which relates to among other things Kirkeby's fascination with the peculiarities of Læsø: the island's landscape attractions, surrounded by beaches and sea and with intact natural systems. The location of the island gave him an ideal place to which he could withdraw, far from the city milieus where both his acquaintances and cultural activities were normally located. There he found time and peace for the observation of nature and a concentrated self-reflection to which he could devote his time undisturbed.

During his long, productive summer stays Kirkeby found himself in a situation of isolation and absence which turned his thoughts in controversial directions.
Not only were most of the bronze sculptures made there, but also a number of pictures that had his partner Vibeke as their theme. The two series of works were closely related. Thus the painting *Vibeke* from 1982 (p. 61) arose concurrently with and as a variant of the "arm and/with head" bronzes. At the same time, in the nature of things, the transposition of the image-figure into a spatial context in relation to the solitary, context-dependent sculptural forms functioned as an effective boundary marker. Kirkeby placed the female figure in the left half of the picture in an indeterminate internal space where some books lying open to the right on the floor speak of his own absence. The subdued colour scheme creates a dark, melancholy mood that suggests strong feelings of longing and loneliness.

Læsø Head II (p. 66) and *IV* seem in a way to have surrendered to these feelings, since they sketch out a pictorial shadow-figure which represents a radical exposure of the female sex. The head is not perceived as suggesting anything portrait-like, but as (im)pure imagination. In these variations on the theme, related to the place where they have arisen, Kirkeby fleshes out – depending on how one views it – the function of the sign-like fragments with a more or less unambiguous erotic excitement.

Læsø Head IV, 1983 / 71 × 44 × 25 cm
→
Large Head with Arm, 1983 / 199 × 82 × 40 cm

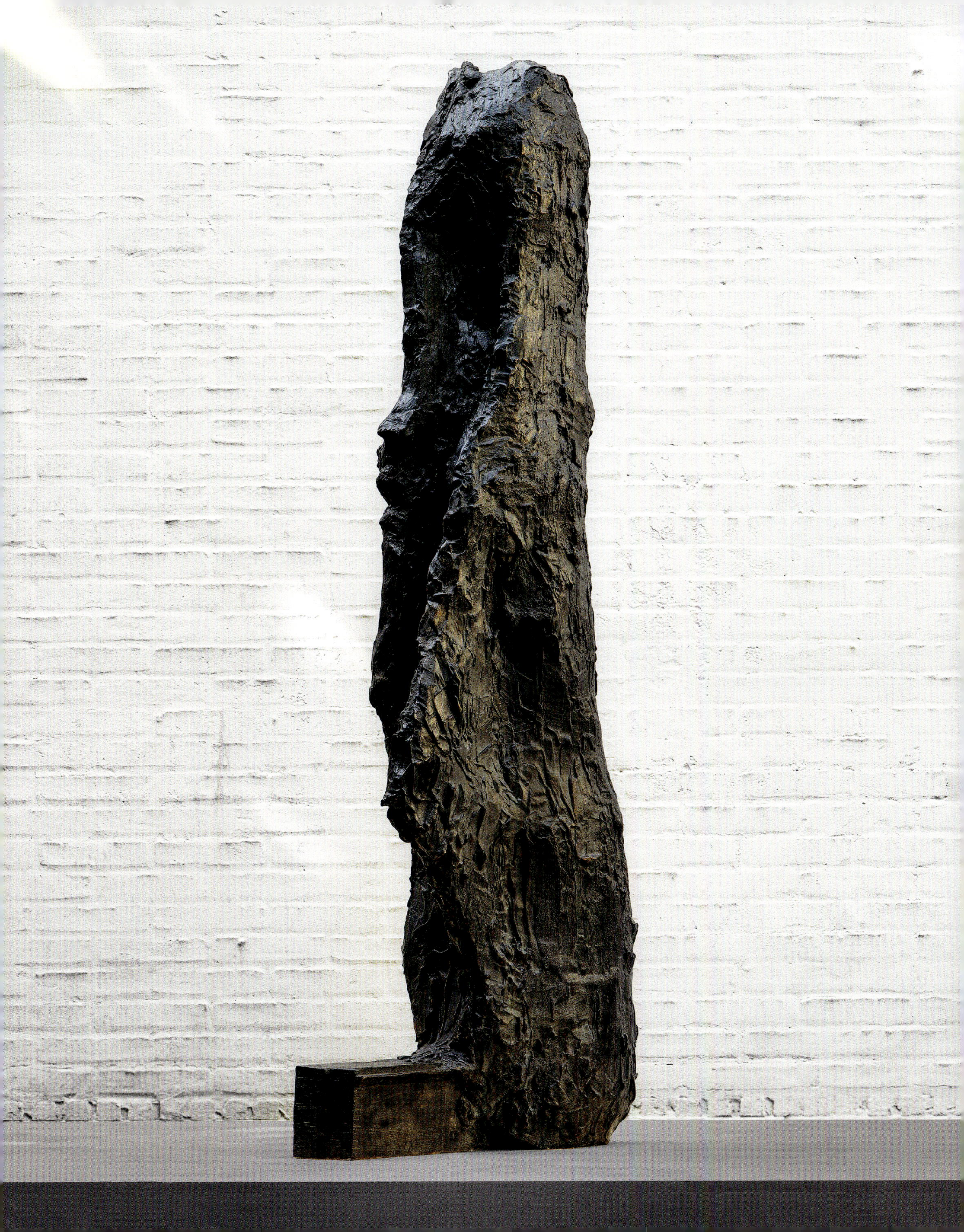

In the suite *19 Sculptures, Læsø* from 1983, Kirkeby has in dry-point etchings improvised on the theme "head and/with arm." With a formulation of the German art historian Michael Semff, "in the most direct way they paraphrase the bronzes" and thus testify to the obsession with which the artist depicts the almost unlimited image-making possibilities that seem to lie hidden in the – in itself simple enough – figuration. In reality these prints represent studies that bring a virtuosic passion to expression. They penetrate the structures and content of the themes, where a spectrum of specific visible bodily characteristics – figure, limbs, head and sex – unfold.

These characteristics also appear in the picture *Summer Night II* (1990), which was also done on Læsø. A female pelvis occupies the foreground as a central motif – an *Origin of the World* from which the outstretched body develops. It is overlaid by a wealth of elements whose origin the observer is hardly able to see. With respect to a "pornographic dimension" in the picture Kirkeby himself spoke of these "many other things" as "the remains of a still-life object" or as "taken from the natural surroundings at the time," and about a "putrefaction mechanism, a piece of a branch or a tree-trunk with a fungus on it." These are vague references to a context in which the erotic motif is embedded: "So the drops run down there and at the bottom is the female lap that is the great drop-catcher."[9]

Kirkeby had an affinity with pornography that always made him restless. It represented an artistic provocation for him, because it was about images. At the same time he regards pornographic images in themselves as uninteresting. The erotic affect that keeps emerging from his works is triggered by a shamelessness in both form and content; a shamelessness that Kirkeby in the final analysis saw as a precondition of his conception of beauty as it can be traced for example in sculptures like *Læsø Head* or paintings like *Summer Night II*: "Sometimes there are images that make the hair on my thighs stand on end. I don't know why, it isn't just an intellectual satisfaction, it's simply direct sensation. That is what is called beautiful."[10]

1 Lars Morell, "Rumbegreber og synsoplevelser", in *Billedkunst*, 1, Silkeborg, April 1999, pp. 12-17. **2** Poul Erik Tøjner, *Per Kirkeby – Maleri*, Forlaget Bjerggaard, 1998, p. 27. **3** Per Kirkeby, *Samtaler med Lars Morell*, Borgen, 1997, p. 121. **4** Ibid., p. 94. **5** Ibid., p. 96. **6** Ibid., pp. 92-94. **7** Ibid., p. 116. **8** Ibid., p. 95. **9** Ibid., p. 174. **10** Ibid.

Ulrich Wilmes is an art historian and former Chief Curator at Haus der Kunst in Munich. He is the author of several books on among others Georg Baselitz and Gerhard Richter.

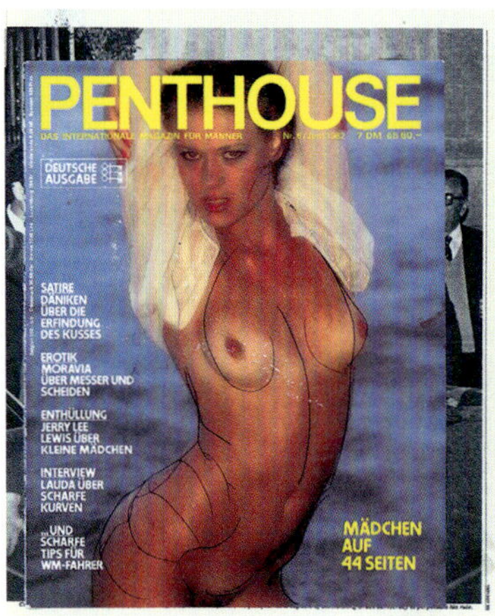

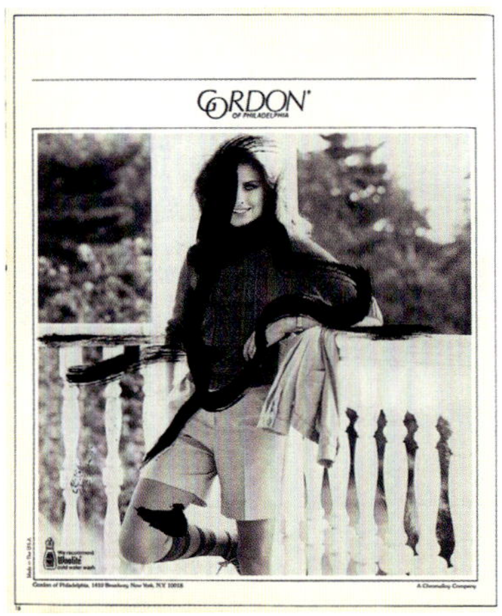

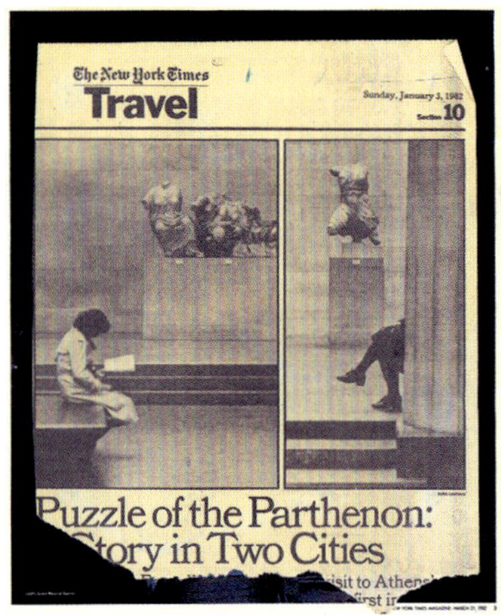

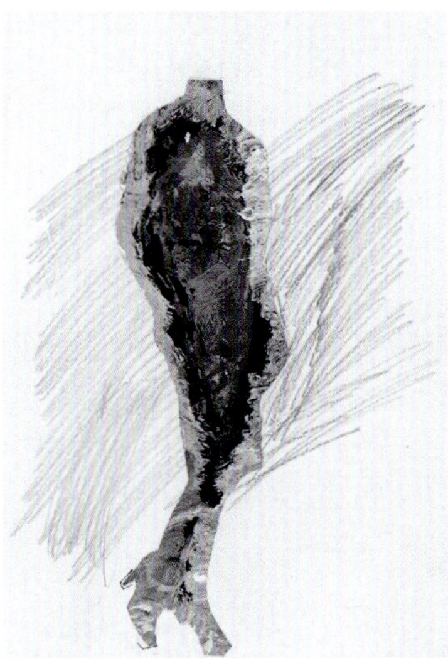

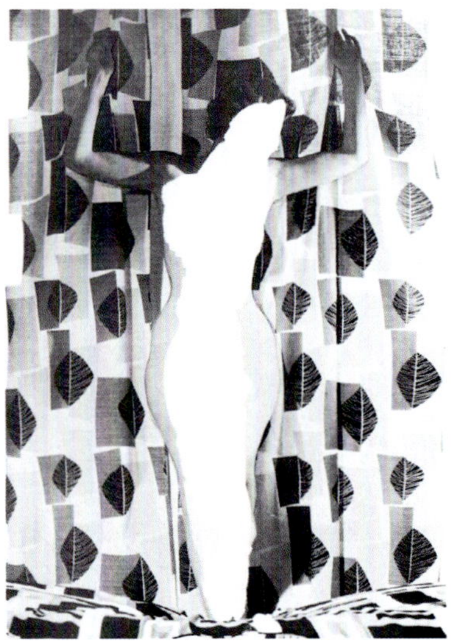

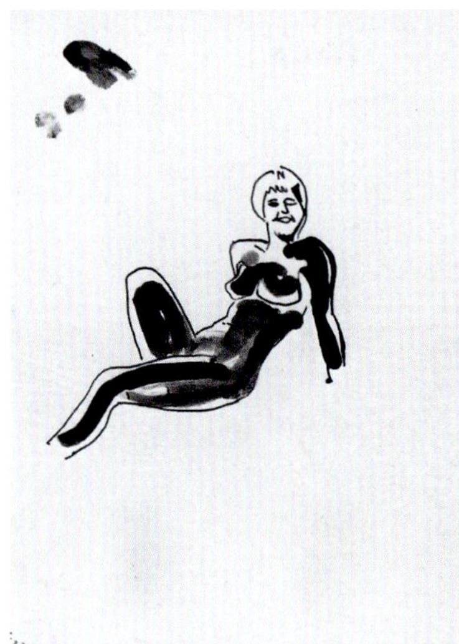

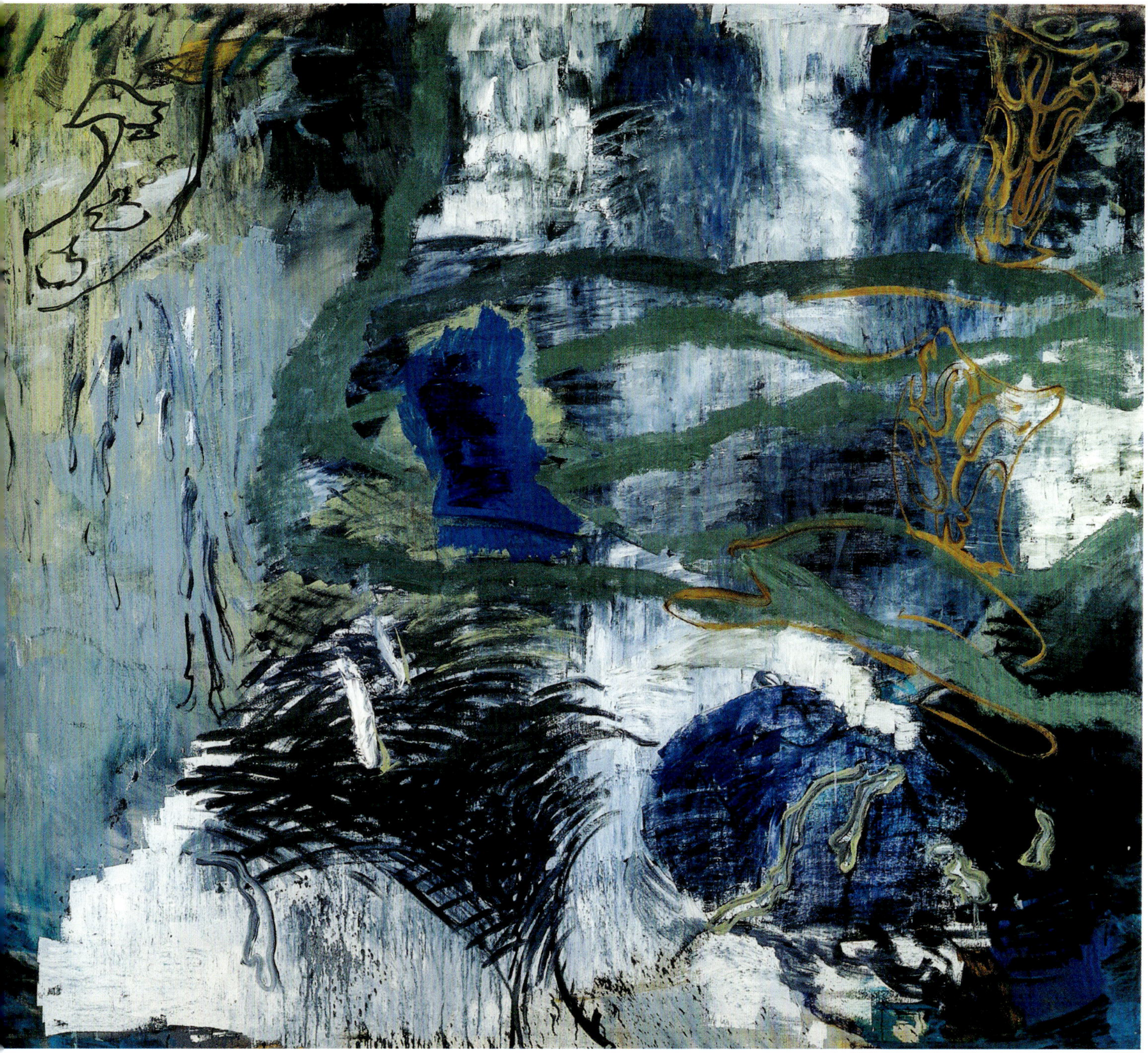

Summer Night II, 1990
Oil on canvas, 200 × 220 cm
←
Sketches and collages, c. 1982
Drawings from *Per Kirkeby:*
Norway – Sweden – Denmark 1975/76

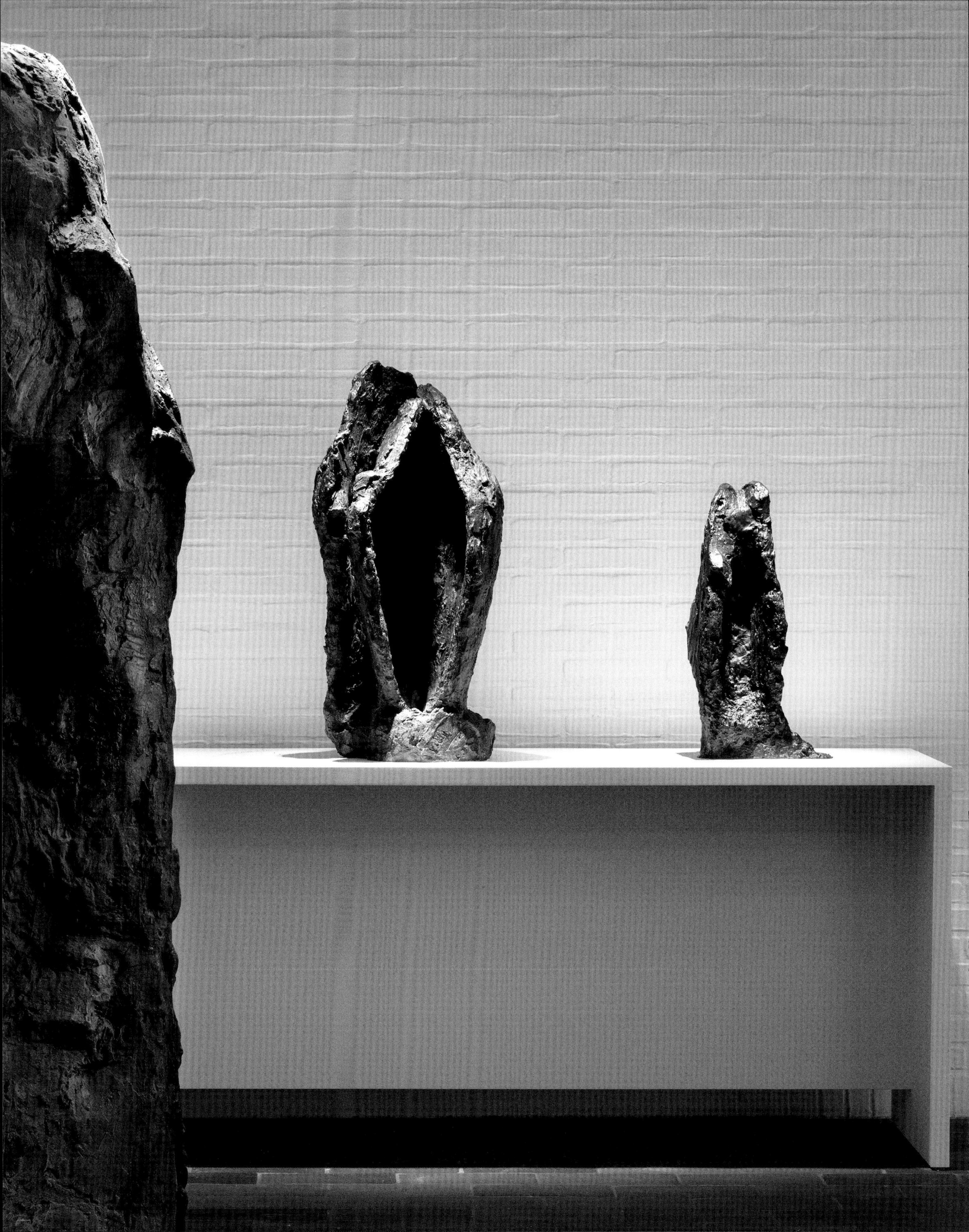

Standing Head, 1986 / 205 × 45 × 70 cm
←
Læsø-hoved II, 1983 / 91 × 38 × 42 cm
Læsø Head IV, 1983 / 71 × 44 × 25 cm

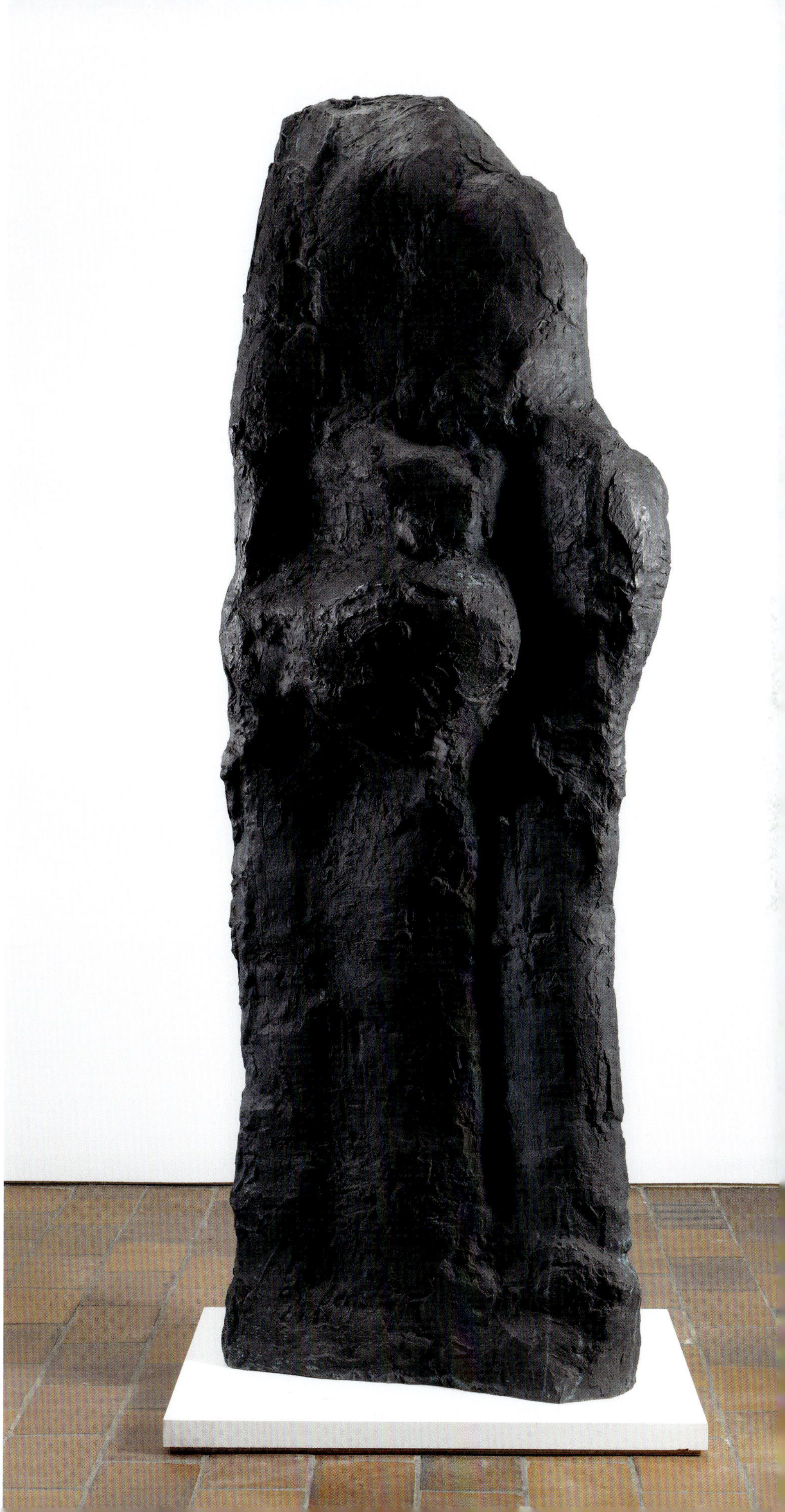

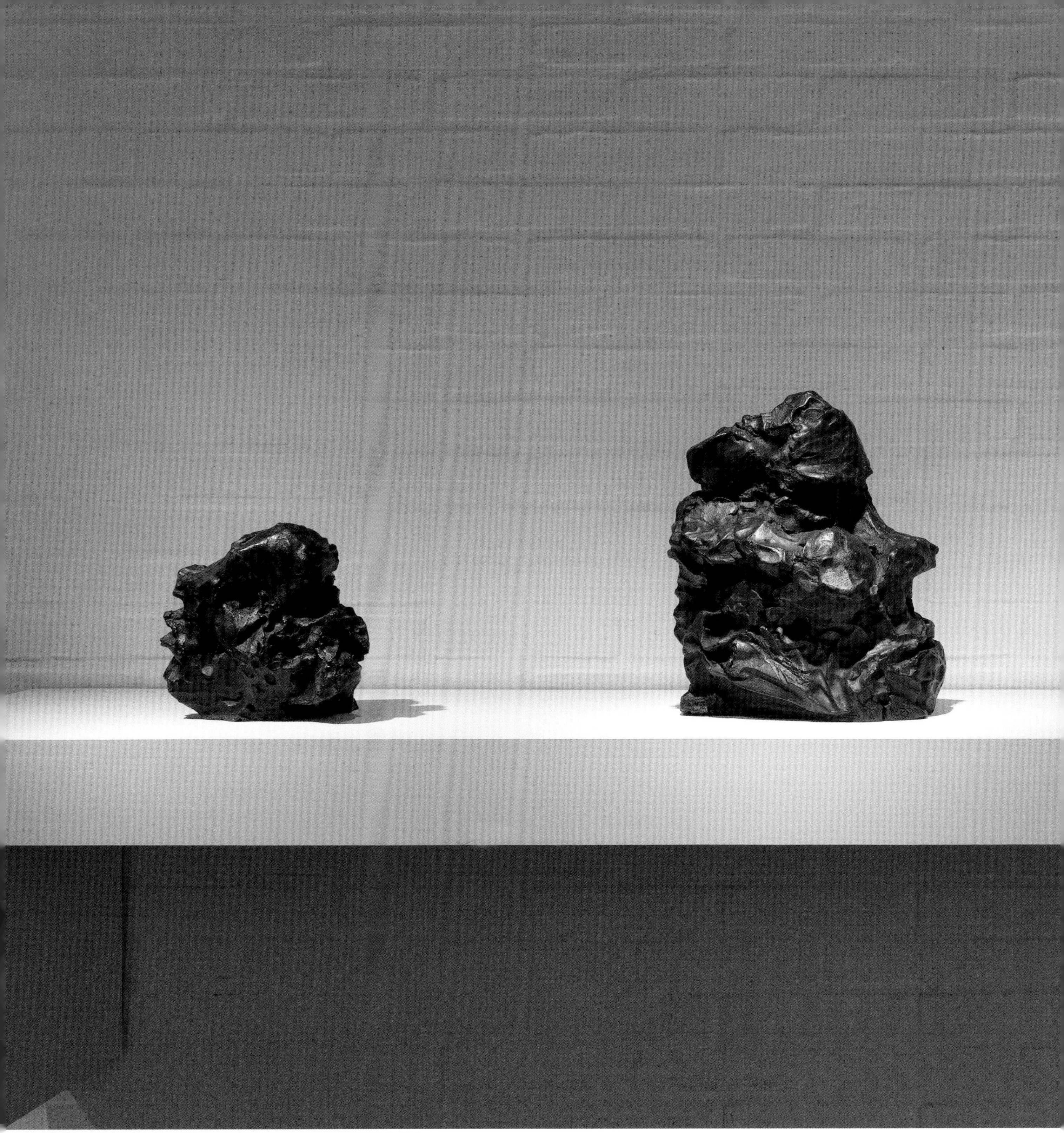

Head at Home IV, 1991-92 / 24 × 21 × 12 cm
Head at Home II, 1991-92 / 37 × 31 × 20 cm
→
Head at Home I, 1991-92 / 28 × 28 × 17 cm
Head at Home V, 1991-92 / 22 × 25 × 19 cm

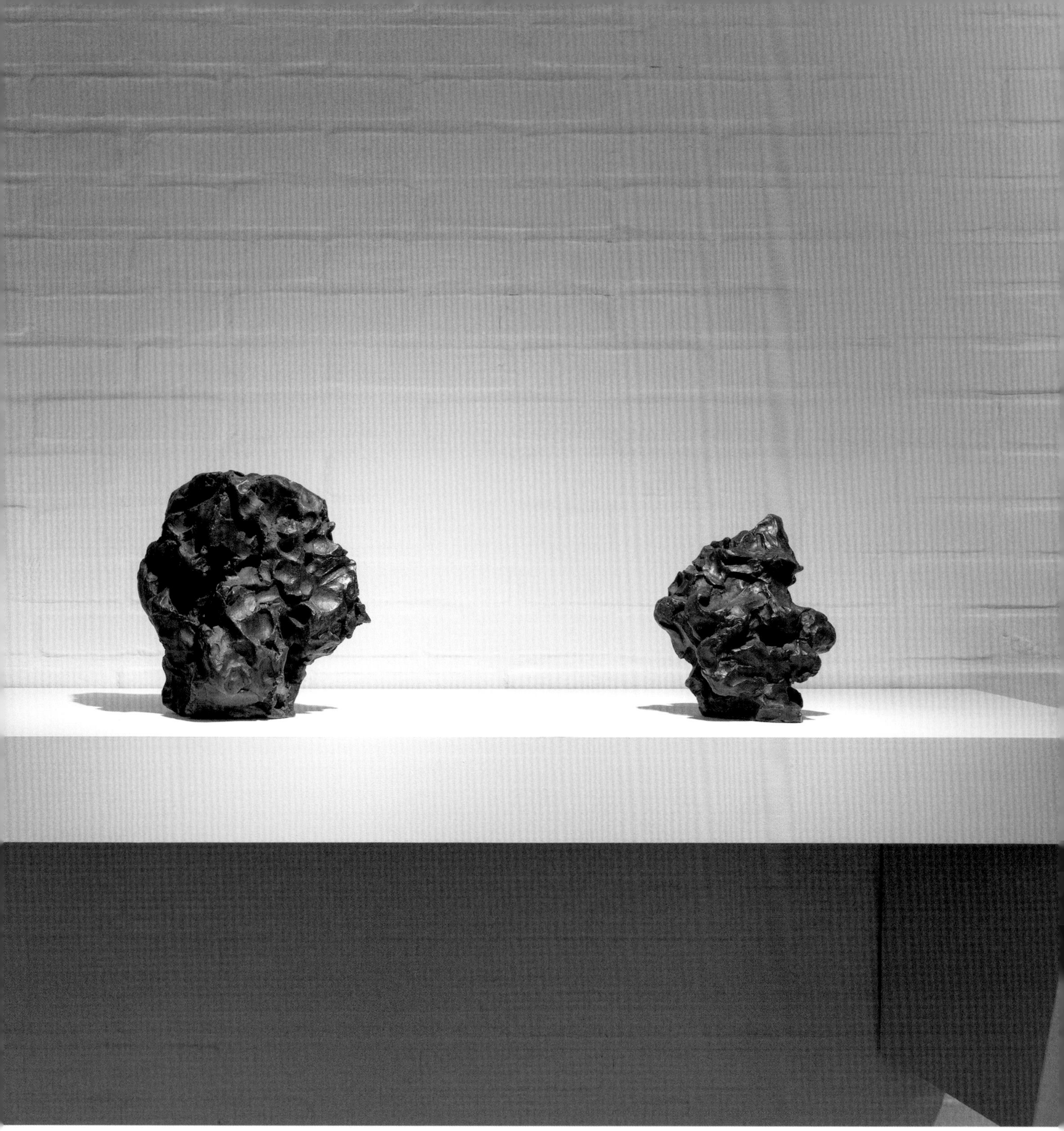

Per Kirkeby's bronze sculptures do not give much away at first glance. Most of them seem dark, impenetrable and reticent, simpler and less insistent than his powerfully coloured paintings despite being physically present and occupying the space around them. Relating to the artist's sculptures requires an effort. Sometimes decoding the work of an artist is easier when their work is juxtaposed with comparable works by another artist – which is maybe what Kirkeby himself was doing in the many texts he wrote on other artists: resolving issues in his own work by allowing such juxtapositions to take effect. In the same way, here the bronze sculptures of Asger Jorn can provide a prism through which to see Kirkeby's sculptures.

Throughout his oeuvre Kirkeby has been in constant dialogue with the art of Jorn. As he explained himself, Jorn was ever-present as "a force of repulsion and attraction, a source of friction in my life."[1] In the 1960s Kirkeby and the Ex-School generation of Danish artists he was part of were dismissive of Asger Jorn because, as Kirkeby writes in the text "Jorn – Externally," they were "up to our knees in an abstract swamp,"[2] which made it easier to lump him together with later Cobra imitators as irrelevant.

Later, Kirkeby admitted that a lot was thrown out with the bathwater – including what he saw as a Nordic tradition for exploring the relationship between figure and matter, and sculpture and painting – in favour of the American minimalism and Pop Art embraced by the Ex-School, and the abstract expressionism that followed in its wake. Kirkeby had to ask himself: "Is it possible to rediscover Jorn, or is the effort wasted?"[3] His bronze sculptures are one of the places he addresses the issues he shares with Jorn most directly. Not that beyond the choice of material their sculptures are much alike.

In 1977 Kirkeby made a biographical film about Asger Jorn, with Jorn's words and music as a soundtrack. The visuals show everything except the paintings Jorn is so famous for. Drawings, graphic and ceramic works, modifications, books and documentary photographs, and the landscapes he inhabited: the windswept countryside of Western Jutland, Himmelbjerget Hill near the lakes of Silkeborg, and his house in Albissola, Italy, where the artist's ceramic reliefs, mosaics and murals unite the house and garden in an organic whole.

Jorn and Kirkeby were both painters who also produced a large number of texts and sculptures, but the path that led them to bronze sculptures differed. Jorn came from the expressive, spontaneous abstract painting of the post-war years, which he transferred to ceramics in the form of platters painted with imaginary figures and sculptures made out of vases. Jorn's interest in ceramics was sparked by craft traditions and the idea of everyday use.

Kirkeby's film about the artist shows him working with a potter in the village of Sorring. We also hear about the earthenware he made for tourists visiting Himmelbjerget Hill[4] and see him transporting his ceramic sculptures in a pram. Elsewhere, Jorn and a group of fellow artists are seen on all fours in Albissola, posing next to ceramic figures or summoning them with gestures, as if coaxing living creatures. Not until 1972 – the year before his death – did Jorn start to cast clay figures in bronze. According to the Danish artist Bjørn Nørgaard, it was the medium that resulted in Jorn's ceramic works always being seen as what he calls "social", whereas his bronze sculptures are "one of the places where Jorn is most alone."[5] Ceramics are widely seen as a quick, unpretentious and functional medium, whereas bronze is associated with seriousness and sole authorship by the artist – with 'real' sculpture. Bronze signals the culmination of the sculptural process, the casting of the ultimate, final form to be put on display in a museum or as a manifestation in public space. Jorn's late bronze sculptures seem to signal the need to be taken seriously, also as a sculptor.

Kirkeby took a different path to sculpture. He came from the deindividualized Pop Art and systemic painting of the 1960s, in which concepts like the figure and expressive form were per definition suspect. His first sculptures were brick sculptures, with one of the earliest from 1966 consisting of a minimalist white-painted house, a blue picket fence, and a brick stele.

The Reification of Brushstrokes

Helle Brøns

In their anonymity and use of prefabricated and untraditional materials, the brick sculptures mark an original expansion of the field of sculpture, as well as a natural progression from Kirkeby's template paintings on Masonite. Whilst his brick sculptures are conceptualised and constructed, Kirkeby's bronze sculptures are individually made by hand, connecting them to the more abstract romantic canvasses he started to paint in the 1980s. Kirkeby's interest in bronze sculptures did not come from the Picasso/Jorn tradition of painted ceramics, but from master sculptors like Wiedewelt, Rodin, Thorvaldsen, Canova and Giacometti. It was in dialogue with these sculptors and his own painting that Kirkeby threw himself into making bronze sculptures.

Whilst Kirkeby made over 100 bronze sculptures over a period of 30 years, and Jorn 24 bronzes in just a year, both of them experienced a mutual exchange between their painting and sculpture, and a constant tension between figure and material.

Model, 1992 / 9 × 20 × 20 cm

Per Kirkeby's first two brick sculptures, originally made for the exhibition *Objects/Sculpture*, Holbergsgade, Copenhagen 1966, reconstructed at the exhibition *The Ex-School*, Museum Jorn, Silkeborg, 2010. In the background a blue fence, recreated from the same exhibition in Holbergsgade, 1966

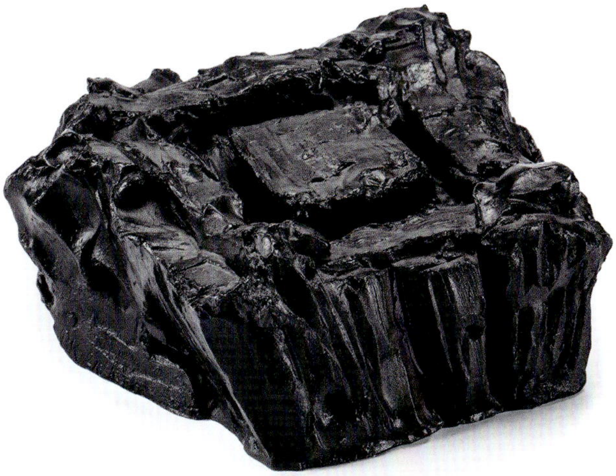

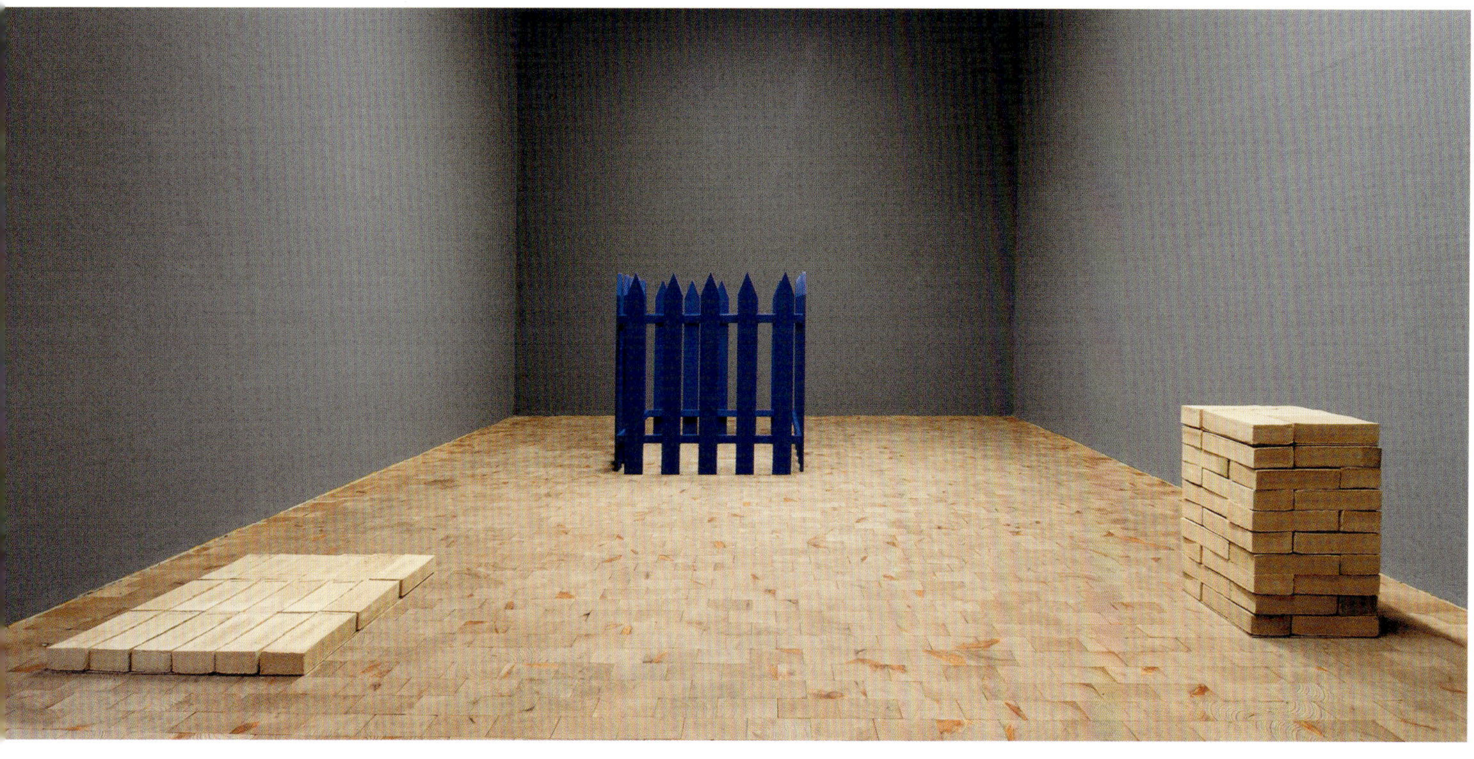

Kirkeby once wrote a short text on the relationship between Jorn's sculpture and painting. This was in 2020, for an exhibition of a selection of Jorn's bronzes and the painting *Scultura Figurata*, all made in 1972. Kirkeby begins with the painting and the recurrent issue of the figure. "Any clear figure sinks beneath the brushstrokes of the paint,"[6] as he wrote, adding that it was impossible to reinterpret the spatiality of a painting when it was bound by the logic of the figure. Kirkeby finds the solution in Jorn's painting, which has no human figures, yet plays with the idea of a painted sculpture in transition. *Scultura Figurata* is a large painting of floating colours coalescing in a composite, amorphous figure – like a sea of plastic, seaweed and oil washed ashore and deposited in small multicoloured islands on the water's edge. Indistinct figures emerge within the main figure: a creature at the bottom of the painting, two mask forms at the top, and other figurations that seem to surface in random formations before drifting away as the gaze shifts.

That the figurative and spatial instability of the painting can be dizzying is something I experienced personally at the opening of the exhibition mentioned above, when I fainted before it. I had tried to fix my gaze on a clear, palpable figure. When that failed, I sought refuge in colour, trying tried to find a path to follow there. When that too failed, I lost consciousness. The episode was not due to any refined aesthetic sensitivity: I was actually just ill. Yet there is something about the experience that relates to the structure of the work and is characteristic of Jorn's late works: the fluid form, the material's tentative metamorphosis into a figure then back again into pure materiality.

Asger Jorn
Seconda Horisonda, 1972
Bronze, 52 × 33 × 30 cm
Private Collection
→
Asger Jorn
Scultura Figurata, 1972
Oil on canvas, 250 × 200 cm
Fænø Gods

This fluid figuration is difficult to transfer to the physical palpability of sculpture. Yet according to Kirkeby, this is precisely what Jorn does: "Jorn's sculptures are the reification of brushstrokes. He lifts brushstrokes out of the painting and gives them free-standing form in the 'real' world. And makes them in bold turn the figures in a painting. This movement in and out of the painting can be sensed as a singular and suggestive difference in the work: Jorn's local version of the tidal movement between painting and sculpture."[7]

Despite being cast in bronze, Jorn's sculptures seem to be in a process of constant metamorphosis. As we move around the sculpture, what from one angle is on its way to becoming a bird disappears and becomes another creature or formless matter. Many of the sculptures stand on some kind of feet, and look as if they are moving. They were made in clay first, and none of them are more than 50-70 cm high, so they could be held, formed, and rotated by hand. Each sculpture often contains multiple suggested or composite creatures that merge from a different angle. Jorn thus retains the openness and ambiguity so central to his visual perception in the solid form of sculpture.

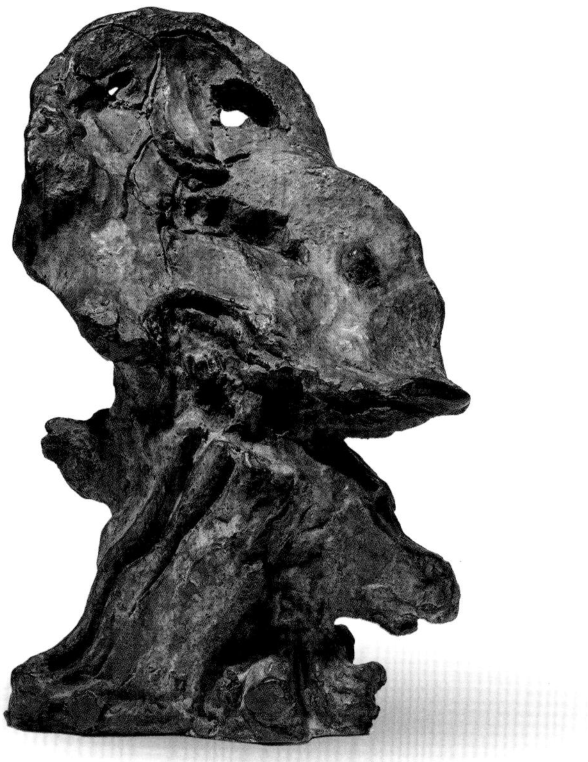

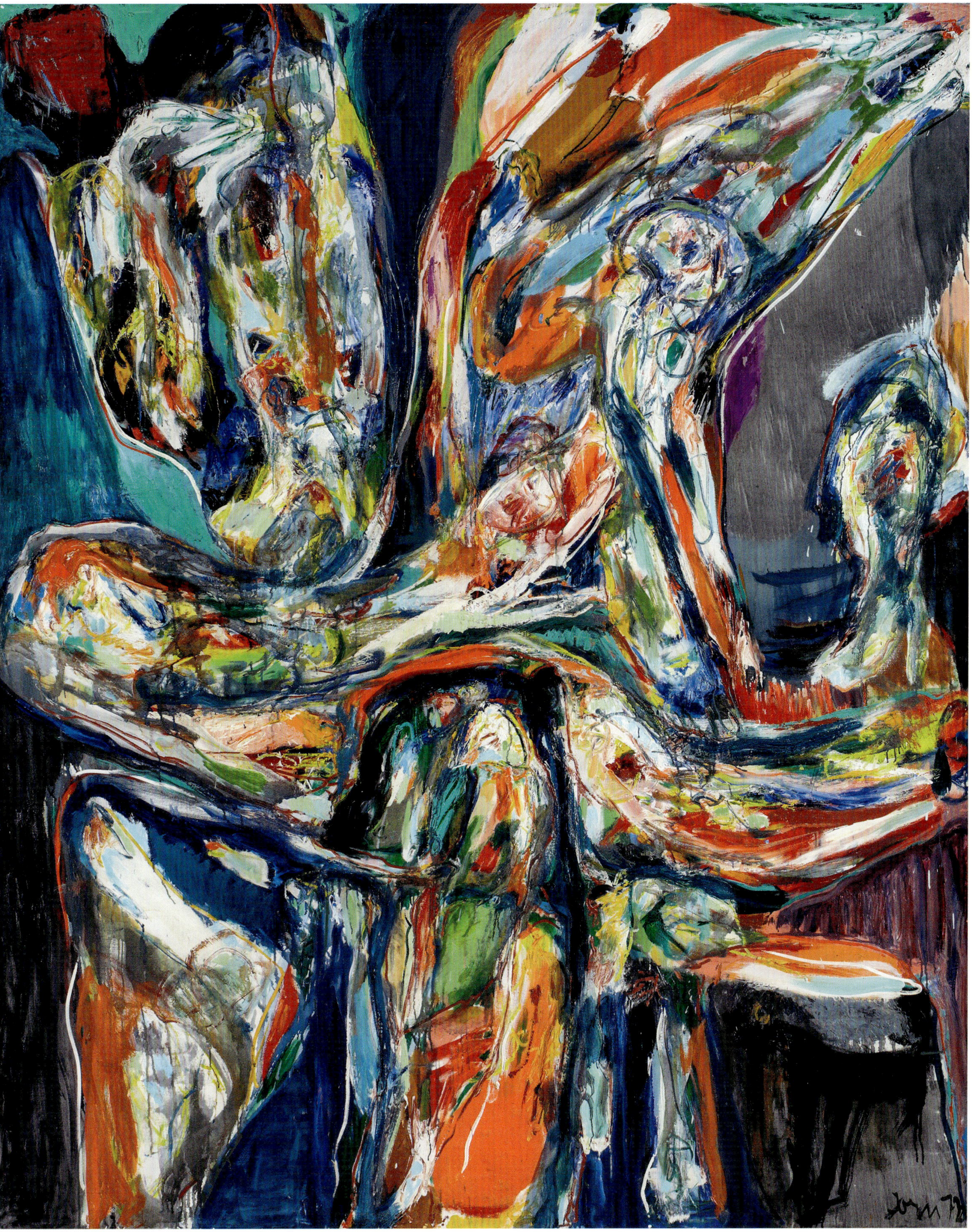

Jorn was interested in what described as "the world of homeomorphism, a plastic universe in which nothing can be added or subtracted [only ever transformed], the informal world."[8] He compared such constantly homeomorphising forms with reshaping a lump of clay, or cartoon characters that are flattened, stretched and squashed without any lasting damage.[9] He focussed on the qualitative characteristics of a figure: whether it is confined, whether it has a rim, whether it has holes, i.e. characteristics that are retained even as the figure morphs, stretches and is deformed over time. Jorn saw matter as a self-structuring force with the capacity to generate meaning of its own.

Sculpture, 1992 / 24 × 13 × 8 cm

Asger Jorn
Dolce dolore, 1972
Bronze, 19 × 20 × 18 cm
Private Collection
→
Untitled, 2010 / 10 × 26 × 18 cm

Asger Jorn
Donna titubante, 1972
Bronze, 40 × 18 × 12 cm
Museum Jorn

The constant malleability of the material, however, could result in a loss of singularity. So he started experimenting with combining the grammar of the material itself with the unique, human generation of meaning. This approach meant constantly allowing chance and the unformed matter of clay to be in dialogue with the control he exerted in shaping the material to nurture a sense of movement and changeability.

He also experimented with shifts and exchanges between painting and sculpture. As Kirkeby points out, Jorn drew figures out of painting into sculpture, then back into painting. "Why does a painter start to make sculptures?" Kirkeby asks, answering: "Because then he can paint works like *Scultura Figurata*!"

As is often the case in Kirkeby's texts on other artists, his description of Jorn's sculpture strikes a chord with his own work and the interplay between sculpture and painting. The two media rub off on each other, and insights gleaned from the one are transferred to the other. Unlike Jorn's sculptures, however, Kirkeby's sculptures are often less dynamic with an obvious back and front, and as such retain a closer connection to painting.

Kirkeby's sculptures, like those of Jorn, are the result of a constant negotiation between medium and form. His sculptures rarely seem to evolve from one figure to another. Instead, fragments of figures seem to arise out of pure materiality. What from one angle appears to be a head or an arm, from another angle dissolves into a shimmering surface marked by the clear traces of human hands. Something smoulders beneath the skin of the sculpture, something rising to the surface and taking shape – or on its way to being absorbed by the materiality of the sculpture.

Like Jorn, in Kirkeby's sculptures we see the brushstroke lifted out of the painting to become sculptural, sitting like a fingerprint on a surface that bears the traces of artistic creation.

As in his paintings, however, the figure is further beneath the surface than in Jorn's works, a disparity that can be seen in the different stages at which the two artists considered a sculpture to be complete. Kirkeby's sculptures have a uniform, black surface, whilst Jorn continued to work on his bronzes after they had been cast, oxidising and patinating their surfaces.

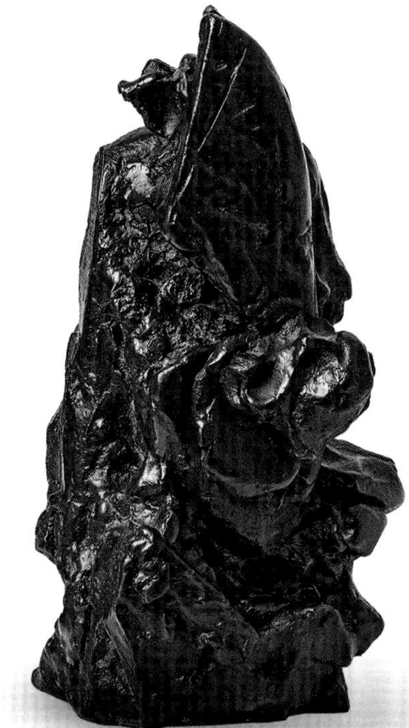

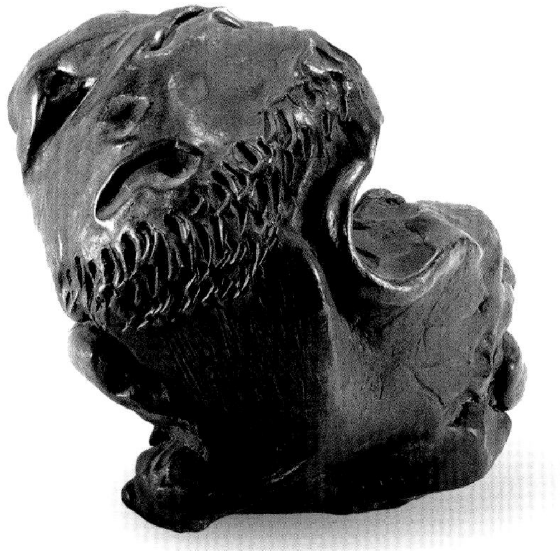

This accentuated differences between rough and smooth and dark and lighter areas, bringing the expressive form of the sculpture closer to the improvisation of his painting, at the same time as making each casting unique. For Kirkeby, on the other hand, even though the surfaces of his sculptures bear the clear imprint of the artist, he wanted to emphasise the resistance of sculpture to intensity and expressiveness, because as he wrote himself: "Sculptures possess to a much greater extent than paintings a kind of hereditary anonymity. To fashion an 'object' is an action that almost transcends the individual. What is given and anonymous comes across that much more clearly in painting, where fear of anonymity may more easily be exorcised by means of tricks endeavouring towards originality."[10] The personal, expressive, originality-seeking dimensions of Jorn's sculptures are thus constantly resisted by Kirkeby, as is the figurative. In several of his bronzes it is as if the sculpture has been draped in cloth – or in a black painting where only the structure of the brushstrokes stands out.

This enveloping, which in some cases almost enshrouds the sculptures, restrains the expressive force of the figure and material, which remain smouldering beneath the surface. One can imagine the sculptures being covered in cloth while they were being made, and that this veiling of their visual and physical articulation inspired allowing sheer mass and scale to come to the fore.

At the same time as being reticent in terms of the figurative, the sculptures are also marked by Kirkeby's constant struggle with the fetishizing of materiality, unlike Jorn, who threw himself into both. For Jorn the emergence and changeability of the figure is an intense, carefree process, whereas Kirkeby's relationship to the figure, in both sculpture and painting, was a more difficult and perilous affair.

Kirkeby's bronzes often deal with intellectual and existential themes that are as weighty as the bronze itself. The sculpture *Resurrection* (1999), for example, unites many of the formal and thematic elements of Kirkeby's oeuvre: the cave, the pyramid, the gateway, the issue of the figure, the weight of the sculpture combined with the flatness of his painting, the lightness of suggestion and the solidity of form. The sculpture, which stands in a cemetery in Frejlev, rises like a rectangular wall – or a large canvas – with a clear front and back. The front is like a dark cave-like tomb.

The rustic pyramid form at the base evokes both a landslide and climbing steps, or as Poul Erik Tøjner writes, the duality of rising/ascension and collapse/ the fall.[11] Both Jorn and Kirkeby's point of departure was Communist and anti-religious. Jorn approached the relationship between spirit and matter from a dialectical, materialist perspective – i.e. Marxist philosophy in which material life conditions form the basis for consciousness – in keeping with which he saw artistic thinking as the product of working physically with the material: "For the materialist artist, a line is the track a certain substance leaves behind as it passes another substance ... It is the pin's or finger's track in clay, and the chisel's track in stone ... He refuses to accept the idealist dogma that 'thought is independent of the material'.

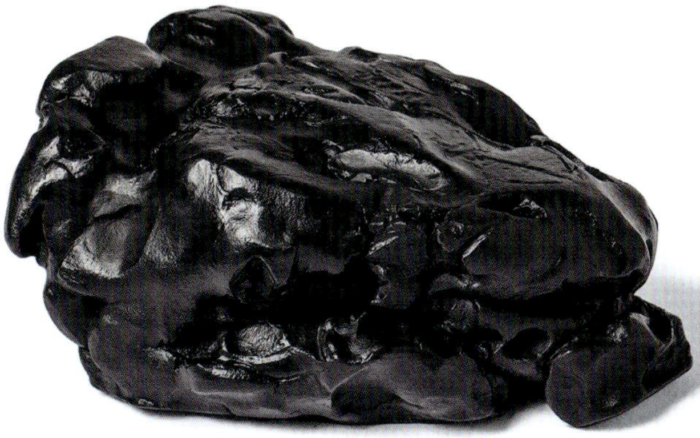

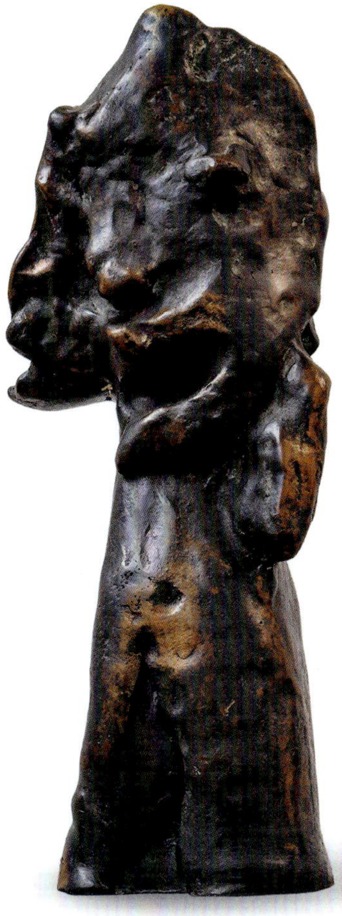

For the materialist artist, human thought processes are instigated by the substances themselves, and are synonymous with the reaction form which these same substances have, because thought (which in itself is immaterial in nature) cannot avoid the natural laws pertaining to matter."[12] In many ways Kirkeby addresses the same issue in numerous works: the inexplicable exchange between the material flesh of matter and a spiritual or intellectual element. In *Resurrection* the relationship is given a more religious framing. As Kirkeby himself explained, religion, especially later in life, became an important frame of understanding in his art: "There are actually a lot of things that cannot be said better than they are in the Bible. That, I am afraid, I have to admit ... an old heathen would hate to come across as a convert."[13] In the work of Kirkeby the material and understated figure thus give shape to inexplicability, emergence and disappearance: birth, death and resurrection.

That Kirkeby's sculptures are more formally and thematically burdened by gravity than those of Jorn is underlined by their function and location. Over the years Kirkeby's sculptures became increasingly site specific or were commissioned for public buildings, public spaces and churches.

As a result they grew significantly in size from the first sculptures, which were only around a metre tall. Jorn's sculptures are smaller and more portable, and therefore often shown in exhibitions mounted on plinths that underline a more traditional and gallery-like presentation highlighted by the bronze itself. That Jorn's intention with the sculptures was very different is obvious when we see the photographs he had taken of them outdoors. Placed in the landscape, Jorn's figures look as if they have been either been pulled out of the earth or (given the artist's partiality to science fiction) landed like aliens in random places on the edge of civilisation. These photographs underline the narrative elements and biomorphic figuration of the sculptures. In comparison, Kirkeby's sculptures become more and more architectural in scale, and in these anonymous, amorphous structures the figure is not present in any narrative sense, but more as an expression of fragmented, incipient hope.

If we return to Kirkeby's question of whether he could still rediscover Jorn, we can conclude that the way he reintroduced the figure and its struggle to break free from the material is rooted in some of the same – perhaps Nordic – art traditions as Jorn.

But whereas Jorn was able to surrender with carefree abandon to imaginative figuration, for Kirkeby making space for the figure without entirely abandoning the anonymous, minimalist art of the 1960s was more of a struggle. And it is this struggle, this issue of the figurative, that emerges as one of the central themes in his bronze sculptures.

1 Per Kirkeby, "Hvad skal man egentlig med kunstnere på film?" in *Fisters klumme*, Borgen, 1995. **2** Per Kirkeby, 'Jorn – Externally' in Asger Schnack (ed.), *Writings on Art: Per Kirkeby,* translated by Martin Aitken, Spring Publications, 2012, p. 125. **3** Ibid., p. 128. **4** Jorn's Himmelbjerg Hill souvenir was a fiasco. The few that sold were bought by his friends. **5** Bjørn Nørgaard, "Skulptøren" in Erik Steffensen (ed.), *Jorn til Folket: Udvalgte værker 1935-1972*, Nordjyllands Kunstmuseum, 1997, p. 93. **6** Per Kirkeby, *Asger Jorn: Scultura Figurata*, Galleri Faurschou, 2002, pp. 2-3. **7** Ibid., p. 3. **8** Asger Jorn, *Ting og Polis*, SISV no. 4, 1964, p. 144. **9** Asger Jorn, "Det dyriske menneske og det menneskelige dyr i kunsten" in *Billedkunst*, Cph, 1967, year 2, no. 3, pp. 13-18. **10** Per Kirkeby, *Evolution* in Schnack, pp. 90-91. **11** Poul Erik Tøjner, *Per Kirkeby – Skulptur*, Forlaget Bjerggaard, 2005, p. 87. **12** Asger Jorn, "What is an Ornament" in Ruth Baumeister (ed.), *Fraternité Avant Tout – Asger Jorn's writings on art and architecture, 1938-1958*, translated by Paul Larkin, 010 Publishers, 2011, pp. 199-201. **13** Anne Wolden Ræthinge, *Jeg er her endnu: Per Kirkeby fortæller til Ninka*, Gyldendal, 2017, p. 227

Helle Brøns is an art historian and curator at Sorø Art Museum. She has written several books and articles as well as her PhD thesis on the art of Asger Jorn.

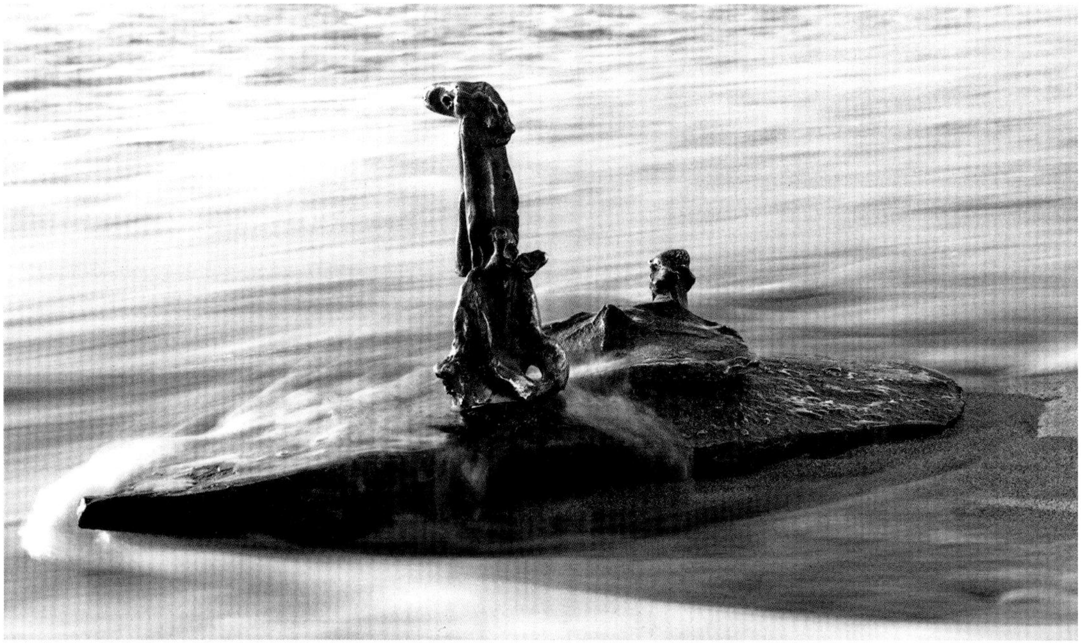

Asger Jorn
Cammino indicato, 1972
Bronze, 22 × 30 × 11 cm
→
Resurrection, 1999 /
290 × 198 × 111 cm

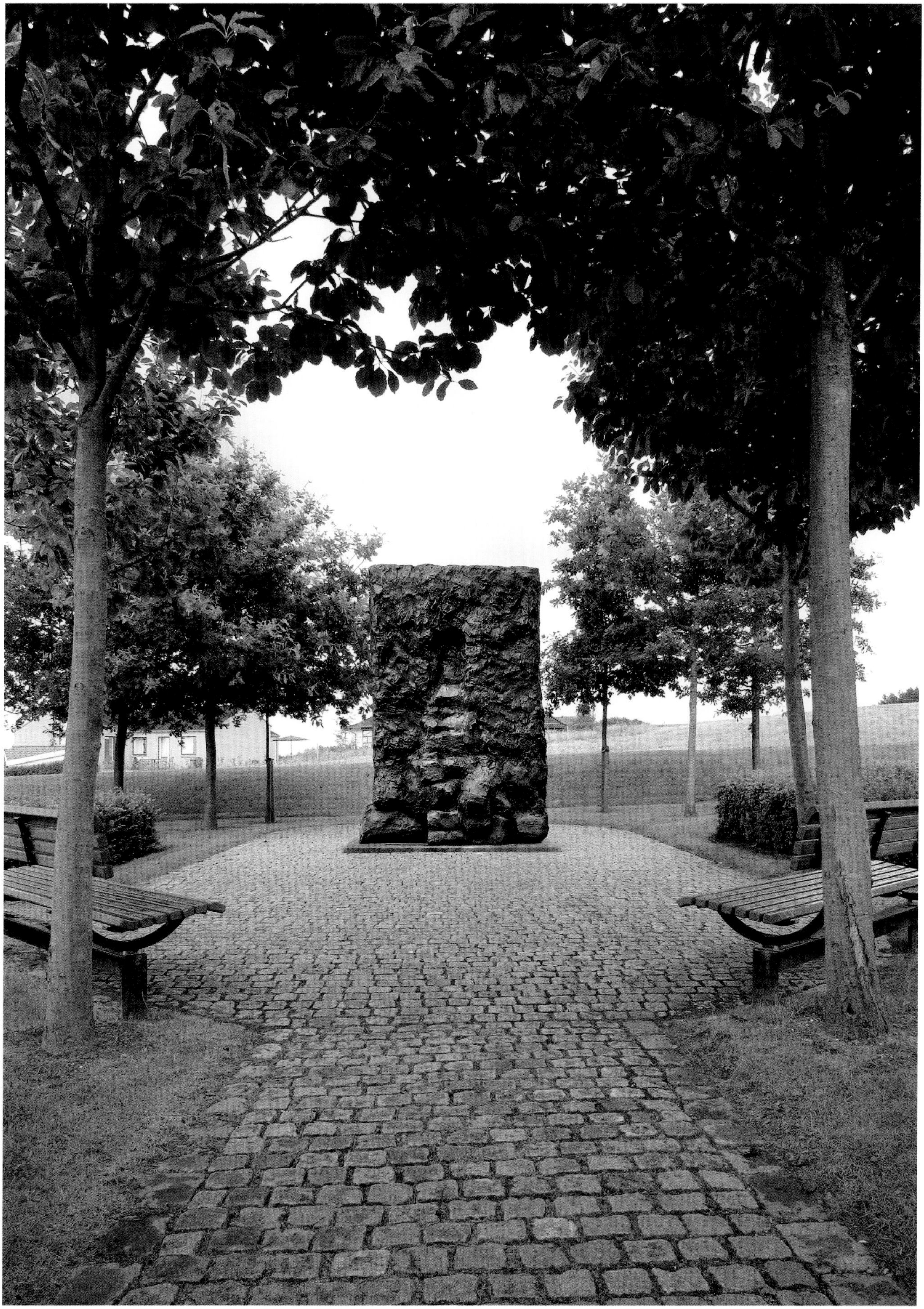

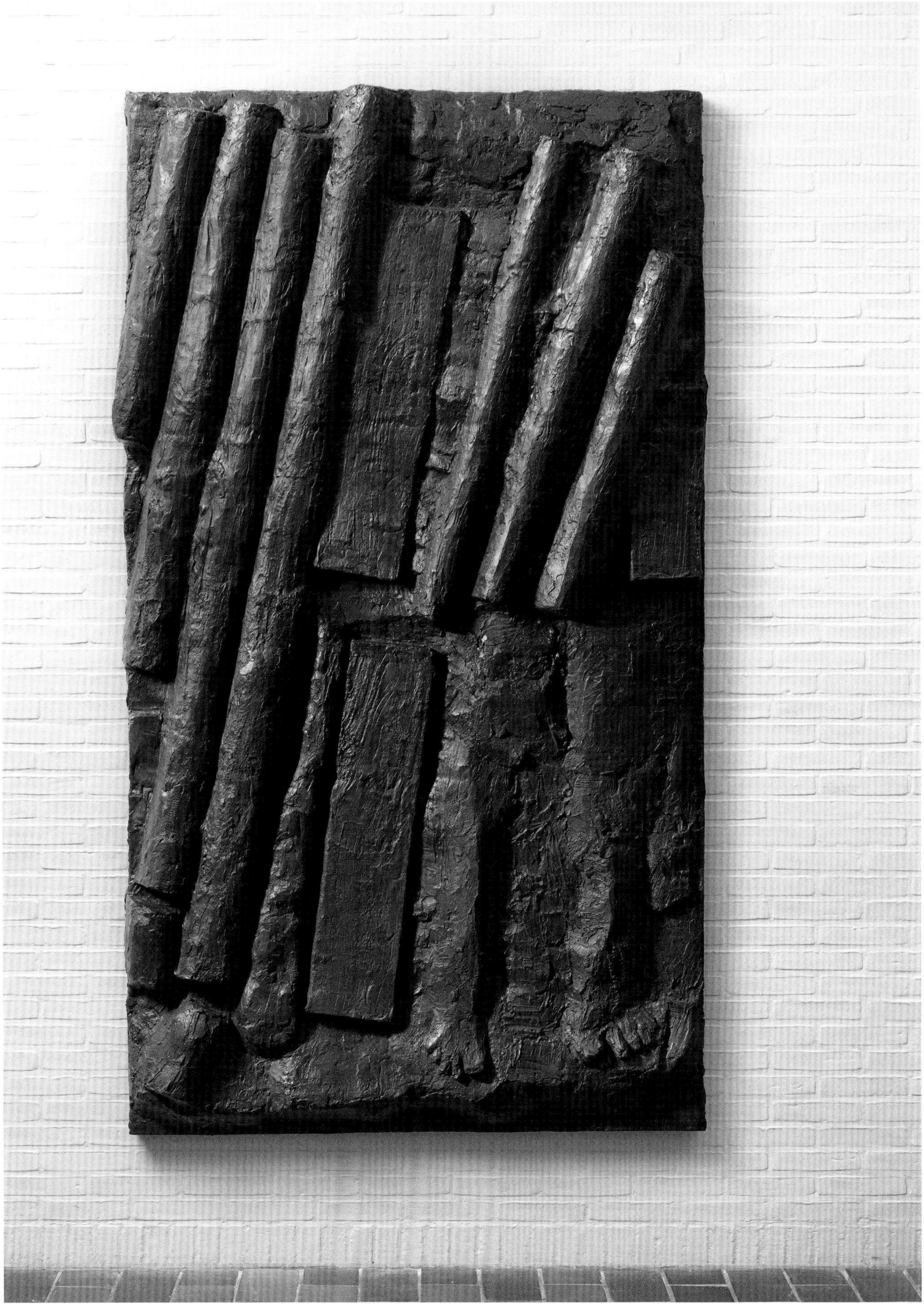

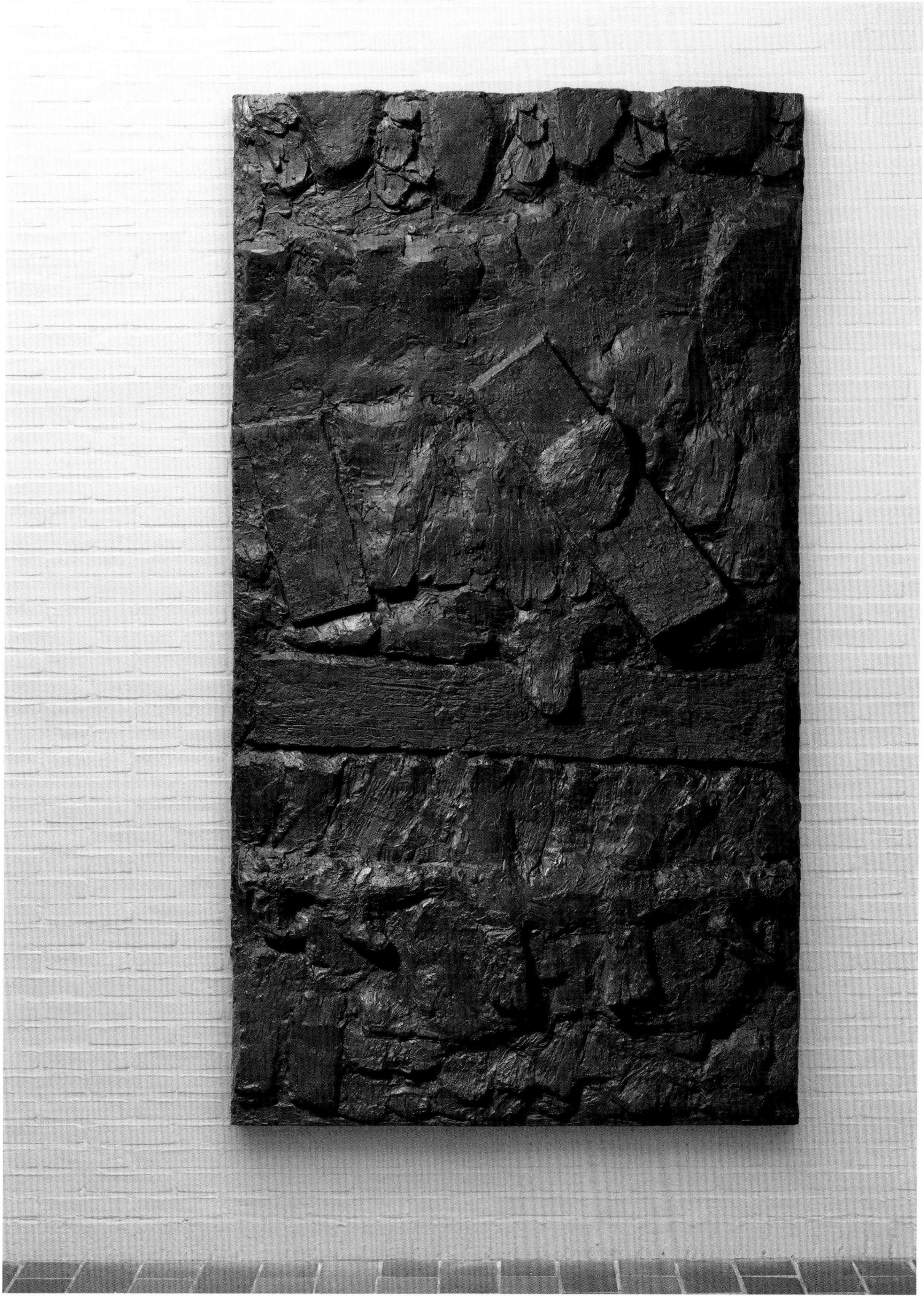

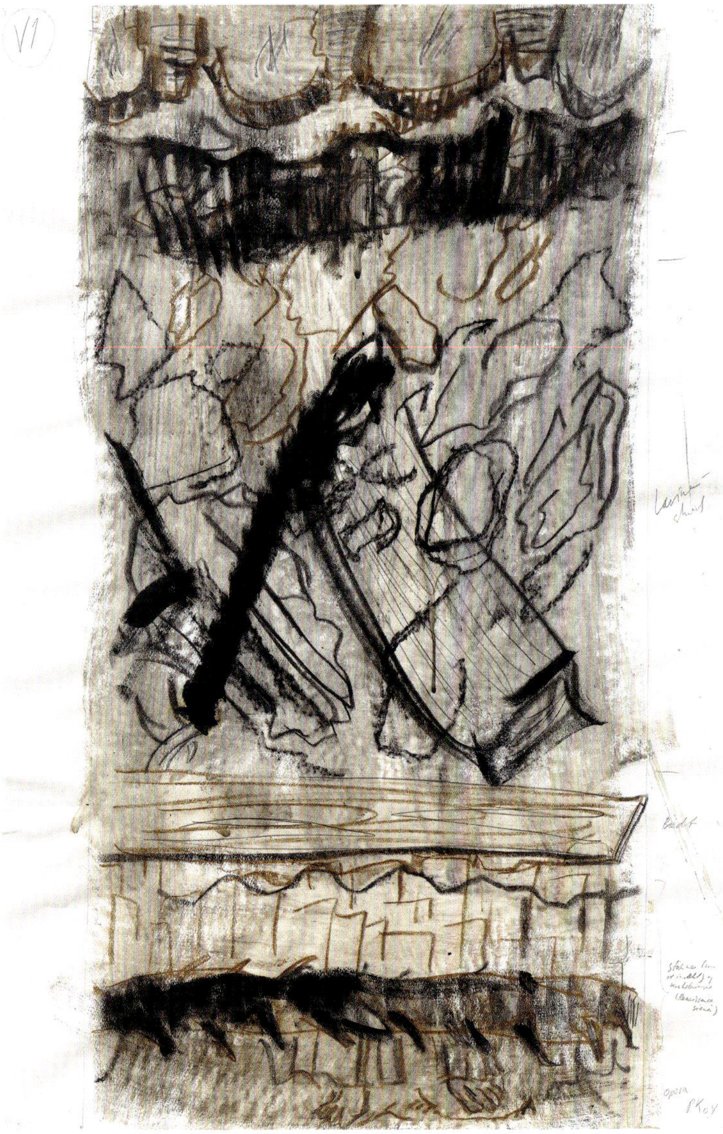

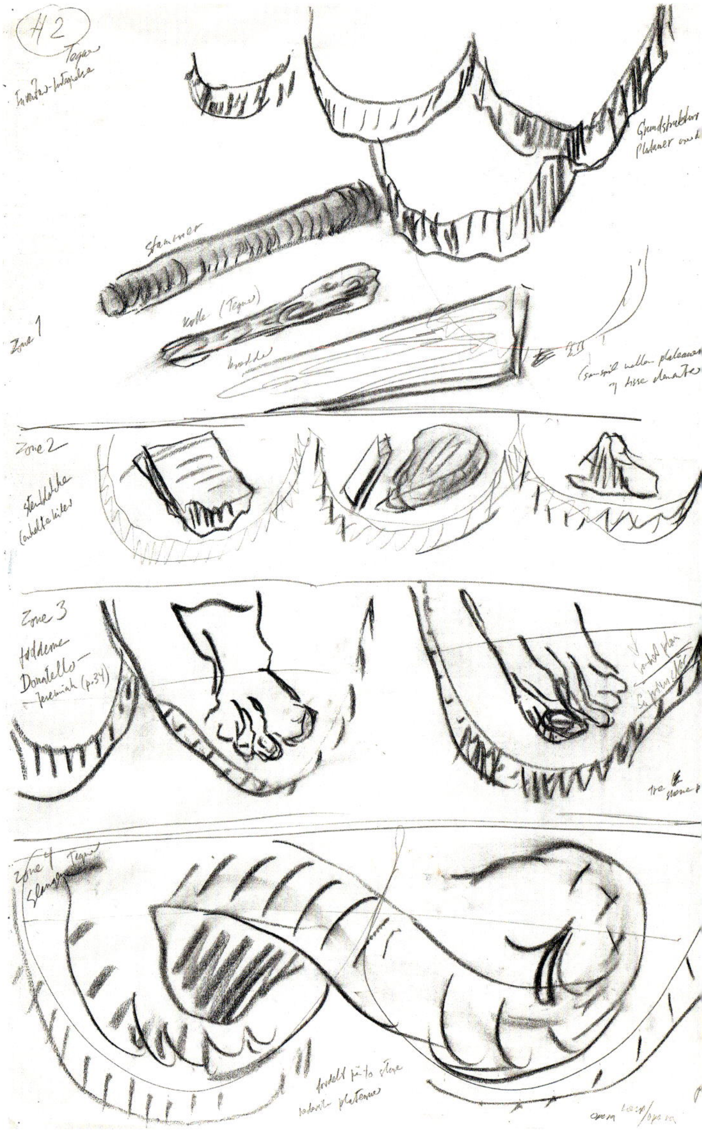

Untitled (Opera), 2004 / 100 × 65 cm. **Untitled (Opera)**, 2004 / 100 × 65 cm

→

Untitled (Opera), 2004 / 100 × 65 cm. **Untitled (Opera)**, 2004 / 100 × 65 cm

←←

Opera Relief I-II, 2004 / 285 × 154 × 40 cm

→→

Opera Relief III-IV, 2004 / 285 × 154 × 40 cm

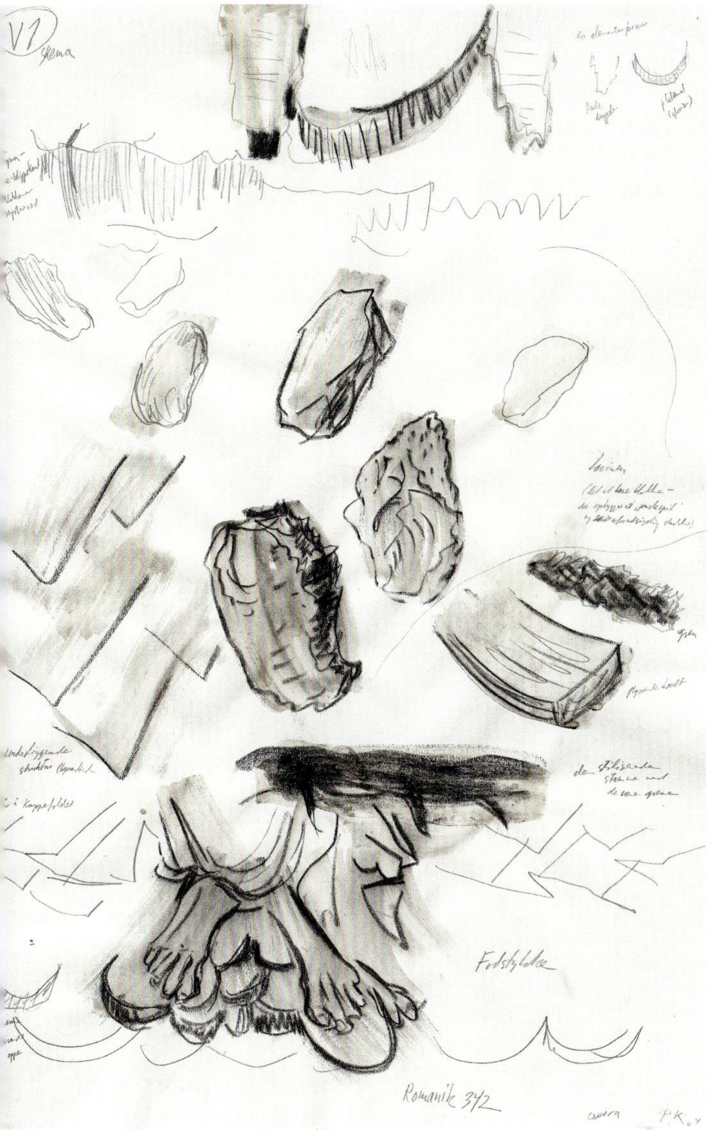

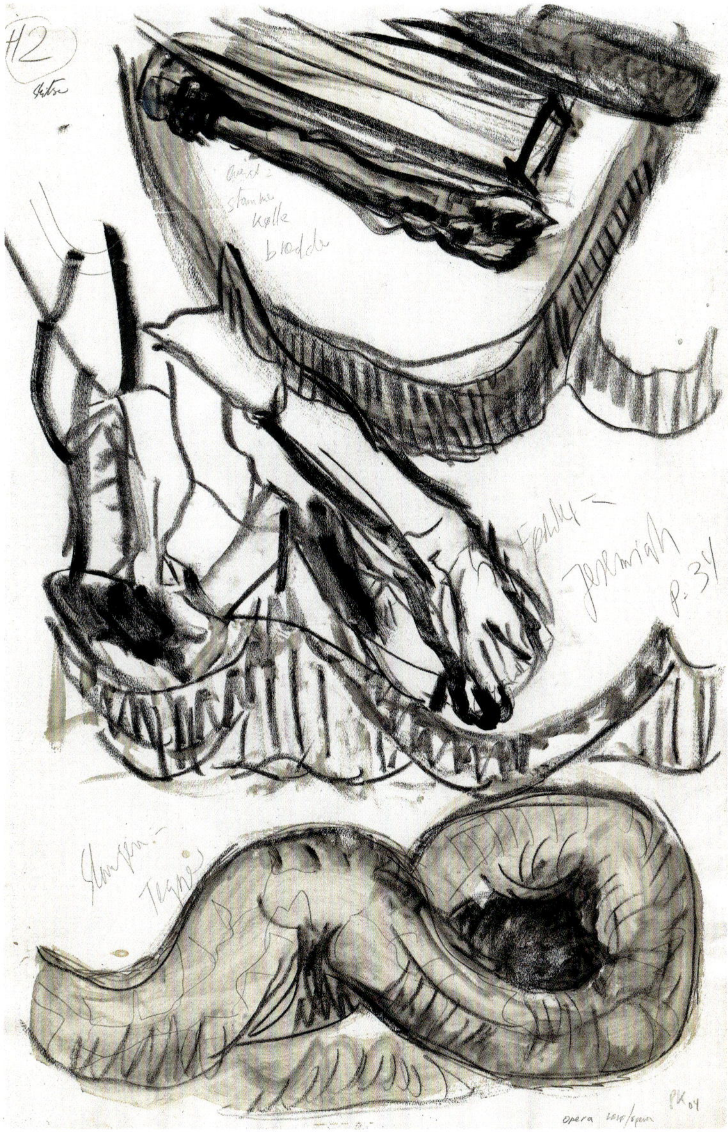

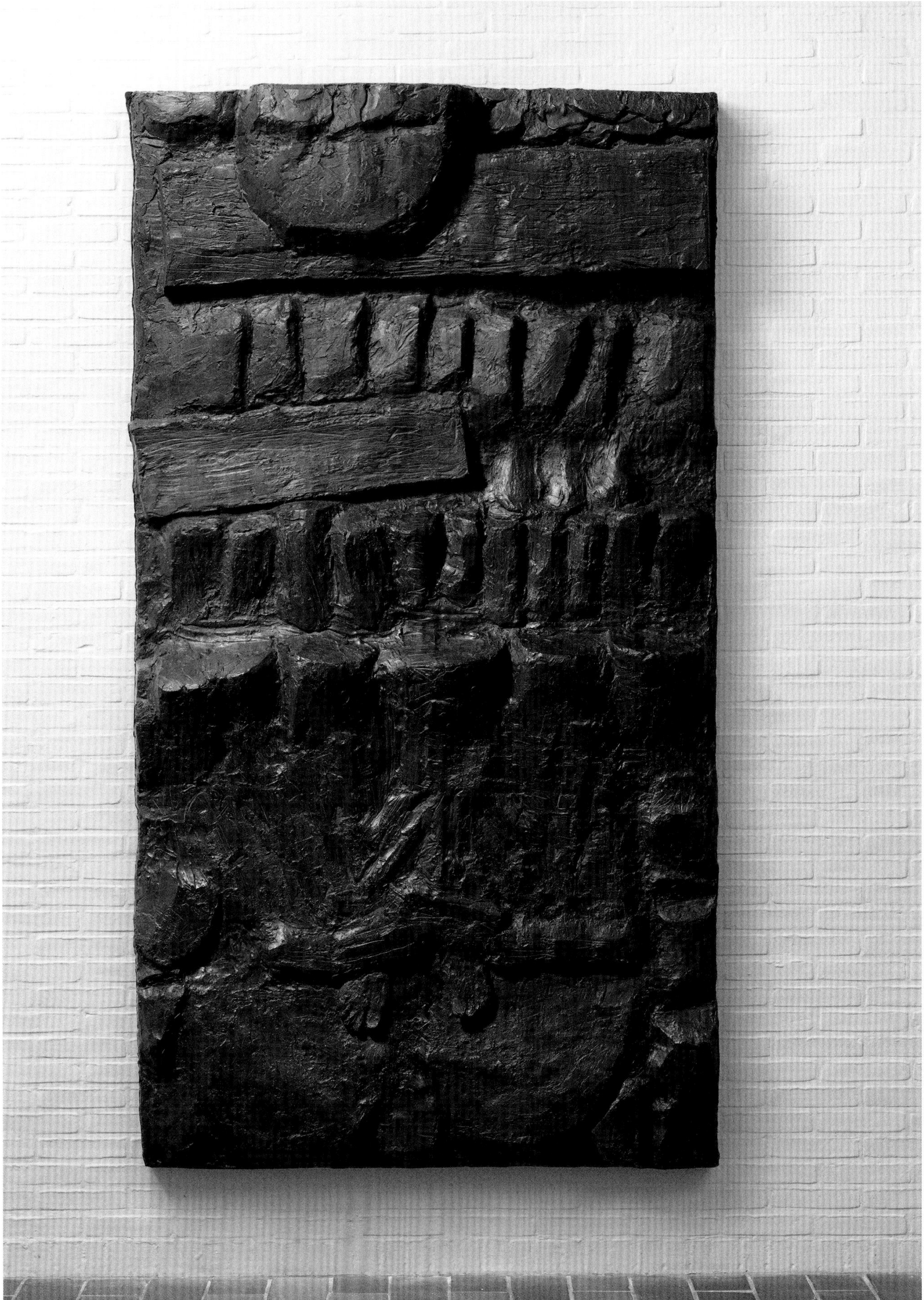

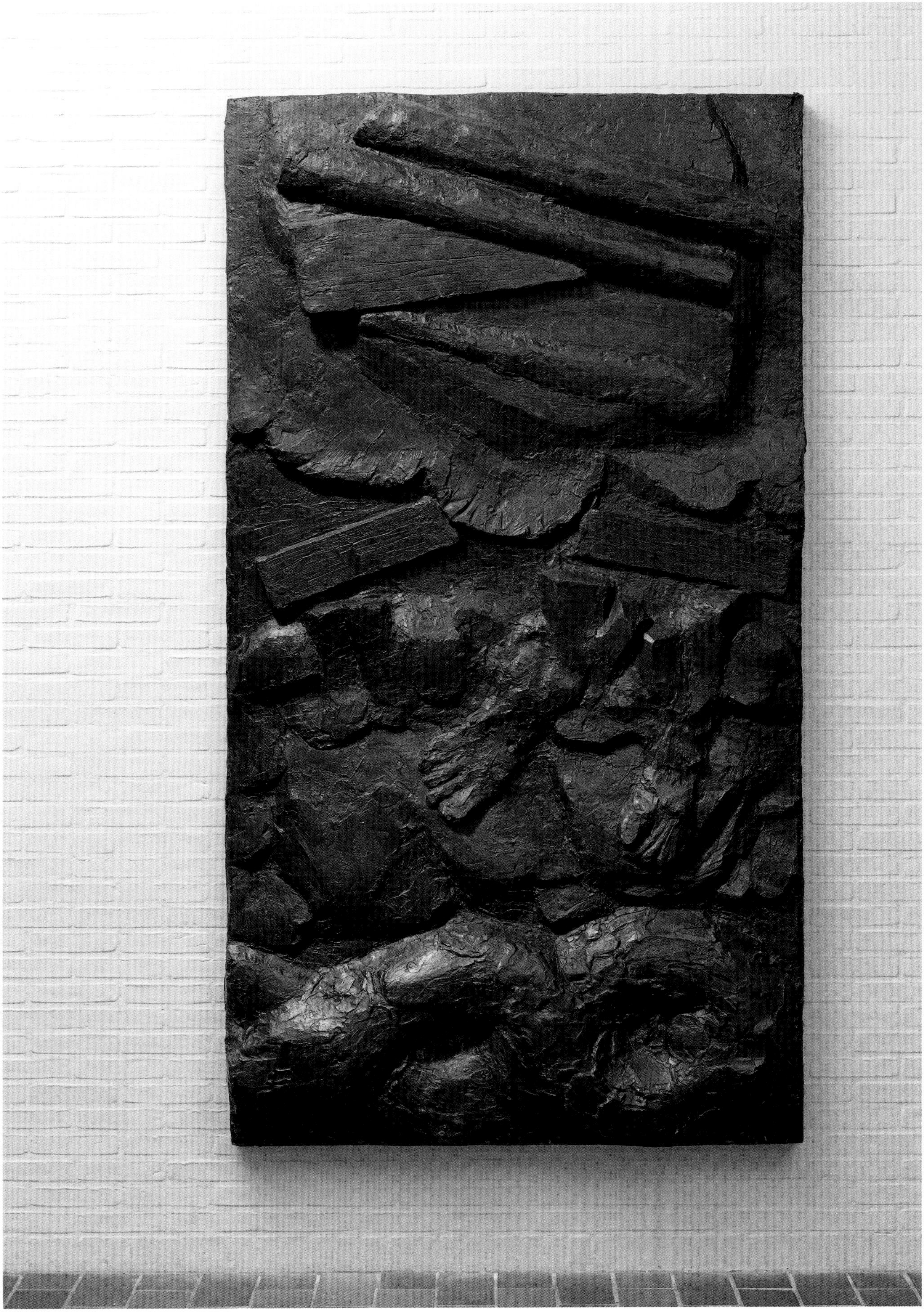

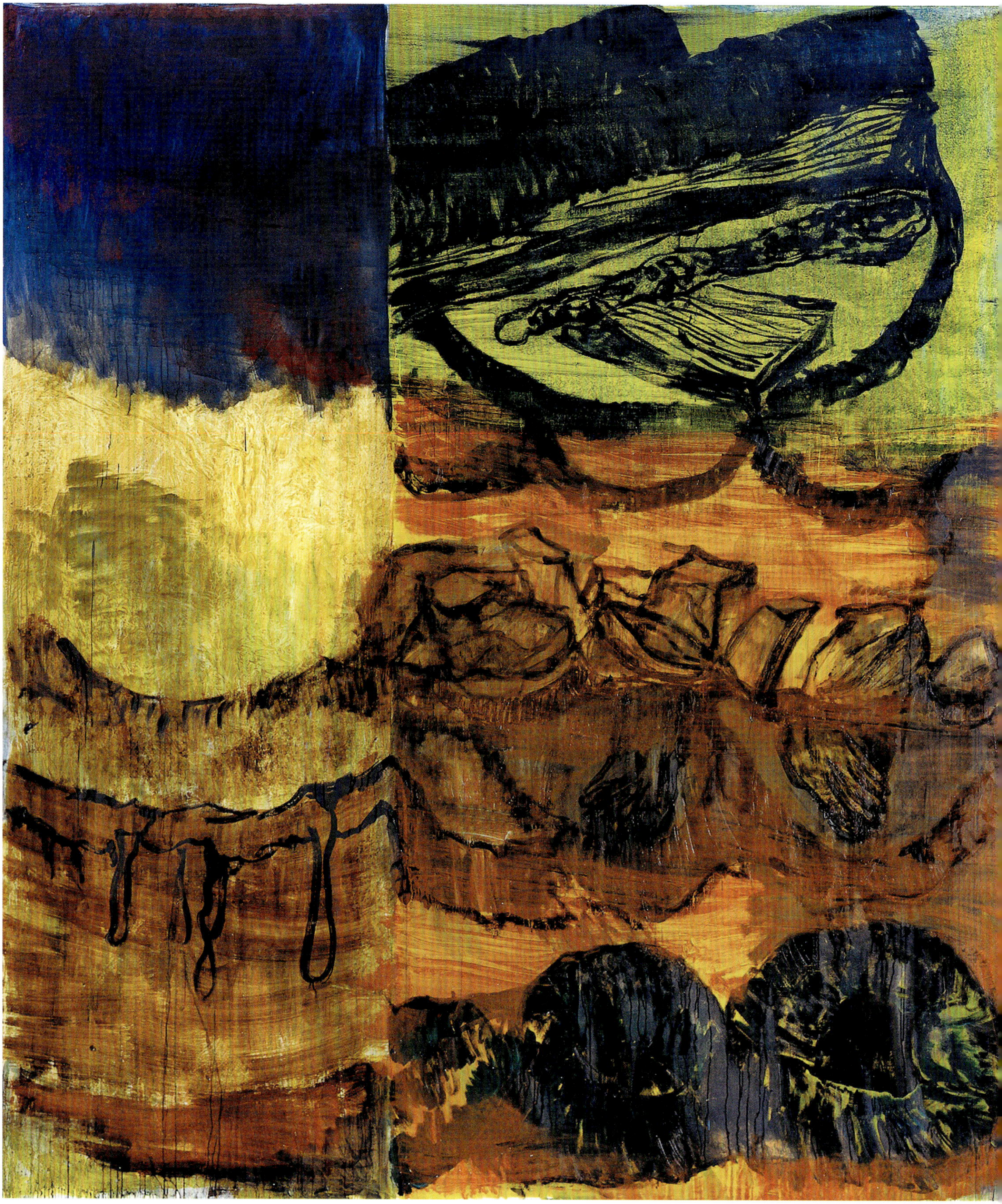

Per Kirkeby in his studio on Læsø, c. 2004

←

Untitled, 2004 / 290 × 245 cm

→→

Untitled, 2004 / 301 × 501 cm

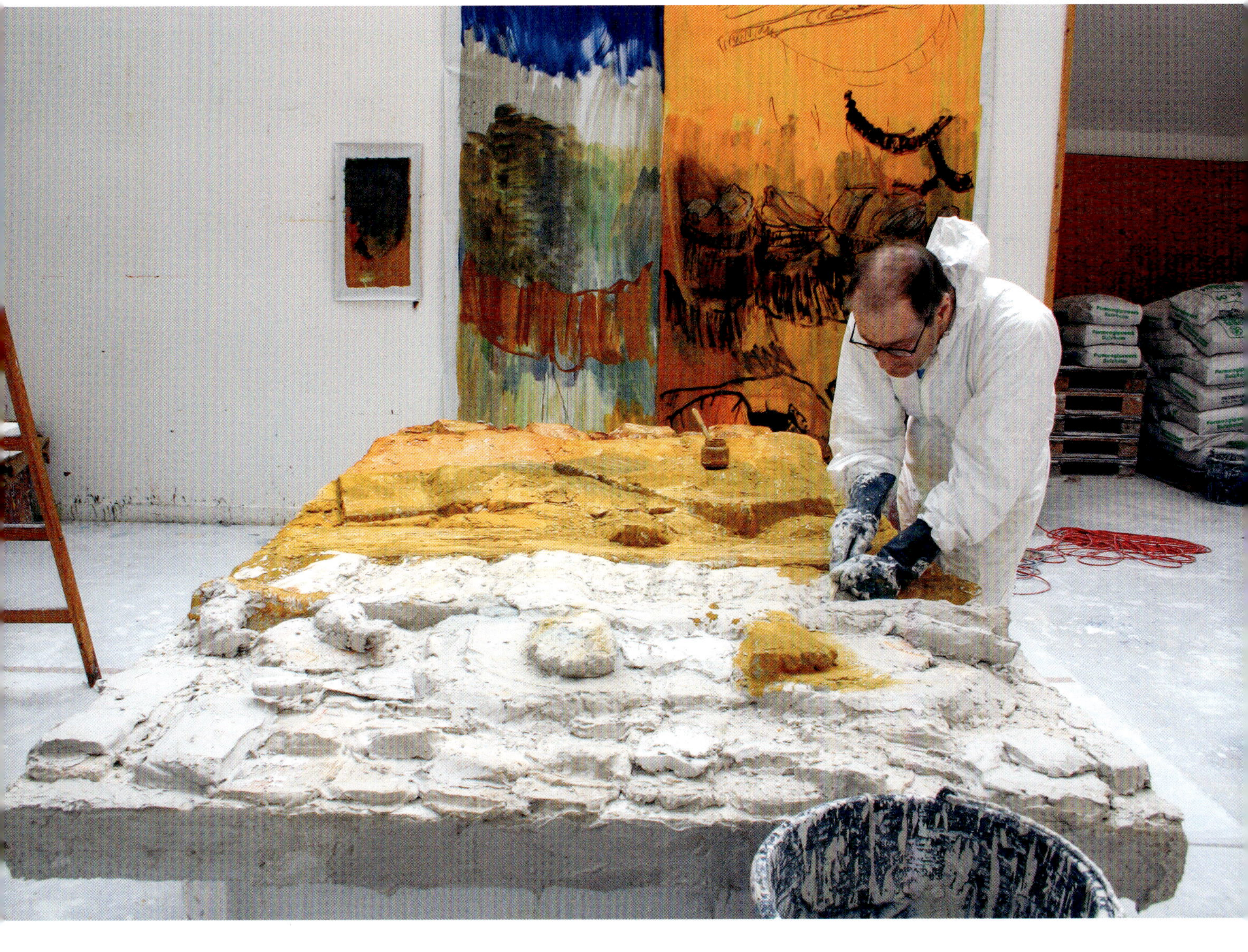

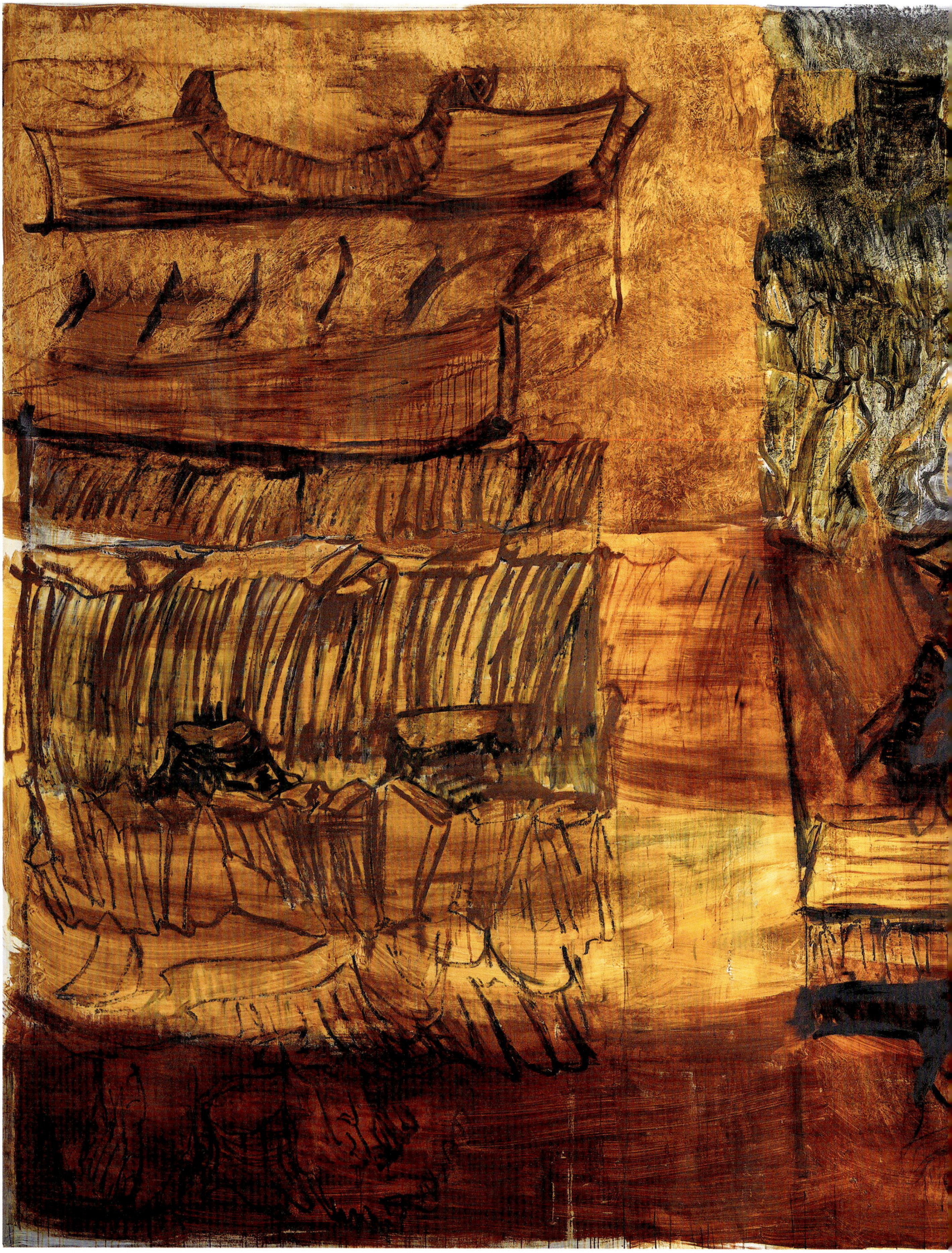

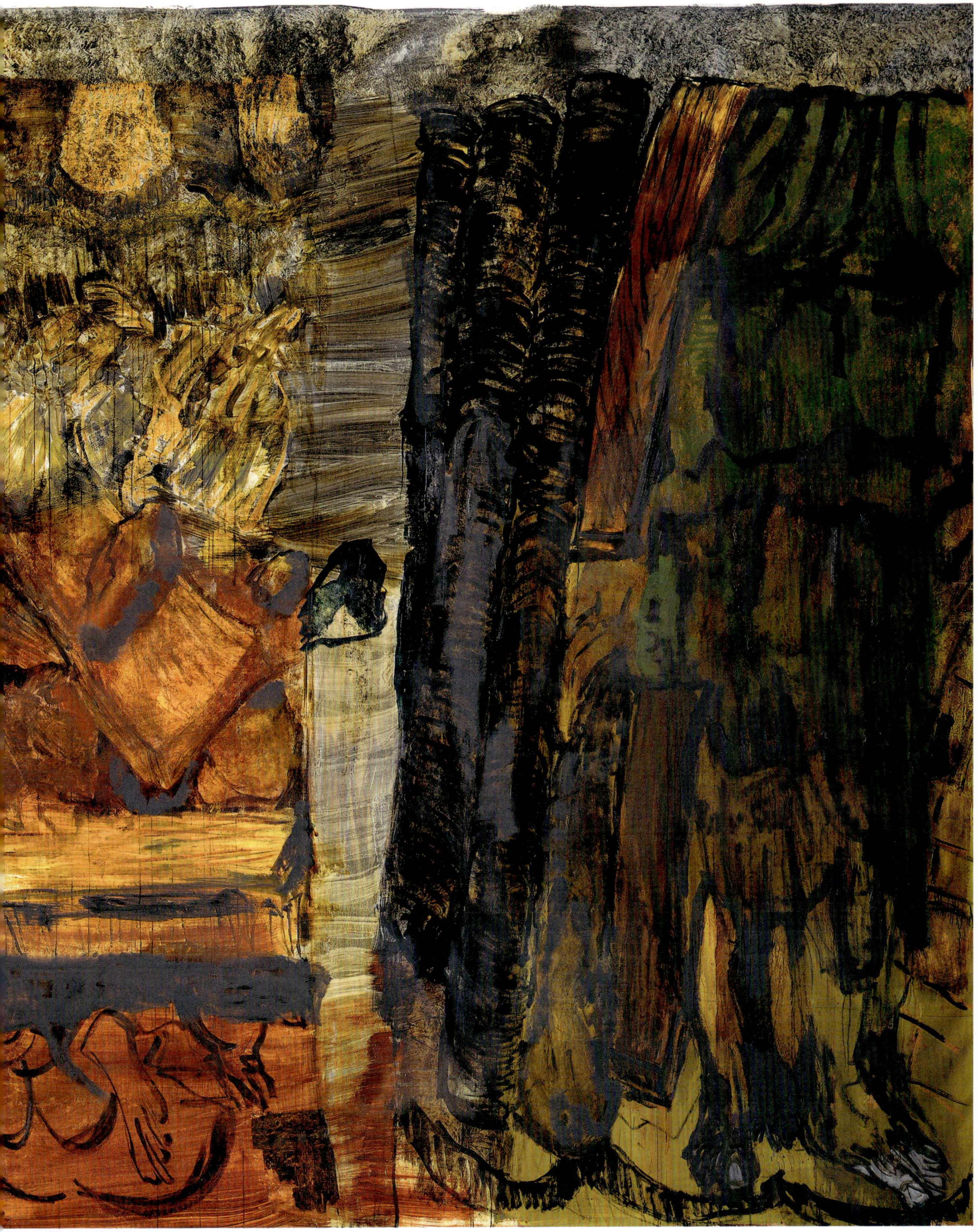

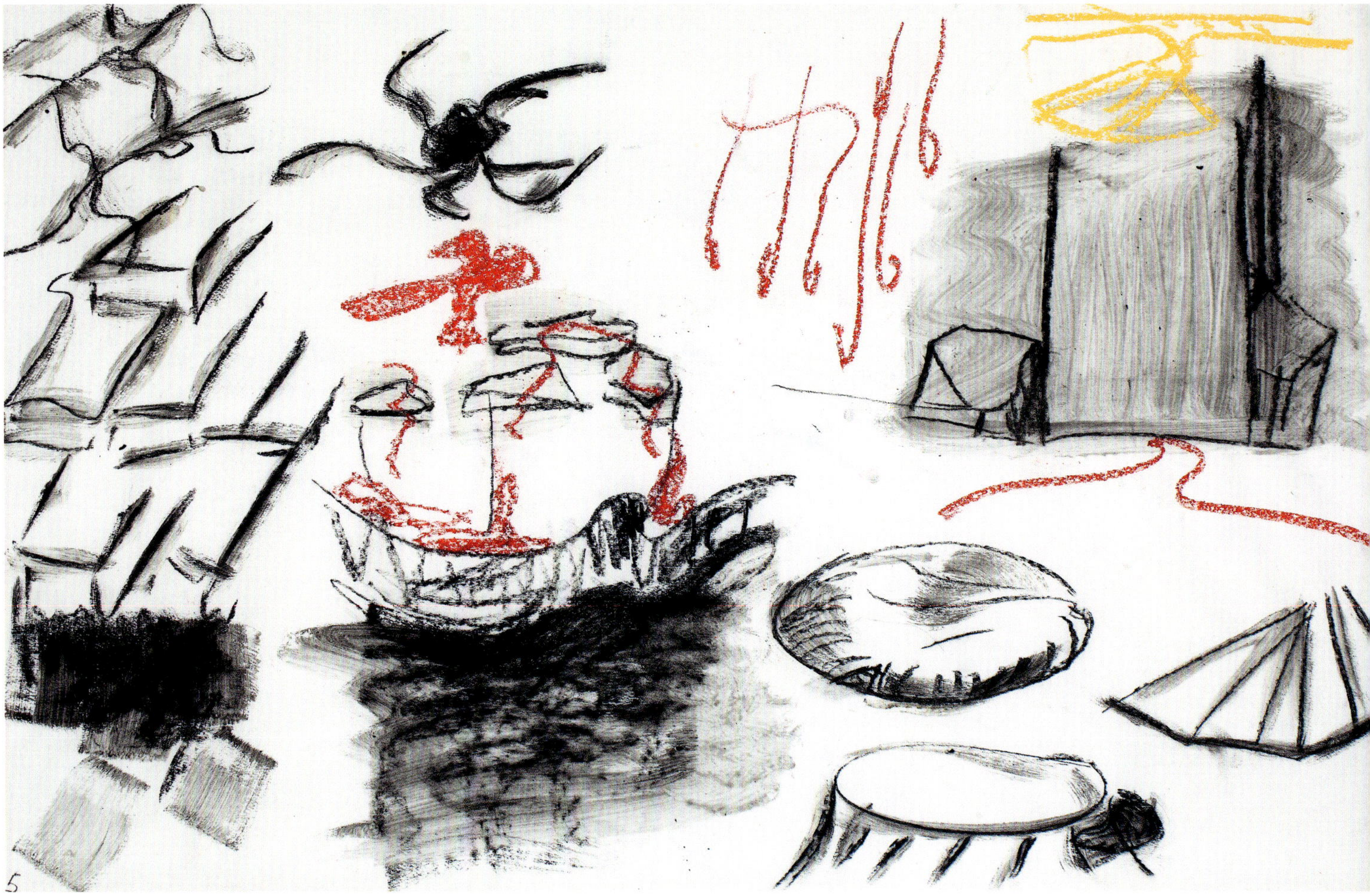

5

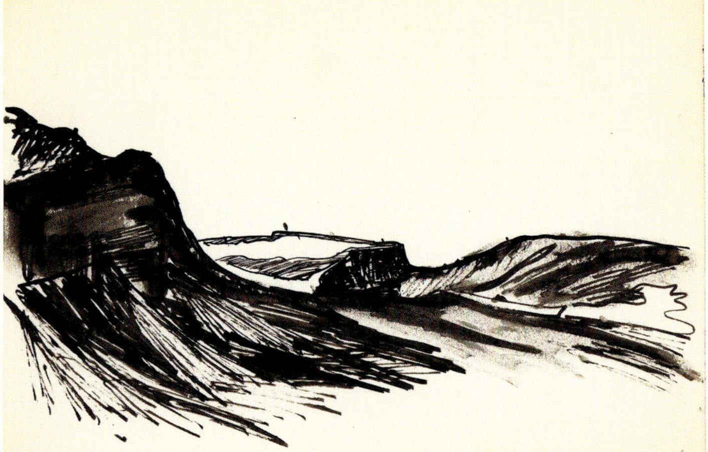

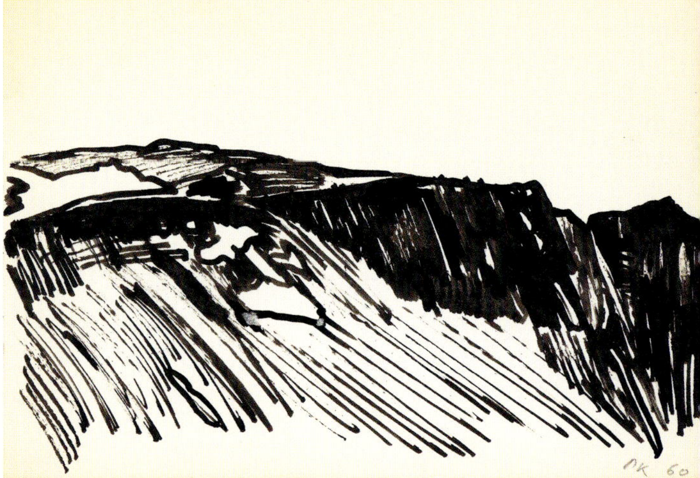

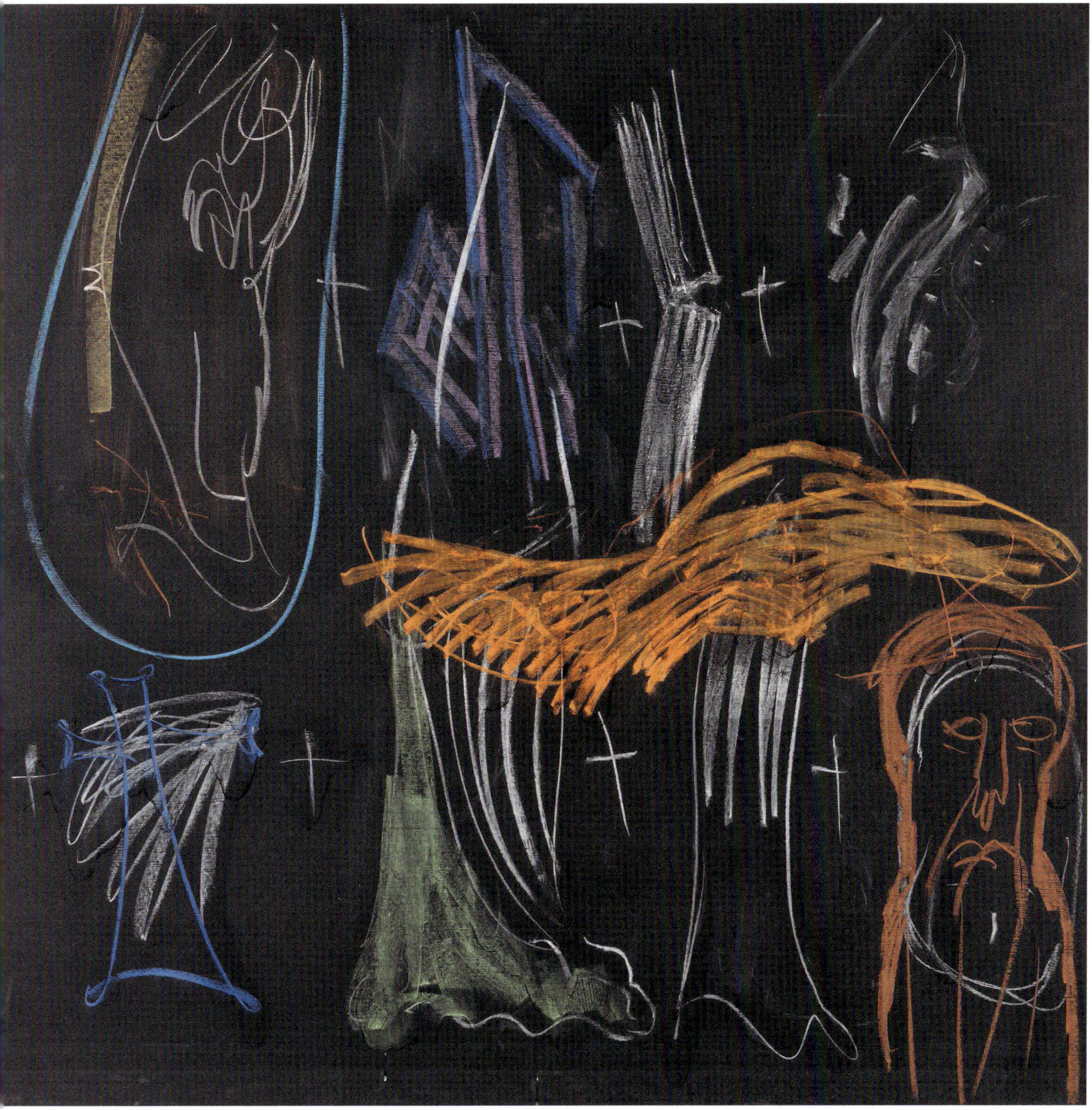

Untitled, 1985 / 122 × 122 cm

←

Untitled (5), 1990 / 70 × 105 cm

Untitled (Greenland), 1960 / 20 × 28 cm

Untitled (Greenland), 1960 / 20 × 28 cm

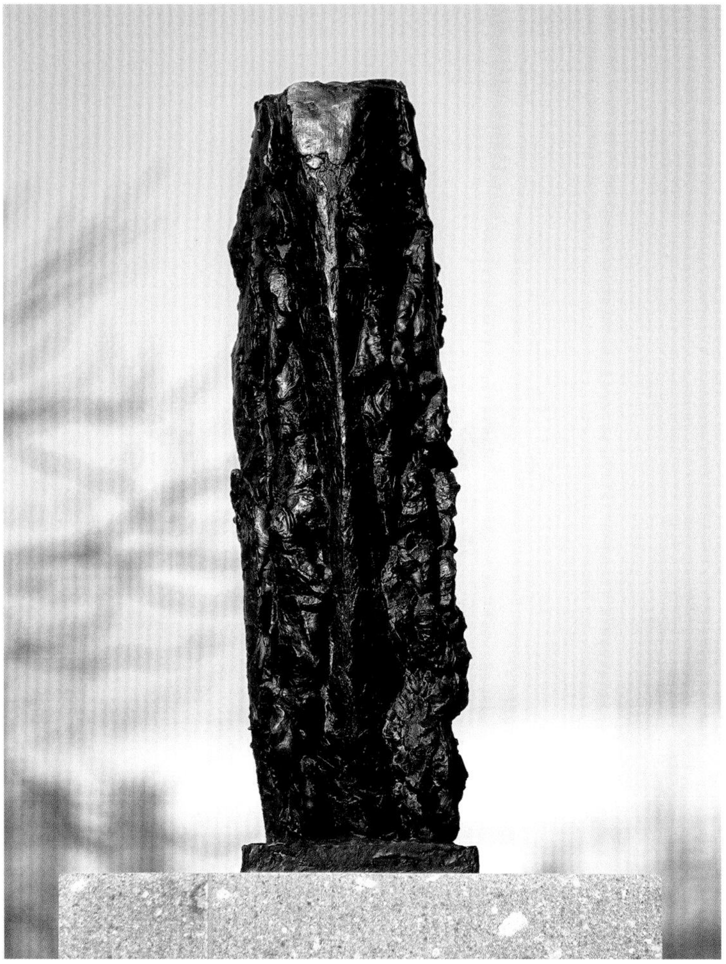

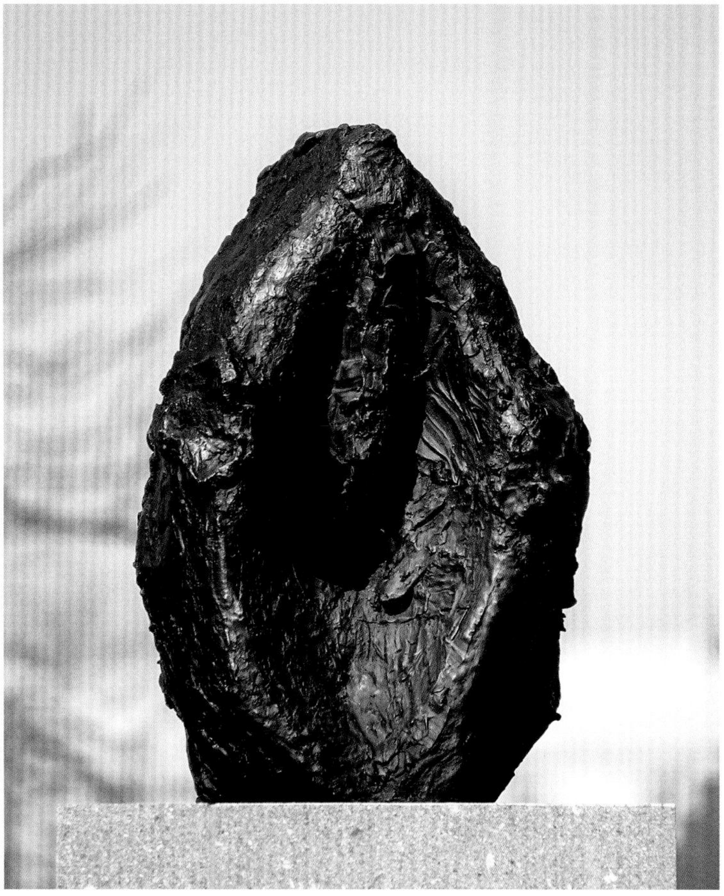

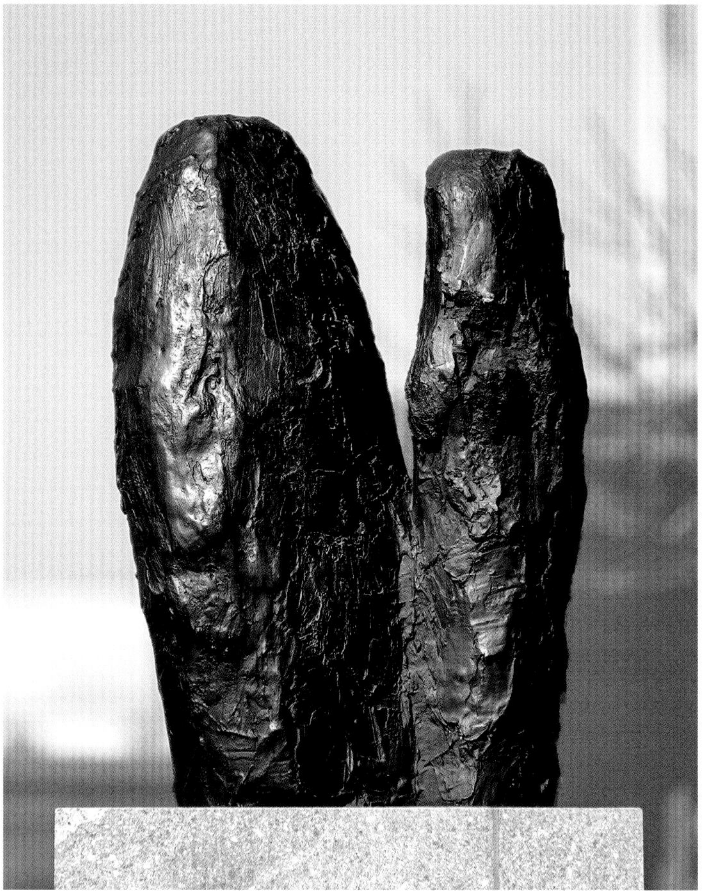

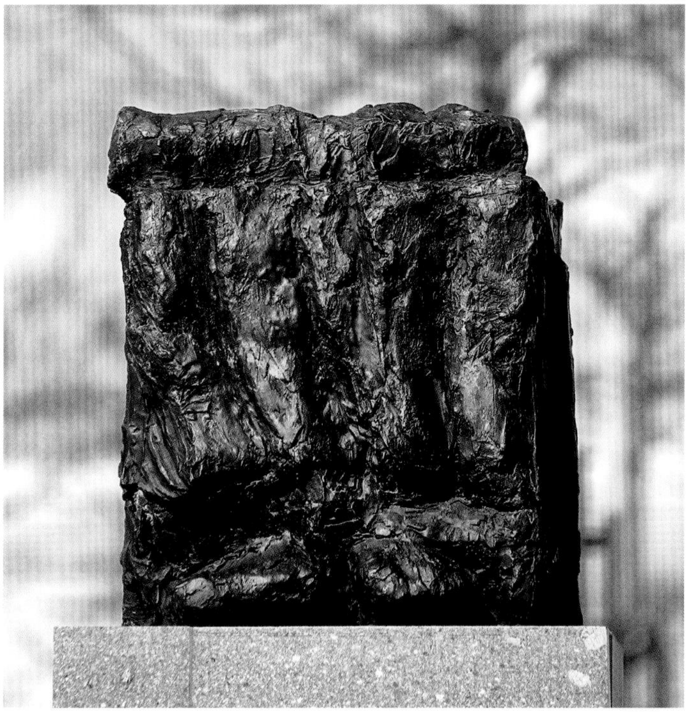

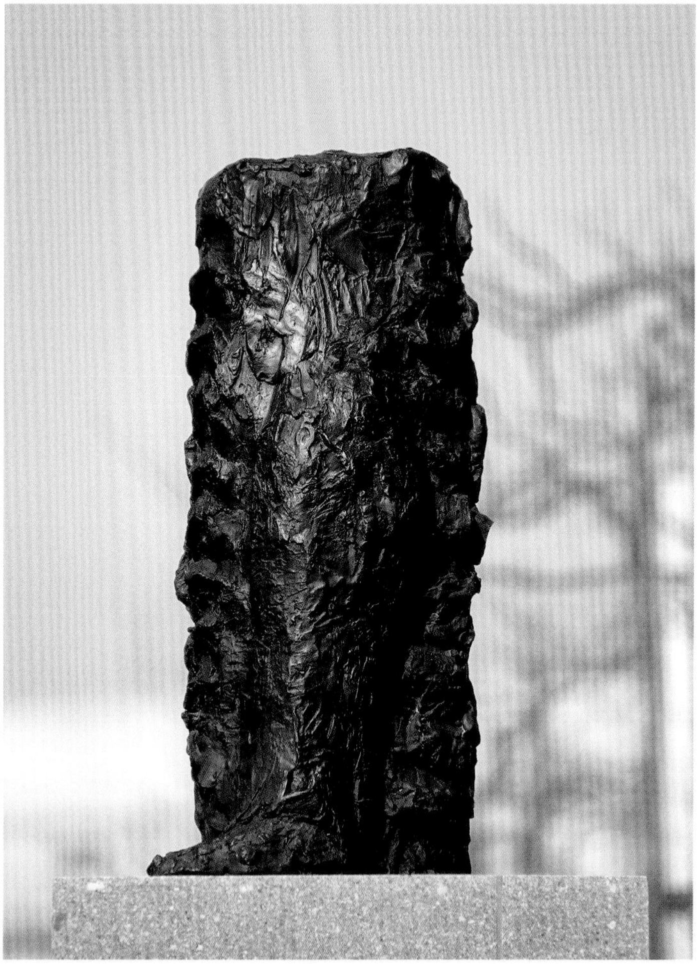

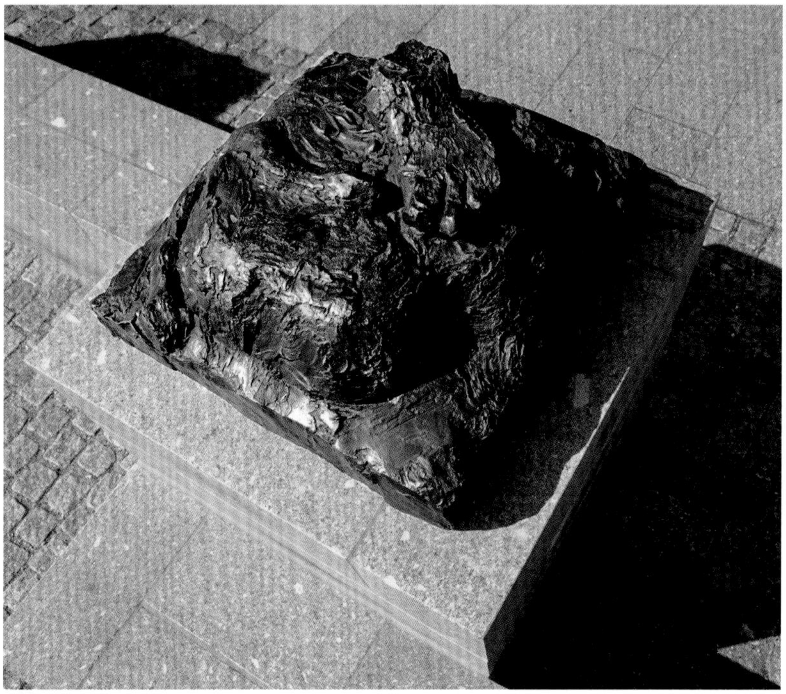

Inventory XX, 2002 / 78 × 68 × 64 cm
Inventory XIII, 2002 / 107 × 49 × 37 cm
Inventory XIX, 2002 / 30 × 60 × 60 cm
←
Inventory XIV, 2002 / 114 × 31 × 61 cm
Inventory XII, 2002 / 92 × 80 × 69 cm
Inventory V, 2002 / 102 × 66 × 55 cm
→→
Installation view, *Per Kirkeby – Bronze*, Louisiana

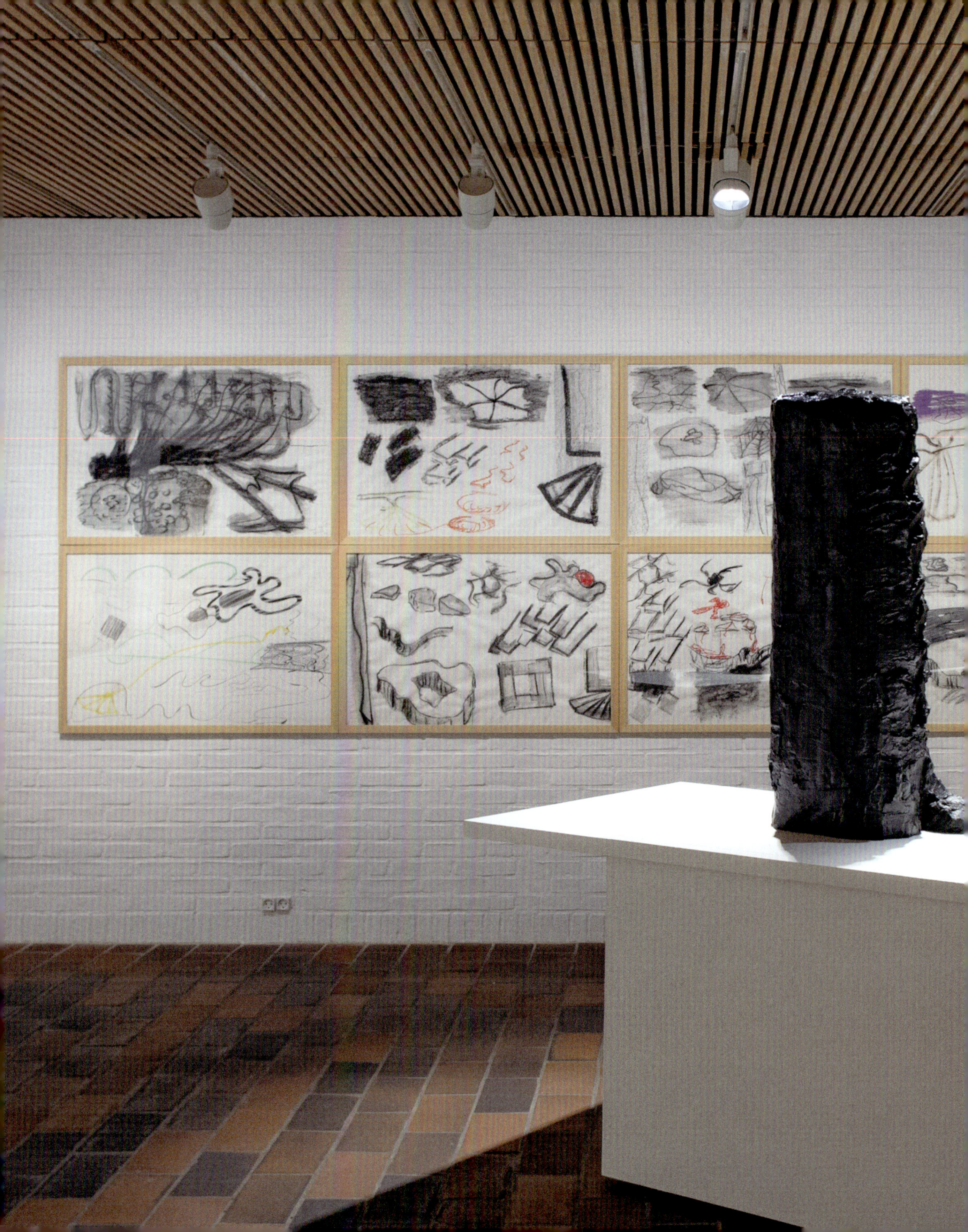

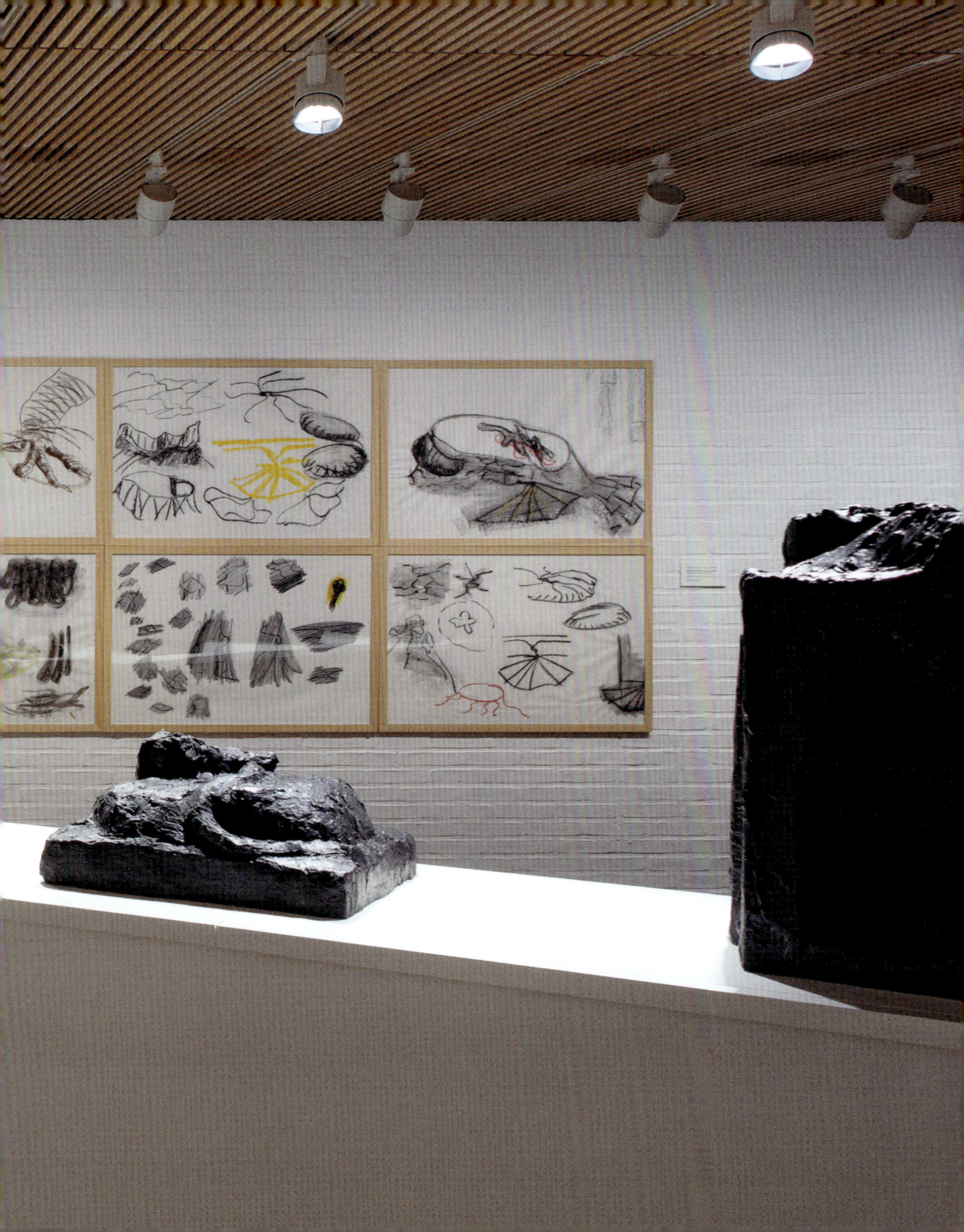

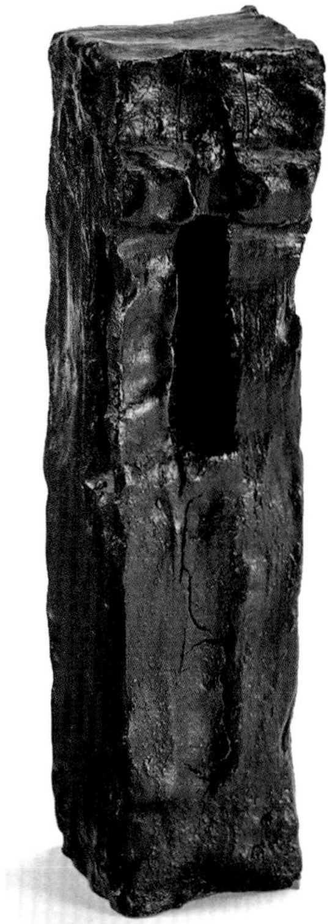

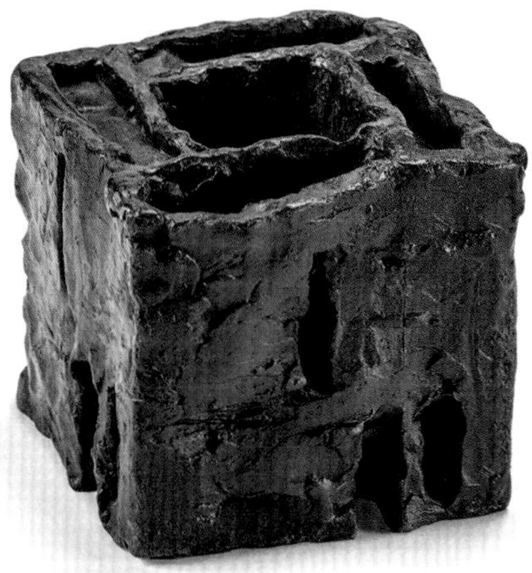

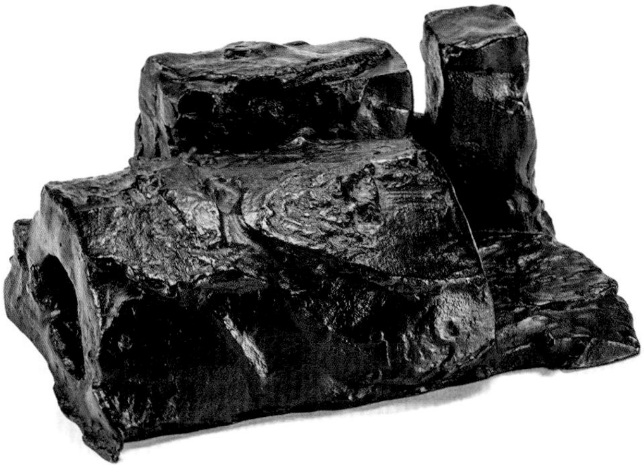

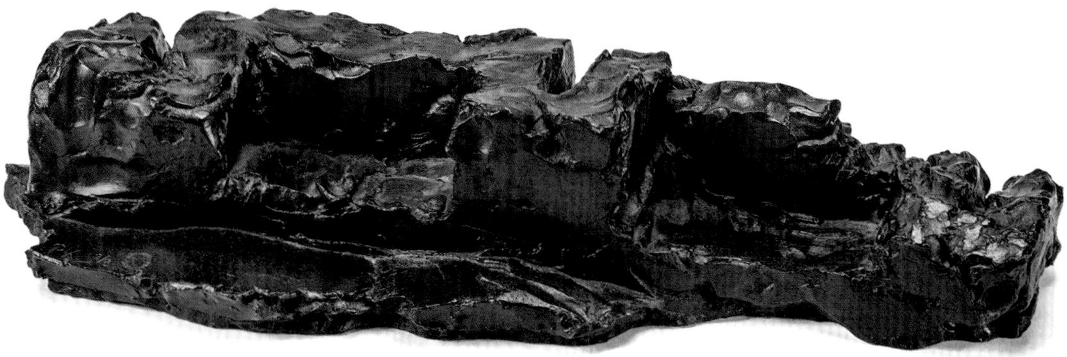

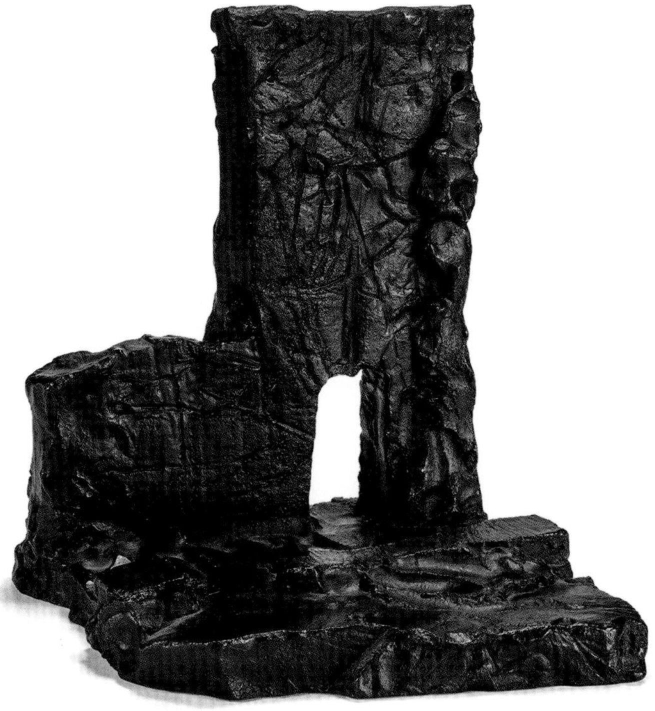

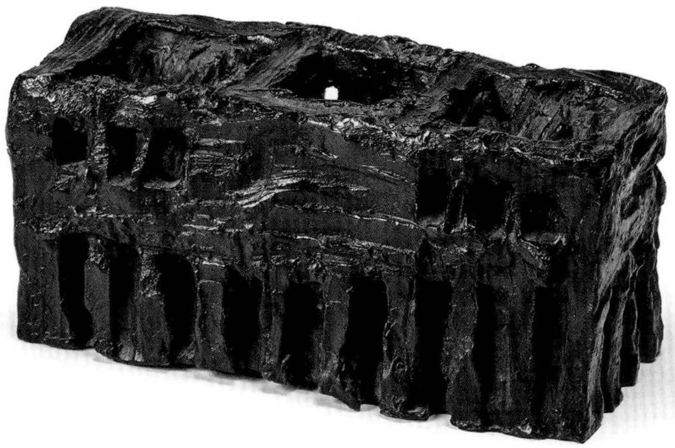

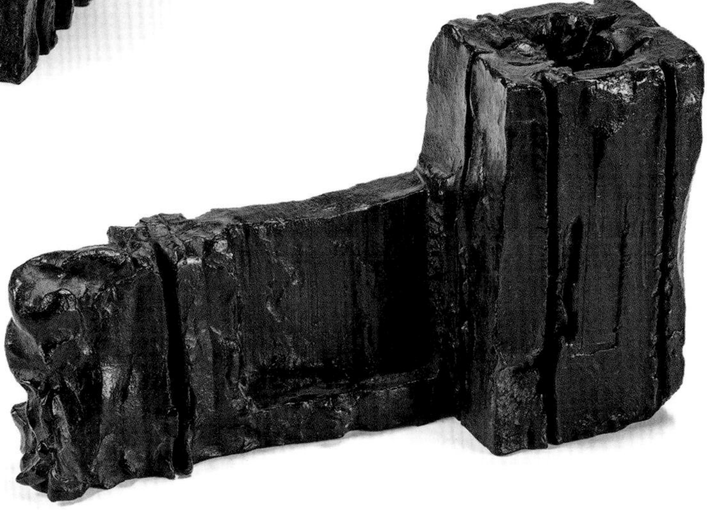

Model, 1989 / 31 × 29 × 26 cm
Model for Louisiana, Humlebæk, 1994 / 10 × 20 × 10 cm
Model for Ballerup, 1993 / 15 × 26 × 9 cm
←
Model II, 1985 / 26 × 7 × 8 cm. **Model**, 1992 / 13 × 13 × 13 cm
Model, 1990 / 11 × 25 × 18 cm. **Model**, 1996 / 10 × 47 × 19 cm
→→
Installation view, *Per Kirkeby – Bronze*, Louisiana

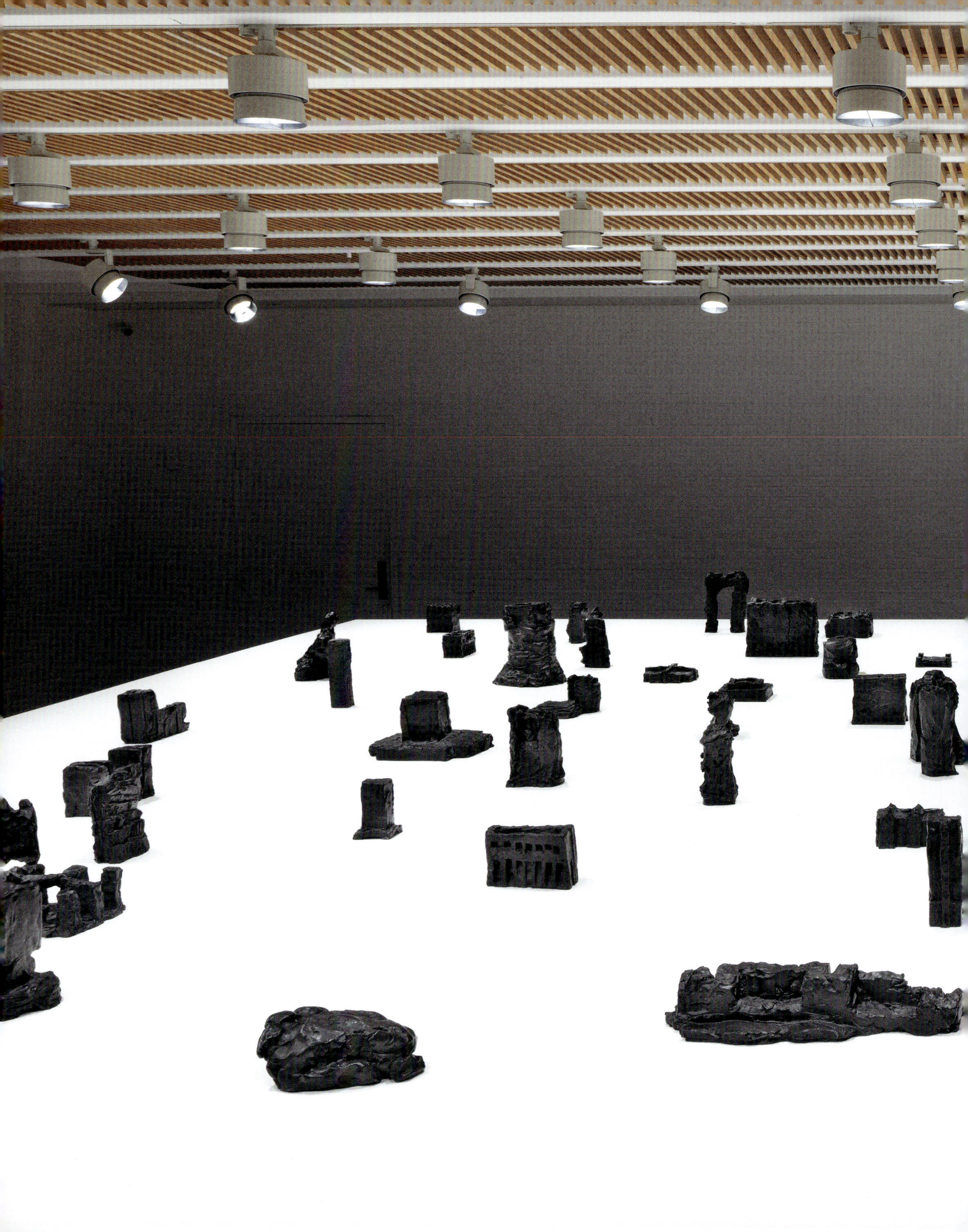

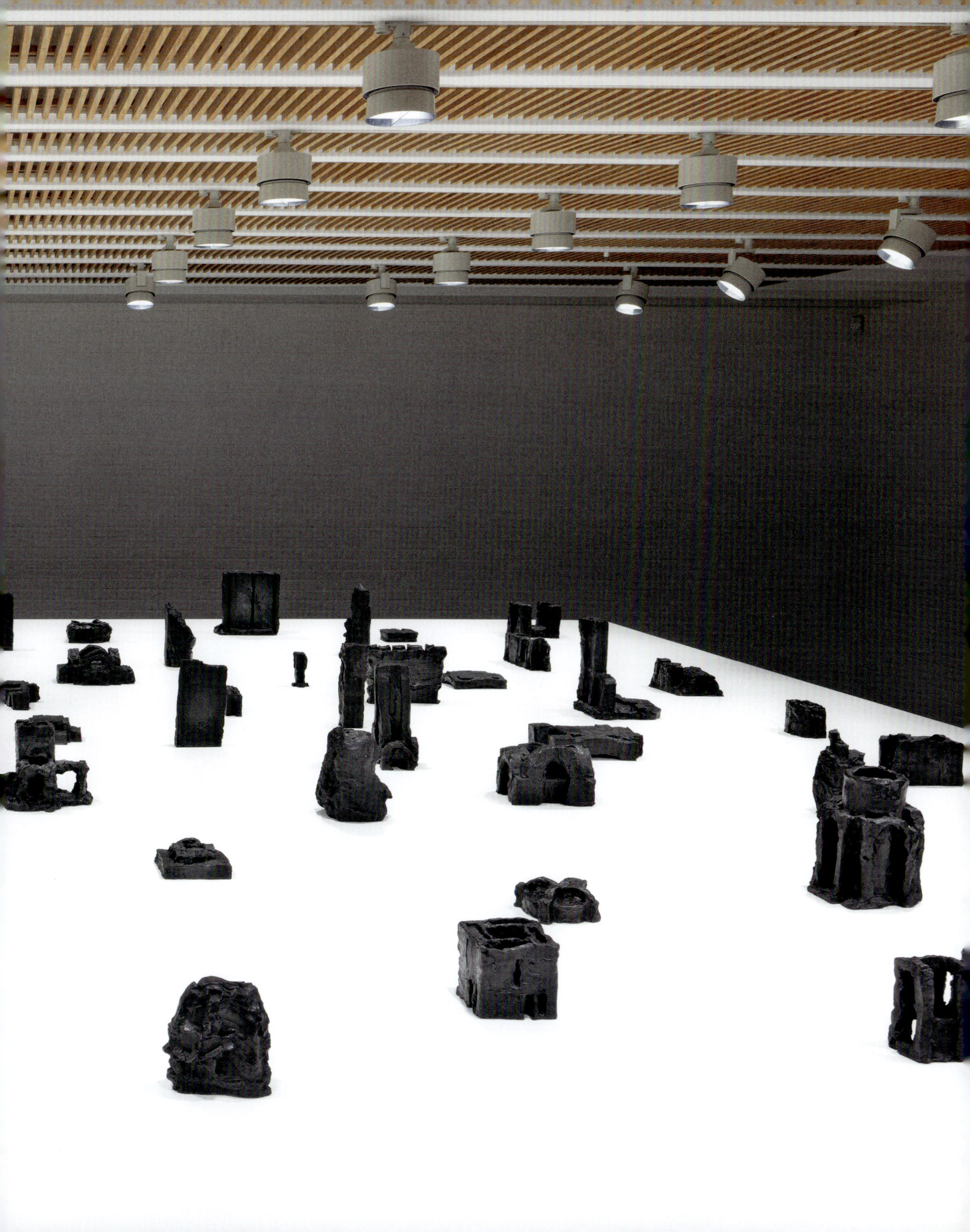

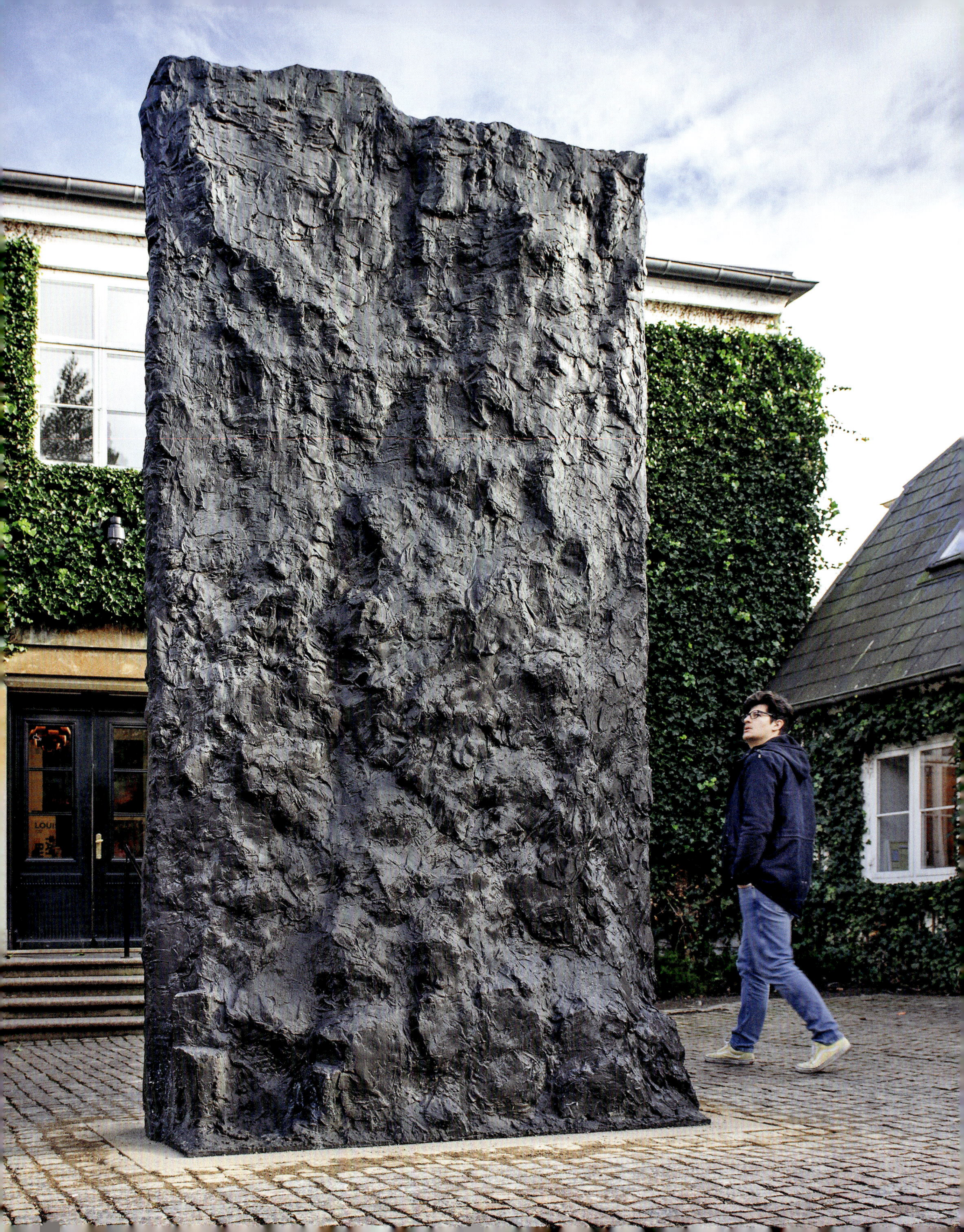

Reference numbers for bronze sculptures and works on paper refer to Galerie Michael Werner and Galleri Bo Bjerggaard's inventory numbers starting with "PK." Paintings and works on masonite are listed in reference to the *catalogue raisonné* numbers of the works in Ane Hejlskov Larsen's *Per Kirkeby Malerier 1978-1989* (Per Kirkeby Paintings, Systime, 2015).

Works by Per Kirkeby

Untitled (Greenland), 1960
Ink on paper, 20 × 28 cm
PK-60-002
Louisiana Museum of Modern Art
Acquired with funding from Museumsfonden af 7. december 1966

Untitled (Greenland), 1960
Ink on paper, 20 × 28 cm
PK-60-009
Louisiana Museum of Modern Art
Acquired with funding from Museumsfonden af 7. december 1966

Untitled (Greenland), 1960
Ink on paper, 20 × 28 cm
PK-60-012
Louisiana Museum of Modern Art
Acquired with funding from Museumsfonden af 7. december 1966

Untitled (Greenland), 1960
Ink on paper, 20 × 28 cm
PK-60-025
Louisiana Museum of Modern Art
Donation: Galleri Bo Bjerggaard

Untitled, 1979
Oil on canvas, 208 × 278 cm
M 395
Louisiana Museum of Modern Art
Donation: Statens Kunstfonds Musealværdiudvalg

Gate, 1981
Patinated bronze, 36 × 24 × 15 cm
PKK3
Louisiana Museum of Modern Art

Small Head with Arm, 1981
Patinated bronze, 35 × 23 × 16 cm
KP 1
Louisiana Museum of Modern Art

Prototype 29, 1982
Ink, wax crayon and pencil on paper, 47 × 34 cm
PKZ 59/00
Galerie Michael Werner, Märkisch Wilmersdorf, Cologne & New York

Prototype 34, 1982
Pencil on paper, 47 × 34 cm
PKZ 64/00
Galerie Michael Werner, Märkisch Wilmersdorf, Cologne & New York

Prototype 40, 1982
Ink, chalk, graphite and pencil on paper, 47 × 34 cm
PKZ 70/00
Galerie Michael Werner, Märkisch Wilmersdorf, Cologne & New York

Prototype 45, 1982
Ink, chalk and pencil on paper, 48 × 34 cm
PKZ 75/00
Galerie Michael Werner, Märkisch Wilmersdorf, Cologne & New York

Vibeke (Naples Yellow), 1982
Oil on canvas, 130 × 100 cm
M 587
Galerie Michael Werner, Märkisch Wilmersdorf, Cologne & New York

Arm, 1983
Bronze, 88 × 16 × 31 cm
PKK 24
Galerie Michael Werner, Märkisch Wilmersdorf, Cologne & New York

Figure, 1983
Bronze, 211 × 49 × 68 cm
PKK 28/6
Galerie Michael Werner, Märkisch Wilmersdorf, Cologne & New York

Landscape, 1983
Oil on canvas, 200 × 200 cm
M 670
Louisiana Museum of Modern Art

Large Head with Arm, 1983
Patinated bronze, 199 × 82 × 40 cm
PKK 25
Louisiana Museum of Modern Art

Læsø Head I, 1983
Bronze, 83 × 27 × 55 cm
PKK 20/0
Galerie Michael Werner, Märkisch Wilmersdorf, Cologne & New York

Læsø Head II, 1983
Bronze, 91 × 38 × 42 cm
PKK 22
Louisiana Museum of Modern Art
Donation: The Merla Art Foundation

Læsø Head IV, 1983
Patinated bronze, 71 × 44 × 25 cm
PKK 23
Louisiana Museum of Modern Art

Mother and Child, 1983
Oil on canvas, 201 × 201 cm
M 652
Louisiana Museum of Modern Art

Torso II, 1983
Bronze, 196 × 122 × 48 cm
PKK 30/2
Galerie Michael Werner, Märkisch Wilmersdorf, Cologne & New York

Untitled, 1983
Oil on canvas, 120 × 101 cm
M 704
Louisiana Museum of Modern Art

Untitled (Karlsruhe), 1983
Oil, pencil and coal on paper, 48 × 36 cm
PKZ 305/00
Galerie Michael Werner, Märkisch Wilmersdorf, Cologne & New York

Untitled (Karlsruhe), 1983
Wax crayon, ink and oil on paper, 48 × 36 cm
PKZ 324/00
Galerie Michael Werner, Märkisch Wilmersdorf, Cologne & New York

Untitled (Karlsruhe), 1983
Gouache and pencil on paper, 48 × 36 cm
PKZ 333/00
Galerie Michael Werner, Märkisch Wilmersdorf, Cologne & New York

Arm and Head no. XIII, 1984
Patinated bronze, 56 × 28 × 16 cm
PKK 32
Louisiana Museum of Modern Art

Head and Arm: Gate, 1984
Patinated bronze, 85 × 83 × 68 cm
PKB 34
Louisiana Museum of Modern Art

Untitled, 1984
Pastel, ink and pencil on paper, 56 × 42 cm
PKZ 180/00
Galerie Michael Werner, Märkisch Wilmersdorf, Cologne & New York

Untitled, 1984
Coal and gouache on paper, 47.7 × 36.1 cm
PKZ 935/00
Galerie Michael Werner, Märkisch Wilmersdorf, Cologne & New York

Untitled, 1984
Watercolour and coal on paper, 21 × 21 cm
PKZ 2343/00
Galerie Michael Werner, Märkisch Wilmersdorf, Cologne & New York

Untitled, 1984
Watercolour, coal and pencil on paper, 21 × 21 cm
PKZ 2344/00
Galerie Michael Werner, Märkisch Wilmersdorf, Cologne & New York

Untitled, 1985
Chalk on masonite, 122 × 122 cm
T 70
Galerie Michael Werner, Märkisch Wilmersdorf, Cologne & New York

Untitled, 1985
Chalk on masonite, 122 × 122 cm
T 76
Galerie Michael Werner, Märkisch Wilmersdorf, Cologne & New York

Standing Head, 1986
Bronze, 205 × 45 × 70 cm
PKK 67/1
Galerie Michael Werner, Märkisch Wilmersdorf, Cologne & New York

Gate I, 1987
Bronze, 220 × 150 × 75 cm
PKK 41/4
Galerie Michael Werner, Märkisch Wilmersdorf, Cologne & New York

Gate II, 1987
Patinated bronze, 256 × 178 × 82 cm
PKK 62
Louisiana Museum of Modern Art
Donation: Ny Carlsbergfondet

Torso Branch, 1988
Patinated bronze, 208 × 158 × 78 cm
PKK 72/1
Galerie Michael Werner, Märkisch Wilmersdorf, Cologne & New York

Torso Offshoot, 1988
Patinated bronze, 220 × 160 × 150 cm
PKK 73/1
Galerie Michael Werner, Märkisch Wilmersdorf, Cologne & New York

Large II (Læsø, August 90), 1990
Chalk and crayon on paper, 70 × 105 cm
PKZ-90-016
Galleri Bo Bjerggaard

Untitled, 1990
Chalk and crayon on paper, 70 × 105 cm
PKZ-90-004
Galleri Bo Bjerggaard

Untitled, 1990
Chalk and crayon on paper, 70 × 105 cm
PKZ-90-013
Galleri Bo Bjerggaard

List of works

Sculpture for Copenhagen
1997 / 410 × 220 × 90 cm

Untitled (1), 1990
Chalk and crayon on paper, 70 × 105 cm
PKZ-90-005
Galleri Bo Bjerggaard

Untitled (2), 1990
Chalk and crayon on paper, 70 × 105 cm
PKZ-90-015
Galleri Bo Bjerggaard

Untitled (4), 1990
Chalk and crayon on paper, 70 × 105 cm
PKZ-90-003
Galleri Bo Bjerggaard

Untitled (5), 1990
Chalk and crayon on paper, 70 × 105 cm
PKZ-90-014
Galleri Bo Bjerggaard

Untitled (6), 1990
Chalk and crayon on paper, 70 × 105 cm
PKZ-90-002
Galleri Bo Bjerggaard

Untitled (7), 1990
Chalk and crayon on paper, 70 × 105 cm
PKZ-90-012
Galleri Bo Bjerggaard

Untitled (8), 1990
Chalk and crayon on paper, 70 × 105 cm
PKZ-90-009
Galleri Bo Bjerggaard

Untitled (11), 1990
Chalk and crayon on paper, 70 × 105 cm
PKZ-90-017
Galleri Bo Bjerggaard

Untitled (12), 1990
Chalk and crayon on paper, 70 × 105 cm
PKZ-90-006
Galleri Bo Bjerggaard

Head at Home I, 1991-92
Bronze, 28 × 28 × 17 cm
PKK 78/3
Galerie Michael Werner, Märkisch Wilmersdorf, Cologne & New York

Head at Home II, 1991-92
Bronze, 37 × 31 × 20 cm
PKK 79/4
Galerie Michael Werner, Märkisch Wilmersdorf, Cologne & New York

Head at Home IV, 1991-92
Bronze, 24 × 21 × 12 cm
PKK 81/3
Galerie Michael Werner, Märkisch Wilmersdorf, Cologne & New York

Head at Home V, 1991-92
Bronze, 22 × 25 × 19 cm
PKK 82/1
Galerie Michael Werner, Märkisch Wilmersdorf, Cologne & New York

Heracles, 1991-92
Patinated bronze, 345 × 254 × 75 cm
PKK 77/1
Galerie Michael Werner, Märkisch Wilmersdorf, Cologne & New York

Sculpture for Copenhagen, 1997
Bronze, 410 × 220 × 90 cm
PKK 116
Galerie Michael Werner, Märkisch Wilmersdorf, Cologne & New York

Resurrection, 1999
Patinated bronze, 290 × 198 × 111 cm
PKB 71
Louisiana Museum of Modern Art
Acquired with funding from The A.P. Møller and Chastine Mc-Kinney Møller Foundation

Inventory V, 2002
Bronze, 102 × 66 × 55 cm
PKB-02-085
Galleri Bo Bjerggaard

Inventory XII, 2002
Bronze, 92 × 80 69 cm
PKB-02-092
Galleri Bo Bjerggaard

Inventory XIII, 2002
Bronze, 107 × 49 × 37 cm
PKB-02-093
Galleri Bo Bjerggaard

Inventory XIV, 2002
Bronze, 114 × 31 × 61 cm
PKB-02-094
Galleri Bo Bjerggaard

Inventory XIX, 2002
Bronze, 30 × 60 × 60 cm
PKB-02-099
Galleri Bo Bjerggaard

Inventory XX, 2002
Bronze, 78 × 68 × 64 cm
PKB-02-100
Galleri Bo Bjerggaard

Large Stele, 2002
Bronze, 420 × 200 × 100 cm
PKB 80
Nykredit

Opera relief I, 2004
Bronze, 285 × 154 × 40 cm
PKB 103
MSJ – Kunstmuseet i Tønder
Permanent loan, A.P. Møller Fonden

Opera Relief II, 2004
Bronze, 285 × 154 × 40 cm
PKB 104
MSJ – Kunstmuseet i Tønder
Permanent loan, A.P. Møller Fonden

Opera Relief III, 2004
Bronze, 285 × 154 × 40 cm
PKB 105
MSJ – Kunstmuseet i Tønder
Permanent loan, A.P. Møller Fonden

Opera Relief IV, 2004
Bronze, 285 × 154 × 40 cm
PKB 106
MSJ – Kunstmuseet i Tønder
Permanent loan, A.P. Møller Fonden

Untitled, 2004
Oil on canvas, 290 × 245 cm
PK 04
Louisiana Museum of Modern Art
Acquired with funding from The A.P. Møller and Chastine Mc-Kinney Møller Foundation

Untitled, 2004
Oil on canvas, 301 × 501 cm
PKI 04-014
Louisiana Museum of Modern Art
Acquired with funding from The A.P. Møller and Chastine Mc-Kinney Møller Foundation

Untitled (Opera), 2004
Gouache, crayon and pencil on handmade paper, 100 × 65 cm
PKZ 2605/00
Galerie Michael Werner, Märkisch Wilmersdorf, Cologne & New York

Untitled (Opera), 2004
Gouache, crayon and pencil on handmade paper, 100 × 65 cm
PKZ 2606/00
Galerie Michael Werner, Märkisch Wilmersdorf, Cologne & New York

Untitled (Opera), 2004
Gouache, crayon and pencil on handmade paper, 100 × 65 cm
PKZ 2607/00
Galerie Michael Werner, Märkisch Wilmersdorf, Cologne & New York

Untitled (Opera), 2004
Crayon and pencil on handmade paper, 100 × 65 cm
PKZ 2610/00
Galerie Michael Werner, Märkisch Wilmersdorf, Cologne & New York

Laocoön, 2011
Oil on canvas, 400 × 200 cm
PK 1295/00
Galerie Michael Werner, Märkisch Wilmersdorf, Cologne & New York

Untitled, 2011
Oil, oil pastel and indian ink on masonite, 122 × 122 cm
PKI-11-010
Louisiana Museum of Modern Art
Acquired with funding from The Augustinus Foundation

Untitled, 2011
Oil, oil pastel and indian ink on masonite, 122 × 122 cm
PKI-11-017
Louisiana Museum of Modern Art
Donation: The New Carsberg Foundation

Laocoön, 2012
Patinated bronze, 220 × 260 × 60 cm
PKK 217/2
Galerie Michael Werner, Märkisch Wilmersdorf, Cologne & New York

Untitled, Undated
Pencil, wax crayon and pen on paper, 29 × 22 cm
PKZ 2263/00
Galerie Michael Werner, Märkisch Wilmersdorf, Cologne & New York

Bronze Models

Model: Two Arms I, 1981
Patinated bronze, 28 × 36 × 19 cm
KP 4
Louisiana Museum of Modern Art

Model: Gate, 1981
Bronze, 30 × 29 × 16 cm
PKK 2/6
Galerie Michael Werner, Märkisch Wilmersdorf, Cologne & New York

Gate II, 1981
Bronze, 30 × 7 × 21 cm
PKM-81-001
Louisiana Museum of Modern Art
Acquired with funding from The Augustinus Foundation and Galleri Bo Bjerggaard

Model, 1984
Bronze, 15 × 14 × 16 cm
PKM 8
Louisiana Museum of Modern Art
Acquired with funding from The A.P. Møller and Chastine Mc-Kinney Møller Foundation and Galleri Bo Bjerggaard

Model for Brick Sculpture, 1984
Bronze, 23 × 7 × 7 cm
PKM 7
Louisiana Museum of Modern Art
Acquired with funding from The A.P. Møller and Chastine Mc-Kinney Møller Foundation and Galleri Bo Bjerggaard

Model I, 1985
Bronze, 32 × 8 × 12 cm
PKM 9
Louisiana Museum of Modern Art
Acquired with funding from The A.P. Møller and Chastine Mc-Kinney Møller Foundation and Galleri Bo Bjerggaard

Model II, 1985
Bronze, 26 × 7 × 8 cm
PKM10 / PKK43
Louisiana Museum of Modern Art
Acquired with funding from The A.P. Møller and Chastine Mc-Kinney Møller Foundation and Galleri Bo Bjerggaard

Model VI, 1985
Bronze, 16 × 18 × 12 cm
PKM 14 / PKK 47
Louisiana Museum of Modern Art
Acquired with funding from The A.P. Møller and Chastine Mc-Kinney Møller Foundation and Galleri Bo Bjerggaard

Model VII, 1985
Bronze, 3 × 18 × 18 cm
PKM 15 / PKK 48
Louisiana Museum of Modern Art
Acquired with funding from The A.P. Møller and Chastine Mc-Kinney Møller Foundation and Galleri Bo Bjerggaard

Model for Kiel, 1985
Bronze, 5 × 19 × 19 cm
PKM 20 / PKK57
Louisiana Museum of Modern Art
Acquired with funding from The A.P. Møller and Chastine Mc-Kinney Møller Foundation and Galleri Bo Bjerggaard

Model for Mönchengladbach, 1985
Bronze, 4 × 20 × 20 cm
PKM 21 / PKK 58
Louisiana Museum of Modern Art
Acquired with funding from The A.P. Møller and Chastine Mc-Kinney Møller Foundation and Galleri Bo Bjerggaard

Model for Paris, 1985
Bronze, 24 × 30 × 16 cm
PKM 18 / PKK 50A
Louisiana Museum of Modern Art
Acquired with funding from The A.P. Møller and Chastine Mc-Kinney Møller Foundation and Galleri Bo Bjerggaard

Untitled, 1985
Bronze, 13 × 20 × 11 cm
PKM-85-001
Louisiana Museum of Modern Art
Acquired with funding from The Augustinus Foundation and Galleri Bo Bjerggaard

Untitled, 1986
Bronze, 14 × 9 × 9 cm
PKM-86-001
Louisiana Museum of Modern Art
Acquired with funding from The Augustinus Foundation and Galleri Bo Bjerggaard

Untitled, 1986
Bronze, 13 × 6 × 7 cm
PKM-86-002
Louisiana Museum of Modern Art
Acquired with funding from The Augustinus Foundation and Galleri Bo Bjerggaard

Untitled, 1986
Bronze, 23 × 13 × 12 cm
PKM-86-003
Louisiana Museum of Modern Art
Acquired with funding from The Augustinus Foundation and Galleri Bo Bjerggaard

Bohr, 1987
Bronze, 13 × 13 × 13 cm
PKM 34
Louisiana Museum of Modern Art
Acquired with funding from The A.P. Møller and Chastine Mc-Kinney Møller Foundation and Galleri Bo Bjerggaard

Model, 1987
Bronze, 4 × 14 × 14 cm
PKM 25 / PKK 65
Louisiana Museum of Modern Art
Acquired with funding from The A.P. Møller and Chastine Mc-Kinney Møller Foundation and Galleri Bo Bjerggaard

Model, 1987
Bronze, 7 × 19 × 20 cm
PKM 26 / PKK 66
Louisiana Museum of Modern Art
Acquired with funding from The A.P. Møller and Chastine Mc-Kinney Møller Foundation and Galleri Bo Bjerggaard

Model, 1987
Bronze, 29 × 15 × 12 cm
PKM 87-001
Louisiana Museum of Modern Art
Acquired with funding from The A.P. Møller and Chastine Mc-Kinney Møller Foundation and Galleri Bo Bjerggaard

Model for Karlsruhe, 1987
Bronze, 7 × 15 × 15 cm
PKM 87-004
Louisiana Museum of Modern Art
Acquired with funding from The Augustinus Foundation and Galleri Bo Bjerggaard

Model for Kröller-Müller Museum, 1987
Bronze, 20 × 27 × 10 cm
PKM 31 / PKK 71A
Louisiana Museum of Modern Art
Acquired with funding from The A.P. Møller and Chastine Mc-Kinney Møller Foundation and Galleri Bo Bjerggaard

Model for Kröller-Müller Museum, Otterloo, 1987
Bronze, 22 × 43 × 22 cm
PKM 32
Louisiana Museum of Modern Art
Acquired with funding from The A.P. Møller and Chastine Mc-Kinney Møller Foundation and Galleri Bo Bjerggaard

Model for Rotterdam, 1987
Bronze, 13 × 29 × 25 cm
PKM 24
Louisiana Museum of Modern Art
Acquired with funding from The A.P. Møller and Chastine Mc-Kinney Møller Foundation and Galleri Bo Bjerggaard

Sculpture, 1987
Bronze, 30 × 10 × 9 cm
PKM-87-033
Louisiana Museum of Modern Art
Acquired with funding from The Augustinus Foundation and Galleri Bo Bjerggaard

Untitled, 1987
Bronze, 7 × 17 × 17 cm
PKM-87-002
Louisiana Museum of Modern Art
Acquired with funding from The Augustinus Foundation and Galleri Bo Bjerggaard

Untitled, 1987
Bronze, 10 × 24 × 24 cm
PKM-87-003
Louisiana Museum of Modern Art
Acquired with funding from The Augustinus Foundation and Galleri Bo Bjerggaard

Untitled, 1987
Bronze, 7 × 28 × 25 cm
PKM-87-005
Louisiana Museum of Modern Art
Acquired with funding from The Augustinus Foundation and Galleri Bo Bjerggaard

Untitled, 1987
Bronze, 5 × 15 × 15 cm
PKM-87-006
Louisiana Museum of Modern Art
Acquired with funding from The Augustinus Foundation and Galleri Bo Bjerggaard

Untitled, 1987
Bronze, 15 × 21 × 20 cm
PKM-87-007
Louisiana Museum of Modern Art
Acquired with funding from The Augustinus Foundation and Galleri Bo Bjerggaard

Untitled, 1987
Bronze, 15 × 13 × 13 cm
PKM-87-008
Louisiana Museum of Modern Art
Acquired with funding from The Augustinus Foundation and Galleri Bo Bjerggaard

Model, 1988
Bronze, 20 × 7 × 8 cm
PKM 36 / PKK 74
Louisiana Museum of Modern Art
Acquired with funding from The A.P. Møller and Chastine Mc-Kinney Møller Foundation and Galleri Bo Bjerggaard

Gate, 1988
Bronze, 30 × 91 × 18 cm
PKM-88-039
Louisiana Museum of Modern Art
Acquired with funding from The Augustinus Foundation and Galleri Bo Bjerggaard

Untitled, 1988
Bronze, 30 × 15 × 12 cm
PKM-88-001
Louisiana Museum of Modern Art
Acquired with funding from The Augustinus Foundation and Galleri Bo Bjerggaard

Model, 1989
Bronze, 31 × 29 × 26 cm
PKM 45
Louisiana Museum of Modern Art
Acquired with funding from The A.P. Møller and Chastine Mc-Kinney Møller Foundation and Galleri Bo Bjerggaard

Model for Groningen, 1989
Bronze, 17 × 27 × 7 cm
PKM-89-001
Louisiana Museum of Modern Art
Acquired with funding from The Augustinus Foundation and Galleri Bo Bjerggaard

Model for Aalborg, 1989
Bronze, 16 × 19 × 21 cm
PKM-89-002
Louisiana Museum of Modern Art
Acquired with funding from The Augustinus Foundation and Galleri Bo Bjerggaard

Model for Karlsruhe, 1989
Bronze, 30 × 25 × 26 cm
PKM 42 / PKK 76A
Louisiana Museum of Modern Art
Acquired with funding from The A.P. Møller and Chastine Mc-Kinney Møller Foundation and Galleri Bo Bjerggaard

Model for (University) Karlsruhe, 1989
Bronze, 7 × 19 × 17 cm
PKM 40 / PKK 75
Louisiana Museum of Modern Art
Acquired with funding from The A.P. Møller and Chastine Mc-Kinney Møller Foundation and Galleri Bo Bjerggaard

Model, 1990
Bronze, 11 × 25 × 18 cm
PKM 54
Louisiana Museum of Modern Art
Acquired with funding from The A.P. Møller and Chastine Mc-Kinney Møller Foundation and Galleri Bo Bjerggaard

Untitled, 1990
Bronze, 18 × 30 × 29 cm
PKM-90-001
Louisiana Museum of Modern Art
Acquired with funding from The Augustinus Foundation and Galleri Bo Bjerggaard

Model, 1992
Bronze, 29 × 27 × 15 cm
PKM 63
Louisiana Museum of Modern Art
Acquired with funding from The A.P. Møller and Chastine Mc-Kinney Møller Foundation and Galleri Bo Bjerggaard

Model, 1992
Bronze, 11 × 21 × 21 cm
PKM 65
Louisiana Museum of Modern Art
Acquired with funding from The A.P. Møller and Chastine Mc-Kinney Møller Foundation and Galleri Bo Bjerggaard

Model, 1992
Bronze, 9 × 20 × 20 cm
PKM-92-002
Louisiana Museum of Modern Art
Acquired with funding from The A.P. Møller and Chastine Mc-Kinney Møller Foundation and Galleri Bo Bjerggaard

Model, 1992
Bronze, 13 × 13 × 13 cm
PKM-92-003
Louisiana Museum of Modern Art
Acquired with funding from The A.P. Møller and Chastine Mc-Kinney Møller Foundation and Galleri Bo Bjerggaard

Model for Ballerup, 1992
Bronze, 14 × 33 × 9 cm
PKM 62 / PKK 114
Louisiana Museum of Modern Art
Acquired with funding from The A.P. Møller and Chastine Mc-Kinney Møller Foundation and Galleri Bo Bjerggaard

Sculpture, 1992
Bronze, 24 × 13 × 8 cm
PKM-92-057
Louisiana Museum of Modern Art
Acquired with funding from The Augustinus Foundation and Galleri Bo Bjerggaard

Sculpture, 1992
Bronze, 25 × 16 × 15 cm
PKM-92-064
Louisiana Museum of Modern Art
Acquired with funding from The Augustinus Foundation and Galleri Bo Bjerggaard

Model, 1993
Bronze, 20 × 29 × 21 cm
PKM 70
Louisiana Museum of Modern Art
Acquired with funding from The A.P. Møller and Chastine Mc-Kinney Møller Foundation and Galleri Bo Bjerggaard

Model, 1993
Bronze, 10 × 16 × 10 cm
PKM 71
Louisiana Museum of Modern Art
Acquired with funding from The A.P. Møller and Chastine Mc-Kinney Møller Foundation and Galleri Bo Bjerggaard

Model for Ballerup, 1993
Bronze, 15 × 26 × 9 cm
PKM 66
Louisiana Museum of Modern Art
Acquired with funding from The A.P. Møller and Chastine Mc-Kinney Møller Foundation and Galleri Bo Bjerggaard

Model for Louisiana, Humlebæk, 1994
Bronze, 10 × 20 × 10 cm
PKM 73
Louisiana Museum of Modern Art
Acquired with funding from The A.P. Møller and Chastine Mc-Kinney Møller Foundation and Galleri Bo Bjerggaard

Model, 1995
Bronze, 12 × 19 × 10 cm
PKM 76
Louisiana Museum of Modern Art
Acquired with funding from The A.P. Møller and Chastine Mc-Kinney Møller Foundation and Galleri Bo Bjerggaard

Model, 1995
Bronze, 9 × 16 × 10 cm
PKM-95-001
Louisiana Museum of Modern Art
Acquired with funding from The Augustinus Foundation and Galleri Bo Bjerggaard

Sculpture, 1995
Bronze, 26 × 15 × 5 cm
PKM-95-002
Louisiana Museum of Modern Art
Acquired with funding from The Augustinus Foundation and Galleri Bo Bjerggaard

Sculpture, 1995
Bronze, 18 × 13 × 8 cm
PKM-95-074
Private Collection

Sculpture, 1995
Bronze, 16 × 16 × 9 cm
PKM-95-075
Louisiana Museum of Modern Art
Acquired with funding from The Augustinus Foundation and Galleri Bo Bjerggaard

Model, 1996
Bronze, 8 × 19 × 6 cm
PKM-96-001
Louisiana Museum of Modern Art
Acquired with funding from The A.P. Møller and Chastine Mc-Kinney Møller Foundation and Galleri Bo Bjerggaard

Model, 1996
Bronze, 10 × 47 × 19 cm
PKM-96-002
Louisiana Museum of Modern Art
Acquired with funding from The A.P. Møller and Chastine Mc-Kinney Møller Foundation and Galleri Bo Bjerggaard

Sculpture, 1996
Bronze, 22 × 15 × 9 cm
PKM-96-079
Louisiana Museum of Modern Art
Acquired with funding from The Augustinus Foundation and Galleri Bo Bjerggaard

Sculpture, 1996
Bronze, 18 × 12 × 8 cm
PKM-96-080
Louisiana Museum of Modern Art
Acquired with funding from The Augustinus Foundation and Galleri Bo Bjerggaard

Untitled (Egebjerggård, Ballerup), 1996
Bronze, 13 × 26 × 11 cm
PKM-96-004
Louisiana Museum of Modern Art
Acquired with funding from The A.P. Møller and Chastine Mc-Kinney Møller Foundation and Galleri Bo Bjerggaard

Untitled (Musikhus Aars), 1996
Bronze, 6 × 26 × 15 cm
PKM-96-003
Louisiana Museum of Modern Art
Acquired with funding from The A.P. Møller and Chastine Mc-Kinney Møller Foundation and Galleri Bo Bjerggaard

Model, 1997
Bronze, 13 × 15 × 6 cm
PKM 82
Louisiana Museum of Modern Art
Acquired with funding from The A.P. Møller and Chastine Mc-Kinney Møller Foundation and Galleri Bo Bjerggaard

Untitled, 1998
Bronze, 25 × 19 × 20 cm
PKM-98-001
Louisiana Museum of Modern Art
Acquired with funding from The A.P. Møller and Chastine Mc-Kinney Møller Foundation and Galleri Bo Bjerggaard

Sculpture, 2005
Bronze, 21 × 12 × 10 cm
PKM-05-083
Louisiana Museum of Modern Art
Acquired with funding from The Augustinus Foundation and Galleri Bo Bjerggaard

Sculpture, 2005
Bronze, 20 × 10 × 9 cm
PKM-05-085
Louisiana Museum of Modern Art
Acquired with funding from The Augustinus Foundation and Galleri Bo Bjerggaard

Sculpture, 2005
Bronze, 14 × 16 × 11 cm
PKM-05-086
Louisiana Museum of Modern Art
Acquired with funding from The Augustinus Foundation and Galleri Bo Bjerggaard

Model, 2010
Bronze, 22 × 19 × 16 cm
PKM-10-002
Louisiana Museum of Modern Art
Acquired with funding from The Augustinus Foundation and Galleri Bo Bjerggaard

Untitled, 2010
Bronze, 10 × 26 × 18 cm
PKM-10-001
Louisiana Museum of Modern Art
Acquired with funding from The Augustinus Foundation and Galleri Bo Bjerggaard

Untitled, 2010
Bronze, 25 × 20 × 12 cm
PKM-10-003
Louisiana Museum of Modern Art
Acquired with funding from The Augustinus Foundation and Galleri Bo Bjerggaard

Untitled, 2010
Bronze, 19 × 21 × 20 cm
PKM-10-004
Louisiana Museum of Modern Art
Acquired with funding from The Augustinus Foundation and Galleri Bo Bjerggaard

Untitled, 2010
Bronze, 13 × 22 × 21 cm
PKM-10-005
Louisiana Museum of Modern Art
Acquired with funding from The Augustinus Foundation and Galleri Bo Bjerggaard

Model IV, undated
Bronze, 25 × 9 × 7 cm
PKM 12
Louisiana Museum of Modern Art
Acquired with funding from The A.P. Møller and Chastine Mc-Kinney Møller Foundation and Galleri Bo Bjerggaard

Other Artists

Francis Bacon
Three Studies of George Dyer, 1969
Oil on canvas, 36 × 30 cm
Louisiana Museum of Modern Art
Donation: Ny Carlsbergfondet

Jean Fautrier
Grand torse, 1928
Large Torso
Bronze, 66 × 28 × 21 cm
Louisiana Museum of Modern Art
Donation: Ny Carlsbergfondet

Alberto Giacometti
Grande tête, 1959-60
Large Head
Bronze, 96 × 34 × 29 cm
Louisiana Museum of Modern Art
Donation: Ny Carlsbergfondet

Asger Jorn
La Double face, 1960
Double Face
Oil on canvas, 116 × 90 cm
Louisiana Museum of Modern Art

Eugène Leroy
Tête blanche, 1990
White Head
Oil on canvas, 129 × 97 cm
Louisiana Museum of Modern Art
Donation: Ny Carlsbergfondet

Markus Lüpertz
Der Mohr (linke Wange rosa, Rechte Wange schwartz), 1983
The Moor (Left Cheek Pink, Right Cheek Black)
Painted Bronze, 45 × 31 × 20 cm
Louisiana Museum of Modern Art

Auguste Rodin
Troisième maquette pour la Porte de l'Enfer, ca. 1881-1882
Third Draft Model for The Gates of Hell
Bronze, cire perdue casting, 110 × 74 × 28 cm
S.06501
Musée Rodin, Paris

Auguste Rodin
Figure de femme à mi-corps, ca. 1910
Half-figure – Female
Bronze, cire perdue casting, 73 × 41 × 64 cm
S.00997
Musée Rodin, Paris

J.F. Willumsen
Tizian døende, 1935
Titian Dying
Oil on canvas, 200 × 250 cm
Inv. 105
Willumsens Museum

Clay and terracotta models in the basement under Per Kirkeby's studio in Hellerup, 1995

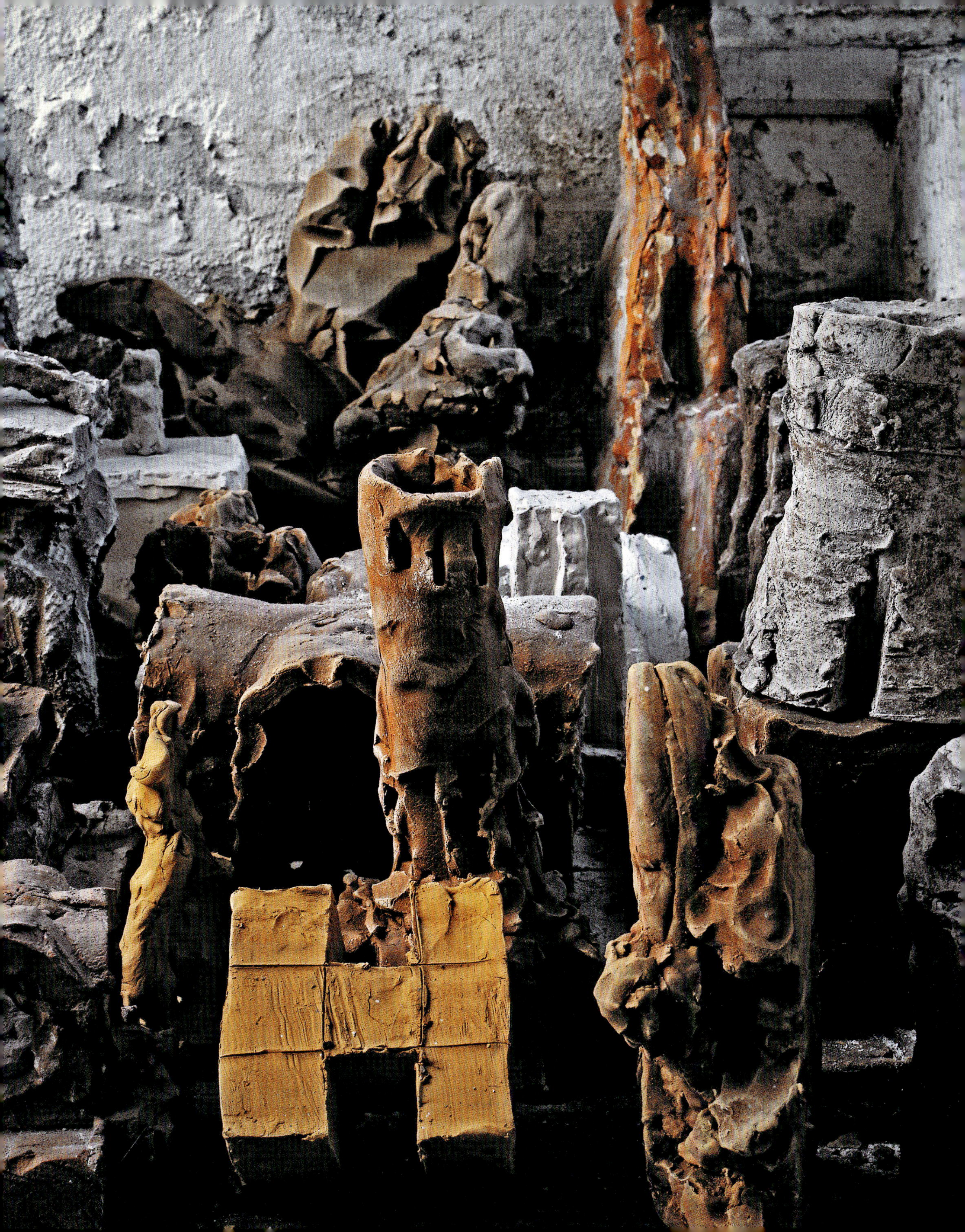

Per Kirkeby – Bronze

Edited by Lærke Rydal Jørgensen and Poul Erik Tøjner
Graphic Design: Michael Jensen
Translations: Glen Garner (Poul Erik Tøjner),
Jane Rowley (Erik Steffensen, Helle Brøns),
James Manley (Ulrich Wilmes)
Proofreading: James Manley
Photo Editor: Sidse Buck and Kim Hansen
Photo: Bjørk Aabech: 3, 38, 41; Jens Bull: 5, 10-11;
Poul Buchard / Brøndum & Co.: 9, 15, 16, 19, 21, 24, 25,
27, 29, 30-31, 42-43, 46-51, 53, 54, 56 bottom, 59, 62,
63, 66-69, 78-79, 82, 83, 86-87, 89, 92-93, 96-97;
Per Kirkeby: 13; Farbanalyse: 14; Jörg von Bruchhausen;
17, 26, 28, 57, 80-81; Hervé Lewandowski / Courtesy
Musée Rodin: 18, 40; Kim Hansen: 44-45, 55, 98;
Anders Sune Berg: 71 bottom; Ole Hein Pedersen: 73;
Marco Recrosio Milano: 76; Jens Lindhe: 103.

Cover, front: Per Kirkeby: *Læsø Head II*, 1983
Patinated bronze, 91 × 38 × 42 cm
Louisiana Museum of Modern Art
Donation: The Merla Art Foundation
Photo: Poul Buchard / Brøndum & Co
Cover, inside: Per Kirkeby in his studio on Læsø, 1983
Photo: Jens Bull
Page 3: Per Kirkeby in his studio on Læsø, 1998
Photo: Bjørk Aabech
Cover, back: Per Kirkeby: *Gate II*, 1987
Patinated bronze, 256 × 178 × 82 cm
Louisiana Museum of Modern Art
Donation: Ny Carlsbergfondet
Photo: Kim Hansen
Endpapers: Per Kirkeby: *Opera-Relief I* (details)
Bronze, 285 × 154 × 40 cm
MSJ – Kunstmuseet i Tønder
Permanent Loan, A.P. Møller Fonden

Litho & Print: Narayana Press
ISBN: 978-87-93659-29-2
Printed in Denmark 2020
www.louisiana.dk

Ecolabelled Printed Matter 5041 0562

MIX
Paper from responsible sources
FSC™ C010651

This catalogue is published
on the occasion of the exhibition

Per Kirkeby – Bronze
Louisiana Museum of Modern Art, Humlebæk
21 February – 21 June 2020

Curator: Poul Erik Tøjner
Curatorial Coordinator/Registrar: Marie Mose Hyllested
Conservator/Exhibition Producer: Mikkel Storch
Graphic Design: Marie d'Origny Lübecker

The exhibition is supported by

BECKETT·FONDEN

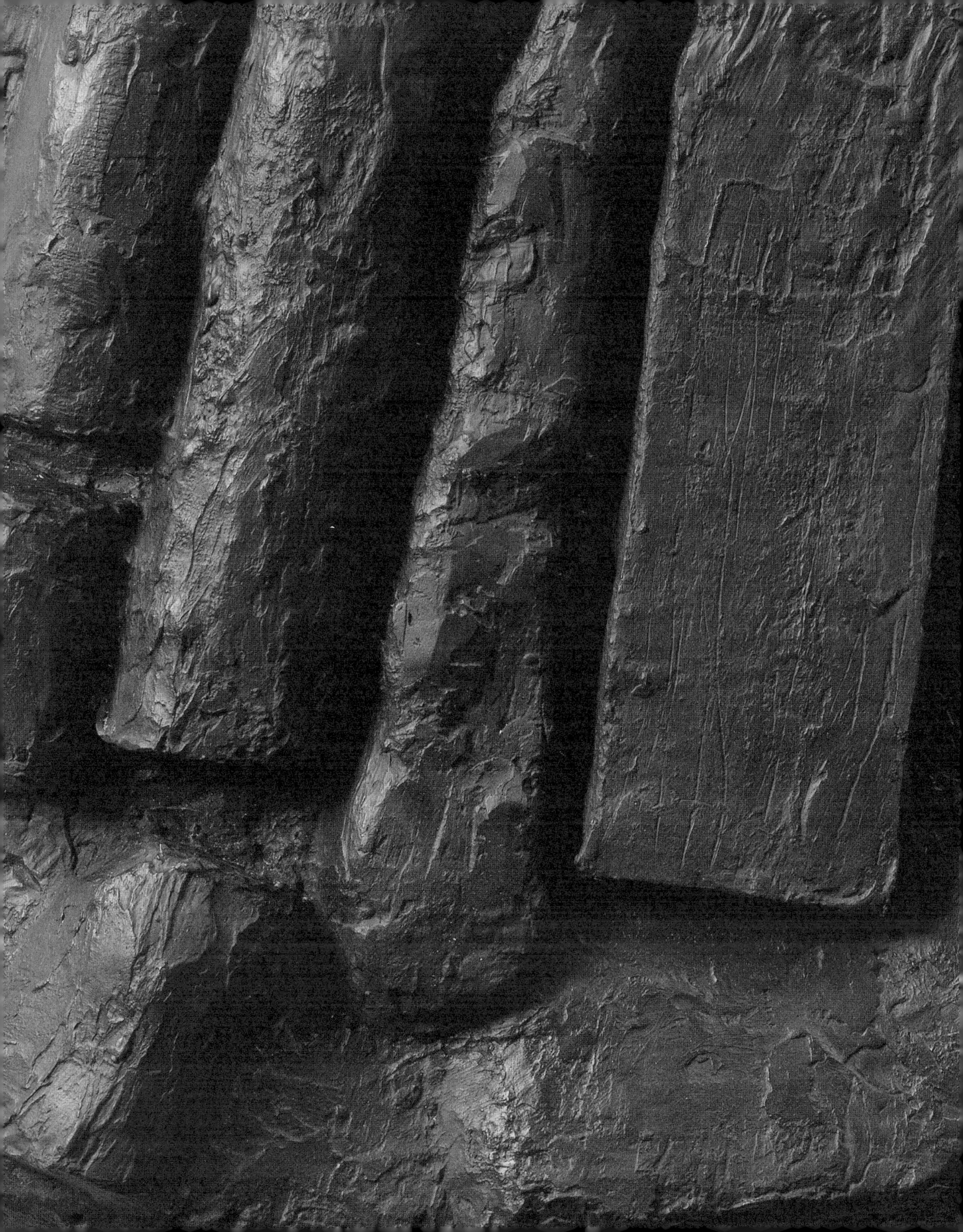

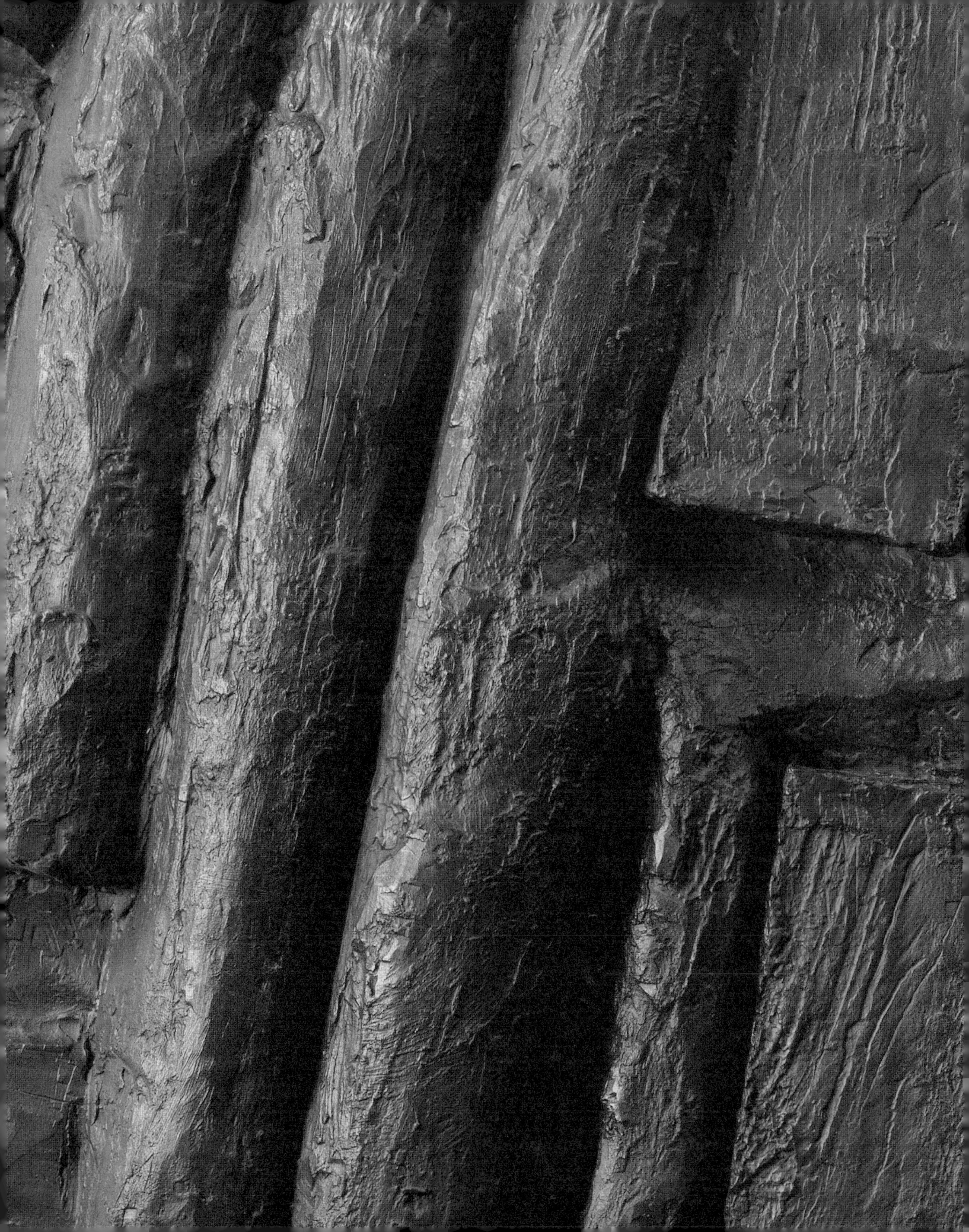